PENGUIN CLASSICS

THE WASPS/THE POET AND THE WOMEN
THE FROGS

ARISTOPHANES, an Athenian citizen, was born in c. 448–445 B.C. and died between 386 and 380 B.C. Little is known about his life, but there is a portrait of him in Plato's *Symposium*. He is presented as a well-liked and convivial person, who 'divides his time between Aphrodite and Dionysus'. His eleven surviving comedies are *The Acharnians* (425), *The Knights* (424), *The Clouds* (423), *The Wasps* (422), *Peace* (421), *The Birds* (414), *Lysistrata* (411), *The Poet and the Women* (411), *The Frogs* (405), *The Ecclesiazusae* (c. 392) and *Plutus* (388).

DAVID BARRETT studied Classics at Cambridge. After the war he was a lecturer in English at Helsinki University for thirteen years. In 1965 he joined the staff of the Bodleian Library in Oxford, where he specialized in Georgian and Armenian books, retiring from full-time work in 1981. He has translated many works from Finnish, as well as Aristophanes' *The Birds* and *The Assembly Women* for Penguin Classics.

ARISTOPHANES

THE WASPS
THE POET AND THE WOMEN
THE FROGS

TRANSLATED
WITH AN INTRODUCTION BY
DAVID BARRETT

PENGUIN BOOKS

PENGUIN BOOKS

Published by the Penguin Group
Penguin Books Ltd, 27 Wrights Lane, London W8 5TZ, England
Penguin Putnam Inc., 375 Hudson Street, New York, New York 10014, USA
Penguin Books Australia Ltd, Ringwood, Victoria, Australia
Penguin Books Canada Ltd, 10 Alcorn Avenue, Toronto, Ontario, Canada M4V 3B2
Penguin Books (NZ) Ltd, 182–190 Wairau Road, Auckland 10, New Zealand

Penguin Books Ltd, Registered Offices: Harmondsworth, Middlesex, England

This translation first published 1964
29 30

Copyright © David Barrett, 1964
All rights reserved

Printed in England by Clays Ltd, St Ives plc
Set in Monotype Bembo

Applications for permission to perform these
translations should be addressed to the League
of Dramatists, 84 Drayton Gardens, London SW10 9SD

To
H.C.O. *and* **C.J.E.**

He spake in Greek, which Britons speak
    Seldom, and circumspectly;
But Mr Judd, that man of mud,
    Translated it correctly.

And when they heard that happy word,
    Policemen leapt and ambled:
The busmen pranced, the maidens danced,
    The men in bowlers gambolled.

JAMES ELROY FLECKER

CONTENTS

INTRODUCTION

Aristophanes, an Athenian citizen, was born round about the middle
of the fifth century B.C. – in 445 B.C. or slightly earlier, since he could
hardly have been less than eighteen years old when his first comedy,
The Banqueters, was produced in 427. His last surviving play, *Plutus*,
was staged in 388 B.C., and he is known to have written at least two
more comedies after this date. Accordingly he is assumed to have
died some time between 386 and 380 B.C.

Very little personal information about him has come down to us,
and what we do know is derived mainly from the text of the plays
themselves. The ancient scholars whose comments on Aristophanes
are preserved seem to have been in much the same position, and such
biographical details as they give are probably based largely on guess-
work. Sculptured portraits representing Aristophanes as an elderly
man with a luxuriant crop of hair are not to be trusted, since the poet
was bald at an early age, as we know from his jocular remarks on the
subject in *The Clouds* and *Peace*.

In *The Acharnians* (425 B.C.) there is a passage which shows clearly
that Aristophanes had some connexion with the island of Aegina,
and was probably living there at that time. Six years earlier this
island, which lay very close to Athens and was strategically important, had been seized by the Athenians; its inhabitants had been
expelled and their land settled by Athenian colonists. It is possible
that Aristophanes' father had been among those who obtained land on
the island, and that the young poet, then in his teens, had accompanied the family to their new home.

For a portrait of the man himself one turns hopefully to Plato's
Symposium – the account of a drinking party at which Aristophanes
was present and actually made a speech. The *Symposium* was written
in the eighties of the fourth century, and the occasion described was
supposed to have taken place in 416 B.C., when Plato was eleven years
old: so that even if such a drinking party was ever actually held, the
details are pretty clearly the product of Plato's imagination. But

Aristophanes was still a well-known figure in the Athens of the nineties and early eighties, perhaps a personal friend of Plato (who composed an admiring epitaph for him); and the portraiture of other characters in the *Symposium*, such as Agathon and Alcibiades, is so brilliantly done that we must assume his portrait of Aristophanes to have been recognizably 'in character'. Unfortunately, much of the subtlety of this portrait is lost on us: it probably contained a good many sly touches which delighted Plato's readers, but which now inevitably pass unnoticed. Nevertheless, it is our only portrait of Aristophanes, and it would be a pity not to deduce what we can from it.

In the *Symposium*, then, he is presented as a well-liked and convivial person, who 'divides his time', as Socrates remarks, 'between Aphrodite and Dionysus'. He appears to be on good terms with his host Agathon and with the other guests, including Socrates, whom he had ridiculed so mercilessly in *The Clouds* seven years earlier. Alcibiades, indeed, is made to quote approvingly from *The Clouds* in Socrates' presence. The guests take it in turn to speak in praise of Eros, or physical love; but when it comes to Aristophanes' turn he is suffering from the hiccups. His neighbour, the physician Erixymachus, suggests various remedies, and agrees to make his own speech while Aristophanes tries them out. By the end of the doctor's speech the hiccups have subsided and Aristophanes is able to make his own contribution to the discussion. His speech is of great interest – it contains the famous definition of love as 'the desire and pursuit of the whole'; but it is not at all clear whether the preposterous 'myth' by which he attempts to explain the origin of sexual attraction is meant to represent the poet's own personal theory – in which case Plato is poking fun at Aristophanes – or whether it is the brilliant and subtle parody we might expect from the author of *The Frogs*. Certainly he begs his listeners, before he begins his speech, to take him seriously: 'it's no good waiting for the funny bits', he says; 'I don't mind being thought amusing – that's my job – but I don't want to be thought ridiculous.' And there is no merry laughter at the end: Erixymachus merely assures him that it was a very nice speech and that he has no intention of making fun of it, as Aristophanes seems to fear. One is left with the impression that while he cannot resist the temptation to enliven his 'myth' with ludicrous anatomical details (he can hardly have expected an eminent physician like Erixymachus to swallow his account of the origin of the human navel), his speech as a whole is meant seriously. We are reminded of the passage in *The Wasps* (p. 91) where he complains that the people who flocked to his trial did so, not out of any real sympathy, but to see if his tormentors would succeed in 'squeezing' a joke or two out of him.

Two more small touches are added to the portrait. At the end of the great speech by Socrates which formed the climax of the discussion, 'everybody applauded except Aristophanes, who was trying to say something about the reference Socrates had made to his own speech' – a reference so brief that it is doubtful whether any of the other guests would have noticed it. (Is this meant merely to illustrate Aristophanes' lack of good manners, or is it another attempt to underline the seriousness with which the 'funny man' took himself?) And when day is dawning, and all the other guests have either fallen asleep or gone home, Agathon the tragedian, Aristophanes the comedian, and Socrates the philosopher are still hard at it, with a bowl of wine in front of them, and Socrates maintaining that the skills required for the writing of tragedy and comedy are essentially the same. But what Aristophanes – or Agathon for that matter – had to say on this subject is unfortunately not recorded.

*

The eleven surviving comedies of Aristophanes are the only complete specimens available to us of what is known as 'Old' Attic Comedy, as opposed to the 'New' style of comedy which replaced it some time in the fourth century B.C., and of which Menander (b. 342 B.C.) was the greatest exponent. It was the New Comedy, with its emphasis on plot and construction and its repertoire of stock situations and type-characters, that set the pattern for Plautus and Terence and, through them, for the modern European comedy of intrigue right down to fairly recent times. Meanwhile, though Aristophanes continued to be read, enjoyed, and admired (chiefly for the sake of his pure Attic Greek), Old Comedy as a form of drama quickly came to be regarded as a crude historical curiosity. To Aristotle (384–322 B.C.), who had strong ideas about breeding and gentlemanly behaviour, the Old Comedy already seemed rough and vulgar, and its humour heavy and lacking in good taste. And even if anyone had wanted to imitate Aristophanes, the conditions under which the Old Comedy had flourished were never to be repeated.

By the time Aristophanes began to write, comedy was already a long-established dramatic form with its own clearly marked conventions and traditions. Contests in comedy had been a regular feature of the Great Dionysian Festival at Athens for at least sixty years; and the tradition certainly went back very much farther than that, though the actual origins of comedy are still a matter of learned dispute. The form seems to have developed gradually, over a long period, from the primitive *komos*, or ritual revel, from which it derived its name. But since little is known of these ceremonies, except what can be deduced from vase paintings and a few vague statements by Greek writers of a much later period, the early stages in the development of Old Comedy are largely a matter of conjecture. By the time that regular contests came to be held there must at least have been some conventional standards by which the work of competing authors could be judged, and to some extent this must have ensured a certain traditionalism and adherence to convention in the writing of comedy. On the other hand, the highly competitive conditions under which comedies were written and produced must have encouraged authors to strive after originality at all costs, and a successful 'gimmick' might itself lead to a modification, or a change of emphasis, in the convention. Aristophanes himself frequently boasts of the originality of his ideas, and occasionally points out (as he does at the end of *The Wasps*, for example) that he is deliberately departing from convention. Since Aristophanes was universally regarded as the greatest, as well as the last, of the Old Comedians, it is possible that he was more daring in his innovations than most of his contemporaries and predecessors: indeed, the latest of his surviving plays, *Plutus*, resembles the New Comedy rather than the Old in style and construction, and in two comedies written later still he is believed to have moved even farther in this direction. Some scholars have seen in this an indication that Aristophanes was the inspirer and begetter of the new style as well as the greatest exponent of the old; my own feeling, however, is that in his last plays Aristophanes was reluctantly attempting to adapt himself to the new fashions that were creeping in.

Since our only complete examples of Old Comedy are the work of a highly original creative genius, who treated the conventions with as much flexibility as the conditions of performance would allow, and who eventually (willingly or unwillingly) abandoned many of them altogether, it is not easy to isolate and define all the traditional elements of Old Comedy as such. We have no real knowledge of the type of *komos* from which comedy was descended, nor do we know by what stages it came to be associated with choral dances, with words specially written for the occasion, and finally with the use of actors and spoken dialogue. But a study of the comedies of Aristophanes does reveal a certain pattern of construction – naturally it is seen more clearly in his earlier works – which seems to represent the 'core' of the traditional comedy, and which may have had its origin quite early in the history of the *komos*. This 'core' consists of (1) a *parodos*, or entry of the Chorus; (2) an *agon*, or contest; and (3) a *parabasis*, or address by the Chorus to the audience. These particular scenes have certain recognizable characteristics, including the regular occurrence of passages in 'long' metres (eight feet to the line) interspersed with shorter lyrics, and a symmetrical ('epirrhematic') structure in which the scansion and number of lines in one metrical passage is exactly reproduced in another – indicating that, originally at any rate, the two passages were danced to the same music.

In the *parodos* the Chorus presents itself in the character chosen for it by the poet – birds, wasps, women of Athens, initiates, or whatever – and performs a series of songs and dances in which it retains this character more or less consistently. The *agon*, as handled by Aristophanes, usually takes the form of a debate or dispute, culminating in the decisive defeat of one of the parties; sometimes, as in *The Wasps*, it is preceded by a preliminary *agon* of a more violent kind – a sort of choreographic battle – which may have been closer to the traditional *agon* of early comedy. In the *parabasis*, the Chorus wholly or partly abandons its assumed character, and addresses the audience directly, speaking as the mouthpiece of the author. The traditional *parabasis* was an elaborate structure in seven parts: (*a*) a prelude; (*b*) the opening address to the audience, usually in anapaests; (*c*) a passage of rapid patter (the 'choker' or *pnigon*); (*d*) the *strophe* or *ode*; (*e*) the *epirrhema*, addressed to the audience, usually in the long trochaic metre; (*f*) the *antistrophe*, corresponding metrically to (*d*); and (*g*) the *antepirrhema*, corresponding in metre and (roughly) in length to (*e*). It will be seen that the *parabasis* of *The Wasps* (pp. 75-9) is a complete example, though in the present translation the metrical correspondence between (*d*) and (*f*) has not been reproduced. That of *The Poet and the Women* (pp. 126-9) is much abbreviated, consisting only of (*b*), (*c*), and (*e*); while that of *The Frogs* (pp. 181-3) has (*d*), (*e*), (*f*), and (*g*). *The Wasps* appears to have what amounts to a second parabasis (pp. 90-1), in the course of which the author is made to speak through the Chorus in the first person, although in the main *parabasis* the Chorus have retained their character as wasps.

Superimposed upon this basic pattern of *parodos – agon – parabasis*, in which the Chorus played the leading part (the involvement of actors in the *agon* had probably been a fairly late development), were the scenes carrying the spoken dialogue. These were written mainly in an iambic metre similar to, but less strict than, the metre of tragedy, and consisted of (*a*) a prologue, enlivened by various forms of verbal humour, in which the protagonist is introduced and his predicament explained; (*b*) (after the *parodos*) a series of comic episodes arising out of, or leading up to, the *agon*; (*c*) a further series of episodes, in which, as a rule, a succession of more or less unwelcome characters are discomfited and driven away. The episodes, when not already separated by the *agon* or the *parabasis*, are often marked off from each other by brief choral lyrics, and the play ends with a choral finale (*exodos*) which may or may not have had a counterpart in the original *komos*.

Some scholars have maintained that the traditional structure of comedy must also have included a *gamos*, or marriage scene. *The Birds* ends in a solemn ceremony in which the chief character is married to the allegorical figure of 'Sovereignty', and in *Peace* another allegorical female, 'Fruitfulness', is presented as a wife to the hero who rescues Peace from her prison and brings her back to earth. In other plays, however, Aristophanes seems to ignore this convention (if it existed) or at most to introduce a token female figure towards the end of the play, such as the flute girl Dardanis in *The Wasps*, the dancing-girl who tricks the Scythian in *The Poet and the Women*, and the 'Muse of Euripides' in *The Frogs*.

*

The Chorus retained its central importance in the structure of comedy throughout most of Aristophanes' lifetime and long after the great tragedians of the period had begun to find their tragic choruses something of an embarrassment. This may have been due partly to the fact that comedy was not expected to tell a story, as tragedy was, and that the songs, dances, and costumes of the comic chorus were regarded as an essential part of the entertainment; and partly to the skill of Aristophanes himself in fitting his new ideas into the traditional 'epirrhematic' structure. Through the *agon*, the Chorus could be integrated into the action of the play in a way which the trage-dians were not often in a position to imitate, unless the plot happened to allow for a contest between the protagonist and a crowd of angry citizens. The *parodos* enabled both Chorus and chorus-trainer to dis-play their virtuosity, and the *parabasis* was doubtless retained for the sake of the opportunity it gave the author to ram home his political message, pat himself on the back, plead for the first prize, satirize the audience, or indulge in scurrilous attacks on his personal enemies. Even as late as 405 B.C., it was the highly political *parabasis* of *The Frogs*, rather than the brilliant and subtle parodies contained in that comedy, that won it the first prize and the unprecedented honour of a repeat performance.

In other ways, too, the Chorus was of vital importance to the author. Before he could put on a comedy at all, he had to be 'granted a Chorus': and the kind of Chorus he got must undoubtedly have had an effect on the kind of comedy he wrote for it. The elderly citizens who formed the main Chorus of *The Wasps* (many of the younger men were busy besieging Scione) could hardly be expected to scurry about like the Chorus of *The Poet and the Women* or execute maenadic dances in honour of Dionysus. In fact Aristophanes gave them no dancing to do at all: the 'battle' scene was a parody of military drill, and at the end of the play they were given three professional dancers to dance in front of them as they marched stiffly out of the orchestra. But it also happened that for *The Wasps* Aristophanes had boys as well as men in his Chorus (or else he had secured the services of an additional Chorus of young boys): of these he made good use in the *parodos* (they probably danced while the old men stumbled and wheezed), and in all probability they reappeared later in the play, first as a comic procession of kitchen utensils and then as a litter of lively puppies.

The procedure by which a poet obtained his Chorus was peculiar. One of the first duties of the 'Eponymous Archon' (Principal Magis-trate) when he took office at the beginning of the year was to nomin-ate the rich citizens who were to undertake, as a compulsory service to the State, the sponsorship of a comic or tragic Chorus for the Great Dionysia. Another of the Archons had the duty of appointing sponsors for Choruses at the Lenaea. Such a sponsor was known as a *choregus*, and he was responsible not only for recruiting the twenty-four mem-bers of the Chorus but also for all the expenses involved in training it,

providing the costumes, and paying salaries to the trainers and professional singers engaged: he probably also paid the flute player and
any additional personnel taken on at the request of the poet, such as
non-speaking actors, castanet players, pipers, professional dancers,
subsidiary choruses, or groups of off-stage singers. Appointment as a
choregus was usually regarded as a great civic and religious honour
and as an opportunity for a display of public-spirited munificence. (If,
however, he felt that another citizen was better able to afford the
expense than he was, the person nominated could challenge this other
citizen either to take over the duties of *choregus* or agree to an
exchange of property. Such exchanges were, in fact, sometimes
carried out.) Meanwhile the poets who wished to compete at the
great festivals had applied to the Archon concerned for the grant of a
Chorus. A new poet would presumably have to submit a sample of
his work, perhaps a complete play. How the Archon reached his decision is not known, nor is it clear whether the poet, on being granted
a Chorus, was put in touch with his *choregus* before or after the
latter had recruited his team. A principal actor ('protagonist'), to be
paid by the State, was assigned by lot to each competing poet: normally only two other speaking actors were employed – we do not
know how the poet obtained their services, or whether their salaries
were paid by the State or the *choregus*. Since the Archons took office
at the beginning of the Hellenic year (mid July) and the great dramatic
festivals, the Lenaea and the Great Dionysia, were held in January and
late March respectively, several months were available in which the
author and the *choregus* could complete their preparations. Officially
the author was competing as 'producer' (*didaskalos*) and not as 'poet',
and at one time it had been usual for authors not only to produce
their own plays but also to compose the music, train the dancers and
singers, and even to act speaking parts. But in Aristophanes' time it
was normal to engage a separate trainer (*chorodidaskalos*) for the
Chorus, and some poets, including Aristophanes himself, made a
practice of handing over the whole business of production to somebody else, even though this meant that his own name would not
appear in the official record. The authorship of the play, as we
can see from some of Aristophanes' *parabases*, was an open secret,
and if a play won the first prize, the prestige was the author's.

*

The rule or convention of employing only three actors (very under-standable if, as is possible, all the speaking actors were paid by the State, and also as a method of ensuring that poets competed on equal terms) had its effect on the structure both of tragedy and of comedy. Occasionally a comic poet was allowed a fourth actor, but only for very small parts which would not affect the structure of the play as a whole. The entire action had to be worked out in such a way that there were never more than three speaking actors (apart from such occasional extras) on the stage at the same time.* Since comedy often required a large number of characters, great ingenuity had to be exercised in allocating them to the various actors and in organizing the action in such a way that no actor was ever required to be on the stage in two capacities at once. Normally the protagonist was given a part that kept him on the stage most of the time; the second actor would perhaps have to play two or three fairly substantial parts; and the third played all the rest. This is the reason why quite important characters often disappear half-way through the play, or fail to appear until the second half; and probably it also explains the stream of visitors who tend to appear in the later episodes of the play, each being discomfited and chased away in turn. Indeed, the second half of an Aristophanic comedy often bears a strong resemblance to the war-time radio show *Itma*, which was produced under rather similar casting conditions, with three or four actors taking a bewildering number of parts. The use of a fourth actor in comedy may have been a fairly late development: in *The Frogs*, a latish work, Aristophanes undoubtedly requires an extra actor, but the other two plays trans-lated in this volume could have been, and probably were, performed strictly to rule, with three speaking actors only. Since an actor, in order to assume a new role, had to do little more than whip off one mask and put on another, lightning changes were possible; and Aristophanes often arranges for these with great ingenuity.

In *The Poet and the Women* the protagonist clearly takes the part of Mnesilochus, who is on the stage practically all the time. The second actor appears first as Euripides, then as First Woman, then as Euripides again, then as the Magistrate (a very quick change, this), and then as Euripides yet again: he also takes the part of Echo,

---

* The Leader of the Chorus did not count as an actor, although he had a speaking part.

probably off-stage. Actor number three has an equally lively time, appearing first as Agathon's servant, then as Agathon (he is given time to change into the special costume required for this part), and then successively as Second Woman (who has to hurry off to the market after making her speech), Cleisthenes, Third Woman, and the Scythian. During his first brief appearance the Scythian is presumably played by a non-speaking actor, but he is promptly sent off to tie up Mnesilochus: 'Third Woman' follows him off and takes over his mask, uniform, and equipment, returning to the stage as the Scythian.

In *The Wasps* the three-actor rule provides the key to the proper allocation of speeches to the two slaves throughout the play. This is very inadequately indicated by the manuscripts, which in most cases either give no indication of the speaker at all, or attribute a speech merely to 'Servant' or 'Slave'. As a result, the slave who appears in the second part of the play is identified by some editors with Xanthias, by others with Sosias. But obviously the slave whom Anticleon summons to 'come round' and guard the waste pipe from the kitchen (p. 44) is being *called off the stage*, so that the same actor can reappear as Procleon, through the chimney, a few moments later. The slave who disappears must be Sosias, because the other slave remains on the stage continuously until Anticleon addresses him by name – as Xanthias – when he distributes the torches (p. 54). It is, accordingly, impossible for Sosias to reappear at all, and the slave in the latter part of the play must be Xanthias. The two 'heavy infantrymen' referred to by Procleon on p. 51 must be Xanthias and Anticleon: the slaves who hold on to Procleon while Anticleon is fetching the torches (p. 54) must be two of the three 'non-speaking' slaves who have just been summoned. The part of First Dog is doubled with that of Xanthias: this probably explains why, in some manuscripts, some of his speeches are attributed to 'Servant'. The situation is neatly exploited by the author when it is Second Dog's turn to speak, and there are already three speaking actors on the stage. 'Why don't you speak?' cries Anticleon. 'Get on with it!' But Second Dog is tongue-tied, and the audience knows why. The Xanthias actor undergoes a rapid series of transformations at the end of the play: Xanthias – Reveller – Baking-Woman – Citizen – Xanthias. The change from Baking-Woman to Citizen appears awkward as it stands, but the mystifying Chaerephon episode may have been designed to cover it in some way.

Readers may find it amusing to work out the casting of *The Frogs* for themselves. The fourth actor appears twice.

*

The actors were highly trained professionals, often skilled in dancing or singing as well as in acting. (The actor who took the part of Agathon in *The Poet and the Women* must have been an exceptionally accomplished singer; in *The Frogs*, Euripides and Aeschylus both had to sing their parodies of each other's lyrics; and the part of Procleon in *The Wasps* demanded an accomplished comic dancer.) The twenty-four members of the Chorus, on the other hand, were probably mostly amateurs, though the singing section seems to have included professional singers (who would have had to be paid), and the Leader, who usually had quite a lot of speaking to do, may have had previous experience as an actor or orator. The training of the Chorus, however, was intensive and almost military in character,* and they were drilled in their movements down to the smallest gesture of hand or arm. No wonder the old men in *The Wasps* boast of their manly prowess 'both in battle and in chorus' (p. 77). When set dances were performed by the Chorus, these were probably of a comparatively simple, folk-dance type, though not necessarily easy to dance without intensive rehearsal. But the fancy stuff, the high kicks and the rest, were left to the professional soloists – Euripides' dancing-girl (impersonated by a male dancer) in *The Poet and the Women*, the 'Sons of Carcinus' in *The Wasps*. The lyrics were probably sung by a section of the Chorus only, the rest accompanying them with dances or rhythmic gestures. Sometimes the words of the lyrics actually include instructions to the dancers (see especially *The Poet and the Women*, p. 134, and *The Frogs*, p. 169). The passages in longer metres were either declaimed by the Leader alone, or in unison, to a set intonation, by the entire Chorus. Occasionally individual members of the Chorus, or the Leader of a section of the Chorus, might be given a few words to speak by themselves, like the Boy in *The Wasps* or the Women's Leader in *The Frogs*, but such lines formed an integral part of the choral passage in which they occurred – they were mere details of 'orchestration'. Only the Leader had a speaking part of any importance.

* The members of the Chorus were, of course, all males, as were the 'flute girls', 'dancing-girls', etc., and the actors of female parts.

The masks worn by the actors were either conventional representations of stock types, gods, or legendary heroes (slave, old man, rustic, flatterer, old hag, Heracles, Hermes, and so on) or actual portraits, in varying degrees of caricature, of known individuals. A clever mask-designer could greatly enhance the humour of a comic episode: in the trial scene of *The Wasps*, for example, the canine mask worn by First Dog must have been strongly reminiscent of the features of Cleon; and an effective new mask probably earned many an actor a burst of applause before he had uttered a word. The use of masks was a factor that had a profound effect on the whole nature of ancient drama: scarcely a scene, scarcely a line even, of Aristophanes would have been written in the same way if the actors had not been masked. A modern actor who tries to act in a mask finds that he has to learn an entirely new technique: unable to make any use of facial expression, he must rely entirely on his voice, delivery, gestures, and movements. Instinctively, a modern playwright writes for an unmasked actor: equally instinctively, Aristophanes wrote for a masked one. This is perhaps one reason why his comedies so often remind us of the comic programmes written for sound radio: in these, too, the actor is unable to grimace at his audience.

Traditionally, the comic actor wore tights over heavy padding (accentuating the grotesque effect to which the mask already contributed), and a tight tunic cut very short so as to reveal an artificial phallus. The evidence is confusing, but it seems probable that this was still used as the basic costume in the time of Aristophanes, although it is clear that a character costume, which might include a longer upper garment, was often worn as well. The phallus, the wearing of which was in full conformity with the ritual aspects of a Dionysian festival, could thus be concealed or displayed as appropriate. In *The Poet and the Women*, Mnesilochus comments pointedly on Agathon's lack of this masculine attribute. Subsequently he is himself dressed up in women's clothes, so that his own phallus is concealed until the famous disrobing scene. In *Peace*, the leading character, who flies up to heaven astride a dung-beetle, uses his phallus as a kind of joy-stick or tiller; and Procleon, in *The Wasps*, offers his to the flute girl as a hand-rope by which to pull herself up on to the stage. (Several episodes seem to imply that the phallus worn by comic actors was, or could be, a long, floppy, flexible affair, and not a *phallus erectus*: this is to some extent confirmed by vase paintings.) One can hardly imagine Aeschylus and

Euripides, in *The Frogs*, conducting their literary debate in so immod-
est a costume; but when Euripides, in the weighing scene, begins to
rummage for something 'strong and big' to throw into the scale,
there can be no doubt as to what the audience expects him to find.
For his burlesque tragic dance in *The Wasps*, Procleon probably
appeared in tights only: the 'flute girl' would be wearing appro-
priately padded tights, with the more interesting anatomical details
painted on. Character costumes were doubtless often colourful and
amusing, but very little is known about them. Many characters could
be identified by their 'attributes' as well as by their masks and costumes: Heracles by his club and lion-skin, Hermes by his *caduceus*,
Perseus (as impersonated by Euripides in *The Poet and the Women*) by
his winged sandals and Gorgon's-head shield.

The costumes of the Chorus, on which large sums were spent, were
certainly regarded as a most important feature of the entertainment.
Choruses representing animals or birds, in particular, offered wonderful opportunities for the design of amusing and colourful masks
and costumes. The Chorus of *The Birds*, in which many different kinds
of birds were represented, must have been a gay sight indeed; and
I find it hard to believe that Aristophanes, if he had any say in
the matter, would have allowed his Frog Chorus to remain invisible, in spite of what an ancient commentator tells us. It must
always have been a tense moment for the *choregus* and his poet
when they watched the Chorus enter the arena and waited for the
thunder of applause that might help to make the play (literally) a
winner.

*

The dramatic performances at the Great Dionysian Festival, and probably also at the mid-winter festival of the Lenaea, took place in the
Theatre of Dionysus, on the rocky southern slope of the Acropolis.
The general shape of an ancient Greek theatre will be familiar to most
readers: in Aristophanes' time, however, the audience was probably
accommodated on wooden benches with earth foundations, and not
on stone seats as in later theatres. There were seats for at least 10,000
spectators – the reference in *The Wasps* (p. 75) to 'countless tens of
thousands' is clearly an exaggeration, but in *The Frogs* (p. 181) we hear
of 'ten thousand men of sense' (literally 'ten thousand intelligences'),
and *Plutus* contains a joke which seems to imply that the actual

number was 13,000. At the foot of the semicircular terraced auditorium was the completely circular arena (known as the *orchestra*, or 'dance floor') where the Chorus performed, with the altar of Dionysus in the middle. Beyond this stood the stage building (*skene*), the exact design of which is still a matter of dispute. Most probably it was at this period a long wooden building containing dressing-rooms, etc., with a painted architectural façade on the auditorium side and one or more doors opening on to the stage. The existence of a raised stage for the actors in the fifth century was for a long time considered doubtful, but there are now signs of a return to the traditional view that a raised stage of some sort was used. It is thought that it probably consisted of a long but fairly narrow wooden platform, about four feet above the level of the *orchestra* and approachable from it by steps. There may also have been ramps or steps at the *ends* of the stage, leading down to the *parodos* – the passage between the stage building and the extreme ends of the rows of seats, providing access to the theatre from outside and leading directly into the *orchestra*. Part of the stage building must have been on two storeys, so that the painted façade could have a window on the upper floor and thus represent a two-storeyed house: for the rest of its length the building seems to have had a single storey with a flat roof, thus providing an upper stage for which both tragic and comic playwrights found a great variety of uses. In *The Wasps* the *skene* would thus have represented exactly what it actually was: a two-storeyed building with a single-storeyed extension; and we can see from this play that the upper level could be reached in two ways – by going up a ladder or a flight of steps leading directly from the stage to the flat-roofed section, or by entering the 'house' by the door and 'going upstairs' inside, so as to appear at an upper window. Actors could make their entrances and exits either by the door or doors in the façade or by the *parodos*, in which case they then had to mount to the stage from *orchestra* level. The actors seem to have been quite free to perform in the *orchestra* as well as on the stage, and, in comedy at least, it looks as if the Chorus could make occasional incursions on to the stage, as appears to happen in the 'battle' scene of *The Wasps*.

The Theatre of Dionysus was equipped with two pieces of stage machinery, devised no doubt to serve the needs of tragedy, but often exploited in the comedies. The first was a device known as the *eccyclema*, enabling scenes to be set behind the visible façade and then 'rolled out' (it is not clear how) on to the stage. It was probably a fairly simple device, such as a large concealed door in the façade with a wooden floor attached behind it: such a door would be hinged at one side, with a wheel or castor at the other so that it could be pushed open easily. (Agathon, in *The Poet and the Women*, has to call for a slave to push him back again.) Another possibility is that the *eccyclema* was on the upper level and was simply pushed out of the 'upper room' on to the flat roof. The second device, known simply as 'the machine', enabled gods and goddesses to make spectacular descents from heaven, as they frequently had to do at the end of a tragedy in order to sort out the mess the characters had got themselves into. Euripides made extensive use of it: at the end of *Medea*, for example, the protagonist and her dead children are wafted away in a chariot drawn by dragons. In *The Poet and the Women* he is given a taste of his own medicine.

*

Assuming the stage arrangements to have been roughly as I have described them (though it must be repeated that many details are matters of conjecture), it is interesting to work out the way in which some of the scenes in the comedies must have been staged, and see how Aristophanes exploited his resources. Often there are cues in the text to help us. Let us take a look, for example, at the opening scenes of *The Frogs*.

Dionysus, puffing and panting, and Xanthias, on his human donkey, enter the *orchestra* by the *parodos*, passing close to a section of the audience, whom Xanthias surveys with disgust. As they mount the steps to the stage, and the conversation turns upon burdens, attention is called to the plight of the 'donkey': 'you'd better change places with him', Dionysus suggests. At last they reach the stage proper, and the door of Heracles' house. ('You see, I've walked the whole way.') Dionysus and Heracles converse, while Xanthias and his mount provide comic business in the background. Eventually the donkey wanders off, via the *parodos*, and re-enters the stage building from the rear. Heracles says good-bye to Dionysus, whips off his mask and lion-skin, lies down on a stretcher, and is carried out of another door as the Corpse. (The ex-donkey is now one of the bearers.) After being intercepted by Dionysus, the Corpse is carried down the steps (this would suggest a descent to the underworld) and out by the *parodos*.

As soon as he is out of sight, the Corpse nips through the back door into the dressing-room, and a moment later returns as Charon, poling his comical boat-on-wheels along the *parodos* towards the *orchestra*. Dionysus and Xanthias, who have had to carry out a bit of business with the luggage to give time for all this, now start their downward journey. By this time Charon, already visible to most of the audience, is just rounding the corner of the stage: Dionysus and Xanthias see the prow of the boat before Charon himself comes into view. They descend to the 'shore': Dionysus gets into the boat, but Xanthias is told that he will have to walk right round the 'lake', i.e. the *orchestra*. This he does, probably by a roundabout route, frequently losing his way among the gangways of the auditorium. Meanwhile the boat is launched, and Dionysus rows right out into the 'open waters' of the *orchestra*. The Frogs now enter, leaping and hopping, by the *parodos* (greeted, perhaps, by a cheer from the audience, who think they are the real Chorus: after all, the title of the play has been announced as *The Frogs*). They dance around the boat, singing and croaking in chorus, until Dionysus succeeds in driving them away. By this time he has rowed right across to the side of the *orchestra* farthest from the stage, and he lands at the feet of his own priest in the centre of the front row of seats. Charon rows rapidly away, and Xanthias rejoins his master. But now the Empusa appears, a fearsome monster which keeps changing its shape: perhaps some of the frog-dancers again, in horrific masks, peeping out in turn from under a blanket. Dionysus, in terror, clutches the skirts of his priest, and then flees up the central gangway, to the delight of the audience. But Xanthias suceeds in exorcising the apparition. They start back towards the stage, but now the real Chorus enters, and they are obliged to crouch down at the edge of the *orchestra*, where they remain until they decide to join in the dancing themselves. The dance brings them back to the foot of the stage steps, and when Dionysus inquires the way to the palace, the Chorus reply 'It's just behind you now' – and so, by Pluto, it is. They have reached their journey's end. Xanthias retrieves the luggage, and Dionysus mounts the steps towards the palace door. Meanwhile the women dancers, who are not going to be needed again (they too, perhaps, are played by the boys of the Frog Chorus), are given their cue to leave the orchestra: 'And I', runs the text, implying a fresh speaker, 'will go with the girls and women.' The men remain, to dance in the meadow of roses and sing of the Mysteries, while Dionysus plucks up courage to knock at the door.

*

Little can be said with absolute certainty about the composition of Aristophanes' audiences. It would be especially interesting to know whether women were allowed to attend the performances, but oddly enough there is no firm evidence either way. There is a joke in *Peace* that can be taken as implying that women were present, and equally well as implying that they were not. (If they were present, the joke in question seems to indicate that they sat separately from the men.) The Chorus of *The Poet and the Women* certainly address the audience as if it consisted only of men, and the masculine flavour of Aristophanes' humour does not suggest the presence of wives and daughters. The Great Dionysia, held in the spring when communications were easy, was attended by foreign visitors to Athens: one assumes, therefore, that resident foreigners, of whom there were a great many (mostly Greeks) were also permitted to attend, though it was only at the Lenaea that a foreign resident could act as Choregus or be a member of the Chorus. The only slaves present would be those serving as attendants, seat stewards, constables, stage hands, and so on. It seems probable that the bulk of the audience consisted of male Athenian citizens, drawn from all classes, but perhaps with a preponderance of the literate upper and middle classes. The 'riff-raff' (*The Wasps*, p. 62) on whom demagogues like Cleon relied for support in the Assembly and the Courts cannot all have been so hungry for culture that they were prepared to spend a public holiday (and two thirds of a juryman's daily pay) watching three tragedies, a satyr play, and a comedy, one after the other. (It is clear from a passage in *The Birds* that if you wanted to see the comedy you had to sit through all the rest first.) It was thus possible for comedies containing violent attacks on such demagogues to win first prize at the Festival without noticeably reducing the influence of these men on the political decisions of the Assembly. It was also possible for a poet to presuppose in his audience an enthusiasm for contemporary drama and even a considerable knowledge of the works of the great Athenian tragedians.

Nevertheless one should guard against over-estimating the literacy of the audience. Ten thousand is a large number, especially if we consider that the dramatic competitions went on for three days – and that the total adult male population of Attica (excluding slaves, but including resident aliens) was only about 75,000 when the Peloponnesian War began in 431 B.C., and decreased as the war went on. Aristophanes often found it necessary, almost in the same breath, to provide low comedy and to flatter the audience with references to its superior culture and intelligence. We do not have to suppose that every member of the audience could follow all the subtleties of his Euripidean parodies or the intricacies of his lyrical metres. When a modern music-hall comedian cries 'To be or not to be!' or 'Lend me your ears!' he gets his laugh. If he says 'Out, damned spot!' he gets an even bigger one. But this does not mean that every member of the audience knows Shakespeare by heart. (Nor does it necessarily mean that the scriptwriter disapproves of Shakespeare.) The Athenian theatre, like the Elizabethan, had its 'groundlings, capable of nothing but inexplicable dumb-shows and noise'; and, like Shakespeare, Aristophanes provided for them handsomely – not without an occasional comment on the necessity to do so.

As a matter of fact, the success of a play in the competition did not depend entirely on its reception by the audience (not all of whom would have been present on all three days of the contest), though the judges must inevitably have been inclined to fall in with the popular verdict. (It was considered a disadvantage to have one's comedy acted on the first day. 'Don't let it tell against us,' say the Chorus of *The Women's Assembly* in their final appeal to the judges, 'that we were put on first: remember it all, and don't break your oath to judge fairly between the Choruses.') The ten judges were chosen by lot when the contest was opened, from a hundred candidates who had in turn been chosen by lot from a larger number still. At the end of the last day each judge placed his verdict in an urn: five of the urns (again selected by lot) were then opened, the rest being ignored. This system made bribery difficult: and if you had arranged to have a friend put on the original list of nominees, there was no guarantee that he would be one of the final ten – even if he was, he might be one of the five whose verdicts were not examined. Another result of the system was that the plays were judged by 'average citizens' and not by experts. There were three prizes for comedy: but since the number of competitors had been reduced from five to three (a wartime measure), a third prize, such as Aristophanes obtained with *The Clouds,* was regarded as the reverse of an honour. In *The Wasps* (p. 76), and in his

rewritten version of *The Clouds* itself (the version we have), he speaks
with some bitterness of this defeat. He won first prize with *The
Acharnians*, *The Knights*, and *The Frogs*; second or first with *The
Wasps*; second with *Peace* and *The Birds*. The placing of his other
extant comedies (*Lysistrata*, *The Poet and the Women*, *The Women's
Assembly*, and *Plutus*) is not known.

*

The comic poets enjoyed very considerable freedom of speech and
a person mocked or attacked in a comedy had no legal means of
redress, though the gentleman referred to in *The Frogs* (p. 171) seems
to have had his revenge by proposing a cut in the poet's emoluments.
But impiety was forbidden, and could be severely punished. The
comedies thus give us an idea of what was regarded as impious and
what was not, and provide a valuable sidelight on the attitude of the
Greeks to religion at this period. Some of the gods – in their capacity
as personified 'characters' – had, it seems, lost much of their sanctity
and could be freely ridiculed: but the divine powers of which these
'characters' were the symbolic representation were regarded with the
utmost reverence, and religious *observances* could only be mocked or
parodied up to a certain point. Thus while Dionysus, in *The Frogs*, can
be presented as an utterly ludicrous figure, Aristophanes is extremely
careful in his treatment of the Chorus of Initiates; and although some
features of the Eleusinian procession are imitated or parodied, there is
no mockery of the Mysteries themselves. Scenes in which the figures
of the gods were made ridiculous were clearly regarded as no more
than harmless fun: naughty, perhaps one might say, rather than
wicked. For obvious reasons, too, some divine figures did not lend
themselves to comic treatment: the great goddesses were seldom or
never treated as figures of fun (as they sometimes were by Homer),
because they had come to be associated with deeper levels of religious
experience. There was nothing very amusing about Apollo; and
Zeus had already lost most of his anthropomorphic character and
become, at one and the same time, the Supreme Deity (who obviously could never be the subject of mockery) and a mere word for use
in everyday oaths or as a synonym for the weather. Thus it is chiefly
Hermes, Poseidon, and Dionysus, along with such minor deities as
Iris and demigods like Heracles, who appear as figures of fun in the
comedies.

One other limitation of the poet's freedom of speech existed: he was not allowed to 'wrong the People' – in other words, to make treasonable statements or insinuations. It was on this charge that Aristophanes was brought before the Council, on the instigation of Cleon, after the production of his second comedy, *The Babylonians,* at the Great Dionysia in 426 B.C. In this play he had not only attacked all the important Athenian officials then in office, and Cleon in particular, but also shown the 'allied' (i.e. subject) cities as a Chorus of Babylonian slaves working on a treadmill – and this in wartime, and before an audience including allied and other foreign representatives. We do not know the details of the trial (to which he refers in *The Wasps,* p. 91), but he seems to have been 'squeezed' of a large fine. After this he learnt to keep within the letter of the law – and continued his attacks on Cleon and his outspoken criticisms of Athenian policy without, as far as we know, getting into serious trouble again. An attempt by Cleon to deprive Aristophanes of his citizenship by proving that he was not of pure Athenian birth was unsuccessful.

*

It is hardly necessary to point out that the conditions I have described were very different indeed from those under which a modern play is written, produced, and performed. But Aristotle was wrong in regarding the Old Comedy merely as a crude predecessor of the New. It is something quite different: something which, like the drama of the Elizabethans, could only have flourished where it did and when it did, and yet, thanks to a writer of genius, can give readers in a later century the illusion of personal participation, a feeling of familiarity with the whole spirit of an age. Reading Aristophanes, we fall under the spell of this illusion: we sit among his audience, indistinguishable from the rest; we laugh when they laugh, are moved when they are moved, hardly conscious that we sometimes have no idea what it is all about. It is not until the performance is over that we look around us and realize what foreigners we are, how utterly we do not belong.

Yet perhaps, in a way, we do belong. Might not Aristophanes himself, from time to time, have found himself similarly at home among an English audience? Do we not, after all, rather pride ourselves on our ability to respond in equal measure to low buffoonery, fantasy, and verbal wit? Are these not, indeed, the essential ingredients of what we regard as 'typically English' humour? And have not we, too, a particular weakness for parody? Shakespeare's mechanicals, performing their tedious brief scene of young Pyramus and his love Thisbe, are true sons of Athens. And if direct imitations of Old Comedy have been rare (*The Knight of the Burning Pestle*, with its brilliant, high-spirited parodies and its Aristophanic *parabasis*, is perhaps the outstanding example), something of the spirit of Aristophanes has found its way even into the most formal of English comedies. If we turn from orthodox comedy to less formal types of entertainment, the kinship between English and Ancient Greek humour becomes even more striking. Could Aristophanes have seen the Crazy Gang in action without wanting to recruit them on the spot for his next comedy? Could he have listened to *Much Binding in the Marsh* without thinking of his own fantasy city of Nephelococcygia – Much Cuckoo in the Clouds? In the music hall, the pantomime, the circus, the sophisticated revue, the Third Programme skit, the television satire, some part of his spirit lives on. But Aristophanes gives us something that these seldom can: a sense of occasion, of urgency, of an intense seriousness underlying all the fun and the bawdry and the wit; a feeling that author, singers, actors, and audience are sharing in an act of celebration, a reassertion of the values which they, as a community, are determined to defend.

It is in the hope of being able to communicate something of this spirit, something of the sense of participation I have mentioned, that these translations have been attempted. They are offered as translations, not as 'adaptations': that is to say, I have aimed at as close an approximation both to the letter and to the spirit of the original text as I could achieve; but where the letter would kill the spirit, it has had to be sacrificed. A style of translation free enough to give the effect of naturalness in another language carries with it certain dangers: the translator finds it necessary at times (it is an important part of his job) to adjust, to expand, to contract, to rephrase, to underline – but if he is not careful he will find himself doing these things for their own sake. In the case of a comedy, full of subtle parody, puns, satirical thrusts, and topical references, written for a living stage by a master of stagecraft and timing, this freedom becomes even more necessary and even more dangerous. I have tried to use it with discretion, and I hope that any errors of judgement on my part will not be put down to mere irresponsibility.

Rightly or wrongly, I have decided that in a version designed to be both readable and actable the dialogue must be converted into ordinary spoken English. To attempt a translation of Aristophanes' iambics into blank verse or heroic couplets would merely make a faithful rendering more difficult : and in any case Rogers' verse translation could never be bettered. As for 'modern' verse, I confess that I do not know the rules. I could, of course, have divided my translation up into lines of varying length, with no capital letters or full stops ; but this would merely have taken up more pages and made the book more expensive.

The lyrics, on the other hand, were written to be sung, and must clearly be translated into singable verse. It is here that the translator of Aristophanes is confronted with his greatest problem. Aristophanes was not only a comic writer : he was also a poet and metrist of great ability. He used the subtle metres of Greek lyric poetry with as much ease and confidence as the great tragedians whose styles he parodies ; and although some of his songs consist mainly or partly of conventional comic patter, the great majority, however witty their content, have an attractive poetic quality which is hard to define and even harder to recapture in translation. Conscious attempts to reproduce the 'charm' of Aristophanes' lyrics have seldom been successful : they tend to result in an ineffectual sort of prettiness which merely dulls the edge of the wit. Where even the great translators have often failed, I have not dared to imagine that I could succeed ; and accordingly I have concentrated on the content rather than on the form of the lyrics, using simple ballad metres such as have always been favoured by writers of light verse in English. I hope that some, at least, of the resulting versions will be found to make up for what they lack in poetic quality by a closer approximation to the wit and point of the originals than I could have achieved in a more flowery rendering.

I have made abundant use of stage directions, chiefly in order to help the reader to visualize the action, or to bring out my interpretation of the text ; where matters of production are involved (I have assumed the use of a modern proscenium stage) they are merely suggestions and could doubtless be improved upon. Similarly the act and scene divisions merely indicate places where a break in the performance would be possible, if circumstances made such a break desirable. Apart from such attempts to bridge the gulf between the ancient and the modern theatre, I have tried to avoid glaring anachronisms. Although the characters speak our language, I have not tried to turn them into Englishmen, but rather to persuade the audience to imagine themselves as Athenians. Since the process of translation itself involves an anachronism, some inconsistency is inevitable, especially when so many of the clichés of our everyday speech are derived from literary quotations. But I have done my best to make the parodies sound like parodies of Aeschylus or Euripides, and not of Keats or Shakespeare.

I have used the standard editions of the text, following Coulon for the most part, but adopting the readings or emendations of other editors where these appeared preferable. I have received great help from a number of annotated editions of the plays, and in particular from Professor W. B. Stanford's admirable edition of *The Frogs*. To Professor Stanford, and to Professor W. K. C. Guthrie of Cambridge, I also owe thanks for their helpful replies to my queries on points of detail. I am deeply indebted to Mr E. F. Watling for the many valuable comments and suggestions he made after reading my first draft of *The Frogs*. And above all I should like to thank the Founder Editor of the Penguin Classics, Dr E. V. Rieu, and his assistant, Mrs Betty Radice (now Joint Editor of the series), for their unfailing patience, kindness, and encouragement.

Helsinki, 1963   D. B.

The publishers acknowledge with thanks permission from J. M. Dent & Sons Ltd to use the poem by James Elroy Flecker on p. 6.

The Wasps

Introductory Note to *The Wasps*

The Wasps was performed in 422 B.C., when Aristophanes was still in his twenties. Athens and her allies had been at war with Sparta for nine years, but at the moment hostilities were in progress only in the north of Greece, where the Spartan general Brasidas was waiting for an opportunity to relieve his beleaguered garrison in Scione.

Since the death of Pericles early in the war, Athens had been without a real leader. Pericles had commanded the respect of all classes and had inspired the Athenians with an intense faith and pride in their own political institutions. But after nine years of war, with no Pericles to guide the counsels of the Assembly, the disadvantages of these institutions were making themselves clearly felt. Not that many Athenians dreamed of blaming the system itself: to do so was to brand oneself as a traitor to democracy, a conspirator, a monarchist, 'a long-haired, tassel-fringed pro-Spartan, hand in glove with Brasidas'. Such movements did exist, especially among the upper classes, but they commanded little support as yet.

The supreme power still lay with the People, whether sitting as an Assembly or as members of the jury-courts, which, in addition to trying ordinary civil and criminal cases, heard the accounts which all office-holders had to render on the expiry of their year of office. In order to exert personal power, a man had to find ways of influencing these bodies. The art of oratory was studied and cultivated intensively: professional speech writers hired themselves to the highest bidder and became experts in wheedling and deception; successful demagogues acquired their network of satellites and informers; and in various ways, if we are to believe Aristophanes, a good deal of public money found its way illicitly into private pockets.

Membership of the Jury Corps was open only to citizens over thirty (middle-age in those days), but no other qualifications were required. The official strength of the Corps was 6,000, members being chosen by lot at the beginning of each year, 600 from each of the ten *phylai*. (Whether as many volunteers as this were normally forthcoming is a little doubtful.) Jurymen wore short brown cloaks and carried staves. On the days when trials were being held, members of the Corps who wished to sit on a jury presented themselves early in the morning and the various juries were selected by lot as required. Important cases were tried by a full court of 501 jurymen, and on exceptional occasions a case might be heard by several 'courts' sitting together. Private lawsuits came before smaller juries, possibly of 201 members. At the time when *The Wasps* was written, the jurymen were still 'organized in swarms' (see p. 79), each juryman having been assigned by lot to one of the ten courts for the whole year. There were thus 100 spare men for each court. It is not known whether jurymen were obliged to attend on a minimum number of days in the year, or what happened if less than 500 presented themselves on a day when a full court was required. Anticleon's calculation of the total annual earnings of the Jury Corps (p. 61) is based on the assumption that each of its 6,000 members attended court on 300 days in the year. The pay was three obols a day – not quite a living wage, but attractive to old people (who regarded it as a sort of pension) and to the very poor. All they had to do was to listen to speeches, record their verdict – guilty or not guilty – and pass sentence. A convicted prisoner could suggest a lighter penalty than that proposed by the prosecutor: on their wax tablets, the jury scratched a long line for the heavier penalty, a shorter one for the lighter; they could not suggest an alternative punishment. The jury were given no legal guidance beyond what the prosecution and the defence saw fit to provide, and they could be influenced, not only by the orators in the court itself, but beforehand, by speeches in the Assembly. Although bribery was difficult, a favourite gambit of the demagogues was to suggest that if sufficiently heavy fines were not inflicted, the exchequer would be depleted and the jury pay might have to be reduced or abolished.

Aristophanes calls his comedy (p. 42) 'just a little fable, with a moral'. But the moral is two-edged. Procleon represents the people of Athens, and his son Anticleon succeeds, not without great difficulty, in convincing him that he has allowed himself to be duped. Even in a democracy, the people are not the real rulers if they allow themselves to be led by the nose. To this extent Anticleon is more clear-sighted than his father; to this extent the opponents of Cleon are rendering their city a service. But this is not enough: what kind of leadership are they providing themselves, with their mania for upper-class luxuries, their drinking parties, their rich clothes and effeminate habits? In the second half of *The Wasps* we see clearly that, for all their simplicity and gullibility, it is Procleon and his fellow-jurymen who stand for the old-fashioned virtues, for the values that made Athens great in the days of the Persian Wars. Their pride, their obstinacy, their severity, their austerity, and above all their courage and virility – can Athenians afford to let these qualities go out of fashion? 'I don't *want* to be given a good time,' says Procleon early on in the play. He is proud of his chilblains, proud of his tattered old cloak that lets the north wind through.

Admittedly, after his one reluctant experiment in luxurious living, he will learn what it is like to appear in court as a defendant: but it will be worth it, if Anticleon has learnt his lesson too. In everything except his gullibility, Procleon is a better man than his son, as the latter learns at last when he finds himself flat on the floor. When Procleon does get drunk, he does it in truly heroic style. And tomorrow, after he has faced his ex-colleagues in court and Anticleon has forked out the money for the fine, not one but two men will be the wiser for their experiences.

CHARACTERS

SOSIAS }
XANTHIAS } *household slaves of Procleon and Anticleon*

ANTICLEON *a young Athenian*
PROCLEON *his father*
FIRST DOG
A REVELLER
A BAKING-WOMAN
A CITIZEN

CHORUS OF OLD MEN (*The Wasps*)
SUBSIDIARY CHORUS OF BOYS[1]

Silent Characters

MIDAS }
PHRYX } *household slaves of Procleon and Anticleon*
MASYNTIAS }

SECOND DOG (*Labes*)
DARDANIS *a flute girl*
CHAEREPHON *the philosopher*
WITNESS *brought by the Citizen*
COOKING UTENSILS *witnesses at the trial of Second*
PUPPIES *children to Second Dog*
REVELLERS
THE THREE SONS OF CARCINUS

ACT ONE

SCENE I: *Outside a house in Athens*

[*The scene opens in darkness, but dawn is approaching. When it becomes lighter, it will be seen that makeshift barricades have been placed in front of the doors and windows, and that the house is enveloped in an enormous net. There is an outside staircase to the flat part of the roof (not covered by the net), where* ANTICLEON *is sleeping. The two slaves,* XANTHIAS *and* SOSIAS, *sit propped against the wall of the house, fast asleep and snoring gently. Suddenly* SOSIAS *stirs, yawns, and stumbles to his feet. He goes across to Xanthias and shakes him by the shoulder.*]

SOSIAS: Xanthias, you old wretch, what do you think you're doing?

XANTHIAS [*waking, with a yawn*]: Relieving the night watch, they call it.

SOSIAS: Earning yourself a few more stripes, you mean. Don't you realize what kind of a monster we're guarding?

XANTHIAS: I know, but I feel like shaking off dull care for a bit.

SOSIAS: Well, that's your own look out. I don't mind. Oddly enough, I'm feeling rather deliciously drowsy myself.

[*They both settle down to sleep again. After a few moments* SOSIAS *begins to toss and mutter.* XANTHIAS *stirs, yawns, and stumbles to his feet. He goes across to Sosias and shakes him by the shoulder.*]

XANTHIAS: Gone into a frenzy, have you? What do you think you are, a blinking Corybant?[2]

SOSIAS: No, just asleep. Though I won't say there was *nothing* Bacchic about it. [*He displays a wine-flask.*]

XANTHIAS [*displaying another*]: Looks as if we're fellow devotees. Talk about sleep assailing the weary eyelids, it was like trying to hold off the whole Persian army. Funny dream I had just now.

SOSIAS: I've been dreaming too, like anything. But tell me about yours first.

XANTHIAS: I dreamt that I saw an enormous eagle swoop down into the Market Square, and it snatched up a coppery sort of snake and flew away with it, right up into the sky. And then suddenly the eagle turned into Cleonymus, and –

SOSIAS: Don't tell me – the snake turned into his shield, and he dropped it![3] Make a good riddle, wouldn't it?

XANTHIAS: What would?

SOSIAS: Cleonymus. 'Try this one on your friends' – just the thing for a drinking party. 'What creature is it that sheds its *shield*, on land, at sea, and in the sky?'[4]

XANTHIAS: Yes, but seriously, I'm worried. It's not lucky, a dream like that.

SOSIAS: Don't give it another thought. No harm in that, I'm sure.

XANTHIAS: No harm, in a man throwing away his equipment? – What was *your* dream, anyway?

SOSIAS: Oh, it was a big thing, mine. All about Athens itself – the whole mighty ship of state.

XANTHIAS: Well, get launched, and let's hear it.

SOSIAS: Well, I'd no sooner fallen asleep than I saw a whole lot of sheep, and they were holding an assembly on the Pnyx: they all had little cloaks on, and they had staves in their hands; and these sheep were all listening to a harangue by a rapacious-looking creature with a figure like a whale and a voice like a scalded sow.

XANTHIAS: No, no!

SOSIAS: What's the matter?

XANTHIAS: Don't tell me any more, I can't bear it. Your dream stinks like a tanner's yard.[5]

SOSIAS: And this horrible whale-creature had a pair of scales and it was weighing out bits of fat from a carcass.

XANTHIAS: Dividing up the body politic – I see it all. Ghastly!

SOSIAS: And then I noticed that Theorus[6] was sitting on the ground at the creature's feet, only he had a head like a raven. And Alcibiades turned to me and said, 'Look, Thothiath, Theowuth ith twanthformed. He'th a waven!'

XANTHIAS: A-wavin' to hith powerful fwendth, of courthe! Good for Althibiadeth!

SOSIAS: Yes, but isn't that a bit sinister, Theorus turning into a raven?

XANTHIAS: On the contrary. Very good sign.

41

SOSIAS: Why?

XANTHIAS: Well, first he's a man, then he suddenly turns into a raven: isn't it obvious what that means? He's going to croak.

SOSIAS: I'll really have to take you on as my personal dream-interpreter, at two obols a day!

XANTHIAS: Now look, I'd better tell the audience what this is all about. Just a few words by way of introduction. [*He turns to the audience.*] You mustn't expect anything too grand: but you're not going to get any crude Megarian[7] stuff either. And I'm afraid we can't run to a couple of slaves with baskets full of nuts to throw to you. You won't see Heracles being cheated of his dinner; we're not going to sling any mud at Euripides; and we don't intend to make mincemeat of Cleon this time – even if he *has* covered himself with glory just lately. No, this is just a little fable, with a moral: not too highbrow for you, we hope, but a bit more intelligent than the usual knockabout stuff. That's our master, the big man sleeping up there on the roof. He's told us to stand guard over his father and keep him locked up inside, so that he can't get out. You see, the old man's suffering from a very peculiar complaint, which I'm sure none of you have ever heard of, and you'll never guess what it is unless we tell you. Would you like to try? [*He waits for suggestions from the audience.*] What's that, Amynias? Mad on dicing? No, it isn't 'cubomania'.

SOSIAS: He's judging others by himself.

XANTHIAS: You're right though, it *is* a sort of mania, an addiction to something. Aha! What's that they're trying to make you say, Dercylus? Dipsomania?

SOSIAS: No, that's much too respectable – all the best people suffer from that nowadays.

XANTHIAS: Nicostratus here wants to know if he's a 'xenophile'.[8]

SOSIAS [*with a meaning look at Nicostratus*]: A lover of guests? I know what kind of guests *you're* thinking of.

XANTHIAS: No, you're all wrong, you'll never get it. – All right, keep quiet, and I'll tell you what the old man's trouble really is. He's what they call a trialophile or litigious maniac – the worst case I've ever come across. What he's addicted to is serving on juries, and he moans like anything if he can't get a front seat at every trial. He never sleeps a wink at night – or if he does drop off, his dreams go fluttering round that water-clock[9] till he wakes up again. He's so used to clutching his voting-pebble that he wakes up with his thumb and two fingers glued together, as though he'd been sprinkling incense for a new-moon sacrifice. Why, if he goes past Demos'[10] house and sees what someone's written on the gatepost – you know the sort of thing: 'Beautiful Demos, what charm you have got!' – he goes and writes underneath: 'Beautiful urn, how I long for your slot!' It's true, honestly. Once he complained that the cock was late calling him – and it was well before midnight! Said the retiring magistrates must have bribed it, because their accounts were coming up for review the next day. Oh, he did have it badly: as soon as supper was over he'd shout for his shoes, and off he'd go to the court, and sleep through the small hours at the head of the queue, clinging to the doorpost like a limpet. And mean! He's so mean that he scratches the long line on his tablet every time they get a conviction – full damages; honestly, he comes home with enough wax under his fingernails to furnish a beehive. He's so afraid of running out of voting-pebbles that he keeps a whole beach of them inside the house here. That's how mad he is: and the more you warn him, the more he goes to court. That's why we've had to bolt him in and guard the house for fear he gets out. This disease of his is getting my young master down. He's tried talking to him, he's tried all kinds of arguments to stop him wearing his juryman's cloak or get him to stay at home: but he wouldn't listen. So then he tried all the usual treatments for madness, gave him a ritual washing and carried out all the purification rites: no use at all. After that he took him to the priests of Bacchus, to see if they could work him up into a Corybantic[11] frenzy, and cure him that way: but the old man escaped and burst into the courtroom, drum and all, to hear a trial. Well, in the end, as none of these rites seemed to do him any good, the young master sailed him over to Aegina and lodged him in the Temple of Asclepius for the night: but next morning, at crack of dawn – there he was at the courtroom door. Since then we haven't been letting him go out at all. But he kept slipping out through the water outlets or the chimneys, and we've had to stuff up every hole we could find with bits of rag. Then he drove a lot of little pegs into the courtyard wall, and hopped up them like a jackdaw and over the top. So now we've covered the whole yard with netting and we're guarding him day and night, By the way, the old man's name is Procleon – yes, believe it or not.

*Pro-*Cleon! And his son's called *Anti*cleon – he's all right, but a bit high-and-mighty at times.

(ANTICLEON *stirs, wakes, and listens attentively.*]

ANTICLEON: Xanthias! Sosias! Are you asleep?

XANTHIAS: Oh, lord! [*He shakes Sosias, who has fallen asleep again.*]

SOSIAS: What's up?

XANTHIAS: It's him. He's awake.

ANTICLEON: Come round to the back, quickly, one of you. My father's got into the kitchen and he's scurrying about in there like a rat. Keep a watch on the waste pipe and see that he doesn't get out that way.

[SOSIAS *runs up the stairs, crosses the roof, and disappears.*]

And you, Xanthias, stand close to the door.

XANTHIAS: Yes, sir.

ANTICLEON: Ye gods, what's all that noise in the chimney?

[PROCLEON'S *head and shoulders appear through the smokehole.*]

Who's there?

PROCLEON: Just a puff of smoke.

ANTICLEON: Smoke? Why, what are they burning?

PROCLEON: Figwood.[12]

ANTICLEON: That accounts for the pungent smell. Pfuh! – Go on, get back inside. Where's the cover? [*He replaces the wooden cover of the smokehole, ramming it down over the old man's head.*] Down you go! I'd better put this log on top as well. Now think of another bright idea. Puff of smoke indeed! They'll be calling me son-of-a-smoke-screen next.

XANTHIAS: Look out, he's pushing at the door.

ANTICLEON: Hold him, push as hard as you can – I'll come and help. [*He runs down the stairs and joins Xanthias.*] Hold on to the latch – and mind he doesn't pull the peg out.

PROCLEON [*within*]: What do you think you're doing? Let me out, d'ye hear? I must get to court, or Dracontides'll get off.[13]

ANTICLEON: That'd be just too bad, wouldn't it?

PROCLEON: When I went to Delphi, the oracle said that if ever I let a man be acquitted I should just dry up and wither away.

ANTICLEON: Apollo preserve us, what a prophecy!

PROCLEON: Come on, please, let me out: do you want me to die?

ANTICLEON: I'm not going to let you out – ever.

PROCLEON: I shall gnaw through the net.

ANTICLEON: You haven't got any teeth.

PROCLEON: I'll kill you, I will: how can I do it, I wonder? Give me a sword – no, give me a juryman's tablet.

[*There is now an ominous silence.*]

ANTICLEON [*as an odd scuffling noise is heard*]: He's up to some real mischief now.

PROCLEON [*innocently*]: No, no, only I thought I'd just take the donkey down and sell him in the market – and the panniers too; it's the first of the month.

ANTICLEON: Couldn't I do that for you?

PROCLEON: No, not so well as I could.

ANTICLEON: Much better, you mean. All right, you can let the *donkey* out.

XANTHIAS: That was a subtle one! Just an excuse to get out.

ANTICLEON: Ha, but it didn't come off: I saw what he was up to. I think I'd better go in and fetch the donkey myself, in case the old blighter slips out. [*He carefully lets himself in, and shortly afterwards opens the door from the inside. He is trying to induce the donkey to come out, but the animal seems reluctant to move.*] Come on, gee up there, what's the matter with you? Fed up at being sold? C'mern there, get a move on: what are you groaning for? Anyone'd think you'd got Odysseus hanging on underneath.

XANTHIAS: Ye gods, but he has! There's somebody under there, anyway.

ANTICLEON: Where? Let me look.

XANTHIAS: Here he is, up this end.

ANTICLEON: Now then, what's all this? Who do you think you are?

PROCLEON [*from under the donkey*]: No-man.[14]

ANTICLEON: No-man, eh? Where are you from?

PROCLEON: Ithaca.

ANTICLEON: Well, No-man, you can get back to No-man's-land, sharp! Pull him out from under there, quickly. Oh, the disgusting old rascal – look where he's stuffed his head. I never thought we'd see our old donkey giving birth to a juryman!

PROCLEON: Leave me alone, can't you, or there'll be a fight.

ANTICLEON: What is there to fight about?

XANTHIAS: He'll fight you over the donkey's shadow, like the man in the fable.

ANTICLEON: You're a nasty, crafty, foolhardy old man.

PROCLEON: Nasty? Me? You don't realize now how delicious I am:
but wait till you've tasted juryman's paunch farci!

ANTICLEON: Get that donkey back into the house, and yourself too.

PROCLEON [*as he and the donkey are pushed back inside*]: Help, help!
Members of the jury! Cleon! Help!

ANTICLEON: You can shout as much as you like once I get this door
shut.

[XATHIAS *helps him to close and rebolt the door.*]

Now, pile a lot of those stones up against the door. Get that peg
back into its socket properly – that's right. Now – up with the bar:
heave! That's it – and now, quickly, roll that big mortar up against
it.

[*They mop their brows.*]

XANTHIAS: Hey, where did that come from? Great chunk of dirt
fell right on my head.

ANTICLEON [*looking up at the eaves*]: Perhaps there's a mouse up
there, knocked a bit of earth down.

XANTHIAS: Some mouse! Somebody's pet juryman, more like it.
Look, there he is, coming up through the tiles.

ANTICLEON: Oh, lord, he thinks he's a sparrow, he'll take wing at
any moment. Where's that bird-net? Shoo, shoo, get back inside!

[*They clamber up and push the old man's head back again, replacing
the tiles.*]

I'd as soon be keeping guard over Scione[15] as trying to keep this old
man indoors.

[*Everything now seems quiet.*]

XANTHIAS [*yawning*]: Ah, well, now we've shoo'd him in again, and
he can't slip past us now. Couldn't we have just a teeny weeny little
sleep?

ANTICLEON: Certainly not. Don't you realize that all the other jurymen'll be along any minute now to call for him?

XANTHIAS: But it's only just beginning to get light!

ANTICLEON [*to the audience*]: Then they must have got up late this
morning. They usually turn up soon after midnight, carrying
lamps and warbling the good old Phrynichean tunes – sweet, sticky,
and antique:[16] that's how they call him out.

XANTHIAS: Oh, we'll soon get rid of *them*: we can throw stones at
them, if necessary.

ANTICLEON: My poor mutt, if you provoke this gang of old geezers

46

it'll be like stirring up a wasps' nest. They've all got sharp stings in their behinds – and they know how to sting too! They shout and hop around and leap at you like sparks from a bonfire.

XANTHIAS: Don't you worry – as long as I've got enough stones I can scatter a whole swarm of jurymen, stings or no stings.

[*Nevertheless they are both soon asleep again. Very soon afterwards a curious buzzing sound is heard: this gradually resolves itself into the wheezing and mumbling of a group of aged jurymen, who form the Chorus. As they clump and hobble on to the stage, guided by small boys carrying rather feeble lamps, they are seen to be costumed as wasps, with vicious-looking stings behind. Over their costumes they wear tattered jurymen's cloaks. As they advance, the LEADER encourages his decrepit companions.*]

LEADER: Come along now, quick march! Pick 'em up there! Comias, old lad, you're getting left behind! Changed a bit since the old days, you have: used to be as tough as leather. Now even old Charinades can walk better than you. Ah, Strymodorus, there you are: my dear old fellow-juryman, how are you? What about Euergides, is he coming along? And old Chabes from Phlya? Ah, here they come – well, well, well, well. All that's left of the old battalion, eh? Remember that night in Byzantium, when you and me was on sentry duty together – we snitched the old girl's kneading-trough and used it for firewood, remember? Nice little bit of pimpernel we had for supper that night – cooked it up ourselves over the fire. [*He smacks his lips reminiscently.*] Well, you fellows, we'd better hurry along, it's Laches[17] up for trial today, don't forget. They say he's got a mint of money tucked away, you know, that Laches. And you heard what the Great Protector said yesterday: 'Come in good time,' he said, 'with three days' ration of bad temper in your knapsacks.' That's what Cleon said. 'You're the ones he's wronged,' he said, 'and you're the ones who're going to punish him.' [*He shakes his head sentimentally at the thought of Cleon's goodness.*] Well, comrades, we'd best be pushing on, if we're going to be there by dawn. And be careful how you go, you still need your lamps: there may be a *stone* lurking somewhere, waiting to trip you up.

BOY: Look out, Dad, it's muddy here.

LEADER: Get a twig and trim the wick a bit, lad, I can't see a thing.

BOY: No, I can pull it up with my finger, look!

LEADER: What are you thinking of, you stupid child, using your
finger like that? Don't you realize there's an oil shortage? [*He
clouts the boy.*] It's all very well for you, you don't have to pay for it.

BOY: If you're going to start using your fists on us, we'll jolly well
blow the lamps out and go home. And you can just jolly well find
your own way in the dark, splashing around in the mud like a lot of
old peewits.

LEADER: I've punished bigger people than you in my time, young
man, and don't you forget it. [*He slips in a puddle.*] Ugh! Now I've
walked right into it. – There's rain on the way; mark my words,
within the next four days there'll be a real downpour. See that
snuff on the wick? It's a sure sign. Ah, well, that'll be good for the
fruit trees; they want bringing on a bit, some of them. A bit of rain
and a north wind, that's what they need. – That's funny: here we
are at Procleon's house, and there's no sign of him. Not like him to
shirk his duties when there's a trial on – he's usually first in the line,
leading the singing: he's a great one for the old songs. Let's stop and
sing to him now, shall we? That ought to bring him out.

CHORUS:
Is there no one at the door?
This has not occurred before!
What has happened to our colleague overnight?
Some disaster, it is clear –
Did his slippers disappear?
Did he stumble as he fumbled for a light?

Did he stub his little toe?
That's a nasty thing, you know,
And may lead to complications if you're old.
If the toe is badly maimed
And the ankle gets inflamed
It may affect the groin, as I've been told.

It's extremely hard to say
What is keeping him away;
He's the sternest, sharpest stinger of us all.
No plea can make him blench
When he's sitting on the bench:
They might as well make speeches to a wall.

48

If I am not mistaken
It's because he was so shaken
By the plea that fellow yesterday submitted.
Of course it was all lies,
But it brought tears to our eyes,
And the bounder very nearly got acquitted.

But we got him in the end,
So cheer up, my dear old friend;
We need you very urgently today:
There's a very juicy case,
A conspirator from Thrace,
And we can't afford to let *him* get away!

LEADER: Get along, boy.

BOY: Dad, can I ask you for something?

LEADER: Yes, of course, what is it you want, son? Marbles, eh?

BOY: No, Dad, I'd rather have figs, that would be nicer.

LEADER: Figs! I'll see you hanged first!

BOY: All right, then, I won't come any farther. I'm going home.

LEADER: Figs, indeed! Don't you realize I have to buy porridge and firewood and meat for the three of us, all out of my jury pay? And you ask me for *figs*!

BOY [*after this has sunk in*]: Dad, suppose they don't summon a jury today, how are we going to buy our dinner? You'd be in rather a tight spot, wouldn't you?

LEADER: Oh, goodness me, what dreadful things you do think of. I'm sure I don't know where our dinner would come from.

BOY:　　Oh why, and oh why was I placed upon the earth,
　　　　And why, tell me why, did my mother give me birth?

LEADER: 'Twas but to give your father a life of misery –

BOY:　　And what is the use of an empty purse to me?

LEADER: Weep and wail, lament in chorus:

BOYS:　Woe, that e'er our mothers bore us.

[*The face of* PROCLEON *is seen at a small upper window, from which he has succeeded in removing part of the barricade.*]

PROCLEON: Oh with what anguish in my soul
　　　　　I've heard you through my tiny hole!
　　　　　How inexpressibly I yearn
　　　　　To join you at the voting-urn!

I long to come to court with you
Some solid, lasting harm to do;
But now, alas, it cannot be,
For I am under lock and key.

Oh would some god, with sudden stroke,
Convert me to a cloud of smoke!
Like politicians' words I'd rise
In gaseous vapour to the skies.

In pity for my sufferings dire
Scorch me, O Zeus, with heavenly fire!
Blow on me with thy breath divine –
And serve with vinegar and brine.

Or turn me, if it be thy will,
To stone – that suits me better still.
Part of the courthouse wall I'd be
And they could count the votes *on me*.

LEADER: Who is it that's keeping you shut up in there?
 [PROCLEON, *putting his finger to his lips, remains silent.*]
 Come on, you can tell us, we're your friends.
PROCLEON: My son. But don't shout so loud – he's asleep out in
 front there. Keep your voices down.
LEADER: But why is he doing it? What's his motive?
PROCLEON: He won't allow me to go to court: [*petulantly*] he won't
 let me do any harm to anybody. He wants to give me a good time,
 he says. I've never heard such nonsense. I don't *want* to be given a
 good time.
LEADER: Outrageous! It's a threat to democracy! He'd never dare to
 say such things unless he was plotting to overthrow the constitu-
 tion. Traitor! Conspirator! – But you must try to find some way of
 escape. Can't you get down to us without him seeing you?
PROCLEON: What way out is there? See if *you* can find one – I'll do
 anything, I'm desperate. If only I could get to court again! [*Lyric-
 ally*] I'm dying to file past the screens again, with the pebble in my
 hand!
LEADER: Couldn't you tunnel a way through the wall and come out
 disguised in rags, like wily Odysseus?

PROCLEON: They've stopped up all the holes: there isn't a chink a gnat could squeeze through. You'll have to think of something else. What do you think I'm made of? Cream cheese?

LEADER: Remember the Naxos campaign, and the way you stole those spits and climbed down the wall?

PROCLEON: Ah, yes, but things were different then. I was a young man, quick-footed and light-fingered; at the height of my powers. And I wasn't under guard: I could get away quite safely. But this place is besieged: there's a whole battalion of heavy infantry right across my line of retreat. There are two of them down by the door, watching every move I make. Anyone'd think I was the cat, trying to make off with tomorrow's joint. They're the ones that have got the spits.

LEADER: Come on, you've got to think up some way of getting out, quickly – it's getting light.

PROCLEON: Well, I'll have to gnaw through the net, I suppose. May Artemis forgive me![18]

LEADER: Spoken like a soldier! Forward to freedom! By the right – close – jaws!

[PROCLEON *gets to work on the net with his few remaining teeth. He has managed to remove a bit more of the wooden barricade, and can now get his head and shoulders through.*]

PROCLEON: I've gnawed a hole in it; but don't make a sound. We've got to be careful Anticleon doesn't catch us.

LEADER: Don't worry about him! One grunt out of him and we'll give him something to grunt about. We'll make him run for his life. That'll teach him to ride roughshod over the ballot box! – Now, tie that cord to the window, and the other end round yourself, and let yourself down. Be brave! Be a regular Diopeithes![19]

PROCLEON: Yes, but what am I going to do if they spot me when I'm half-way down and try to haul me back inside?

LEADER: Don't worry, we'll come to the rescue – won't we, boys? 'Hearts of oak are we all, and we'll fight till we fall' . . . They'll never be able to keep you in: we'll show them a thing or two.

PROCLEON: All right. [*He attaches the cord.*] Here I come – I'm relying on you. And [*emotionally*] if anything should happen to me – lift me gently, and spare a tear for my corpse. And bury me under the dear old courtroom floor.

LEADER: Nothing's going to happen to you, don't worry. Come along down like a brave fellow, with a prayer to your very own patron god.

[*From the folds of his clothes* PROCLEON *produces a statuette of the hero Lycus, in the form of a wolf.*[20] *This he now addresses in prayer.*]

PROCLEON:

O Lycus, lord and hero, let me turn to you in prayer:
It really is remarkable how many tastes we share.
You love the tears of suppliants, no sound can please you more,
And that is why you choose to live close by the courtroom door.
Have pity on your neighbour now, and lend your aid divine,
And I'll promise not to piddle in the reeds around your shrine.

[*Leaving the image behind him in the room, he climbs out and begins to descend, hanging on to the cord and feeling about with his feet for a foothold on the net.*]

ANTICLEON [*waking suddenly*]: Wake up there!

XANTHIAS: What's the matter?

ANTICLEON: I thought I felt a sort of noise. Is the old man trying to slip past you again?

XANTHIAS [*looking up and seeing Procleon*]: No, by heaven, he's letting himself down on a rope!

ANTICLEON: Here, what are you doing, you wicked old rascal? Don't you dare come down! [*To Xanthias.*] Quick, get up the rope and whack him with that harvest-festival affair. That ought to send him hard astern.

PROCLEON [*now half-way down*]: Stop him! Anyone got a case coming on this year? Smicythion! Tisiades! Chremon! Pheredeipnos!

[ANTICLEON *has meanwhile entered the house by the front door. He now appears at the upper window and starts to tug at the rope.*]

Quick, to the rescue, or they'll have me back inside!

[*The* CHORUS *prepare for battle as* XANTHIAS, *half-way up the rope, whacks Procleon from below with the harvest wreath, and* ANTICLEON *tugs from above.*]

CHORUS:

Comrades, why are we delaying[21]
When we should be up and slaying?
Turn, your deadly stings displaying,
Wave them in the air!

Let no reckless fool provoke us,
From our nest attempt to smoke us –
We will stand no hocus pocus!
    Let our foes beware!

Vengeance we agree on!
Run, boys, run to Cleon!
Raise a shout, and fetch him out:
    We know whose side he'll be on!

Here's a man who's roused our fury –
Wants-to-stop-us sitting on the jury;
But we wasps will soon make sure *he*
    Never sits again!

[*The* BOYS *run off, shouting. The* CHORUS *mill around like angry wasps, buzzing noisily.*]

ANTICLEON [*trying to make himself heard*]: Gentlemen! GENTLEMEN! Listen to me! And stop buzzing like that!

LEADER: We'll buzz as much as we like!

ANTICLEON: Because I don't propose to let him go.

CHORUS [*severally*]: Shame! – Scandalous! – Bare-faced tyranny! – Long live Athens! – Long live Theorus!

XANTHIAS: Help, they've got stings – look, sir.

ANTICLEON: They have indeed: as Philippus found at his trial.[22]

LEADER: And as *you're* going to find in a minute. Wasps! About . . . turn! Present . . . *stings*! By the right, in reverse, quick . . . *march*! Keep in line there!

    [*They close in on Xanthias.*]

Now then, let him have it! Put some spite into it! Show him what a wasps' nest he's stirred up!

    [XANTHIAS *hastily drops to the ground.* PROCLEON *follows him down, but* XANTHIAS *seizes him and uses him as a shield.*]

XANTHIAS: I don't fancy a fight with this lot, I must say. I don't like the look of those spikes of theirs at all.

LEADER: Let go of that man, or, I warn you, you'll wish you were a tortoise, with a nice thick shell.

    [XANTHIAS *releases Procleon.*]

PROCLEON: Now then, my fellow-jurymen, my savage-hearted

wasps! Some of you go for his backside: give it him hot, that's the way! You others surround him; jab at his eyes and fingers.

[*The* CHORUS *attack.* XANTHIAS *tries to seize Procleon, but is surrounded.* PROCLEON *makes a dash for freedom.*]

ANTICLEON [*from the window*]: Midas, Phryx, Masyntias! Here, quickly, get hold of him!

[*Three* SLAVES *rush from the house and grab Procleon.*]

And don't you let him go, d'you hear, or it's chains and no dinner for you. Don't mind them – they make a lot of noise, but it doesn't mean anything. All sizzle and splutter, like rissoles in a pan.

[*He withdraws from the window.* PROCLEON *struggles wildly, but is overpowered by the* SLAVES, *two of whom obtain a firm grip on his arms.*]

LEADER: Let him go, or we'll run you through.

PROCLEON: Oh, Cecrops, Lord and Hero![23] As a true Athenian, with the serpent blood in your veins – from the waist down, anyway – are you going to stand by and see me mauled by barbarians? Men who've had nothing but the best from me – *six* of the best, every time.[24]

LEADER: Such are the miseries of old age. Look at these two now, laying violent hands on their old master, without a thought for all he's done for them: the leather jackets, the shirts, the caps he's bought them, and all the care he's shown for their feet in the winter-time, making sure that they're nice and warm. No respect for old ... footwear at all.

PROCLEON [*to one of the two slaves holding him*]: Let me go, you brute! Have you forgotten what happened when I caught you stealing grapes? Didn't I tie you to the nearest olive tree and give you a hiding that made you the envy of the whole neighbourhood? Have you no sense of gratitude? Come on, let go of me, both of you, before that son of mine comes out again.

LEADER: You wait, my lads, you're going to pay heavily for this. And you won't have to wait long, either. You'll find out what it is to come up against men like us – sour-faced and stern and passionate.

[ANTICLEON *rushes from the house with an armful of smoking torches, which he distributes to the slaves.*]

ANTICLEON: At them, Xanthias, drive them back, away from the house!

XANTHIAS: Just watch me!

ANTICLEON [*to one of the other slaves*]: Come on, you too! Smoke 'em out! – Shoo, shoo! Go away! Buzz off! – Go on, hit them with it! What we need is Aeschines,[25] to gas them into a coma.

[*After a choreographic battle the* CHORUS *is beaten back.*]

XANTHIAS: There, I knew we'd beat them off in the end.

ANTICLEON: Lucky for you they've been training on Phrynichus and not on some of these modern songs. You'd have been overcome by the fumes!

CHORUS [*in disorder, taking refuge in derision*]:
Treason and treachery! Now it is clear!
Typical tyranny! Strikes from the rear!
See how this ruffian glories in wrong:
We have our hair cut short, his is cut long!

Who do you *think* you are? Simply because
You think you're somebody, *you* flout the laws!
Totalitarian, *that's* what you are!
Down with all tyranny! Shame on you! Yah!

ANTICLEON: Couldn't we drop all this fighting and shouting? Why don't we talk things over? Perhaps we could come to some agreement.

LEADER: Agreement? With you? An enemy of the people, a monarchist, a long-haired, tassel-fringed pro-Spartan, hand in glove with Brasidas?

ANTICLEON: Honestly, I'd just as soon do without a father altogether as embroil myself in this kind of altercation day after day.

LEADER: 'Embroil myself' – hark at him! If it's fancy phrases you want, let me tell you this: you ain't got past the trimmings yet – you're still picking at the parsley. Wait till the prosecutor flings these same charges at you in court: 'conspiracy' is the word *he'll* use.

ANTICLEON: Are you going to go away and leave me in peace, or stand here bickering all day?

LEADER: I'll not leave while I've a drop of blood left in my body. You're plotting to establish a monarchy.

ANTICLEON: It's 'monarchy' and 'conspiracy' all the time with you people: however trivial the offence, it's always the same charge – 'monarchism'. The word hasn't been heard in Athens for donkey's years, and now it's suddenly become as common as salted fish:

you can't even walk through the market without having it flung
at you. If you buy a perch instead of sprats, the man at the sprat
stall mutters 'Bloody monarchist!' If you ask the sardine man to
throw in a couple of spring onions, the woman at the vegetable
stall gives you a nasty sidelong look. 'A monarchist, that's what
you are,' she says. 'Do you expect the city to pay you a tribute of
onions?'

XANTHIAS: Like that tart I had yesterday, down town. I just happened to say, 'Come up on top, let's play king of the castle.' 'Cut
out that king stuff,' she says, 'we're democrats here.'

ANTICLEON: And these people [*he indicates the Chorus, but includes the
audience in his sweeping gesture*] lap it all up. Just because I want
my father to give up leading the life of a miserable snooping litigious early-morning prowler and live like a gentleman, I'm accused
of being a conspirator and a monarchist.

PROCLEON: Well, that's what you are. I wouldn't give up the life
I'm leading, not if you fed me on peacock's milk for the rest of my
days. I'm not interested in your lampreys and your eels in aspic –
give me a nice juicy lawsuit, done to a turn.

ANTICLEON: I know, I know – you've developed a taste for that sort
of thing. But if only you'd keep quiet and listen to me for a bit, I'm
sure I could convince you that you're quite wrong.

PROCLEON: Wrong, to sit as a juryman?

ANTICLEON: Worse than wrong: you don't realize how you're
being bamboozled by these men you almost worship. You're a
slave, without knowing it.

PROCLEON: Oh, ho, I'm a slave, am I? I hold the supreme power.

ANTICLEON: You think you do, but you don't. You're a lackey all
the time. Oh yes, I know – as an Athenian you can squeeze the
Greek world dry. But are you prepared to explain what *you* get out
of it personally?

PROCLEON: Certainly I am. Let these gentlemen decide between us.

ANTICLEON: All right, I agree to that. Let him go.

[*Procleon is released*].

PROCLEON: What's more, I'll speak on oath. Fetch me a sword.

[*One of the* SLAVES *fetches a sword and hands it to* PROCLEON,
who holds it stiffly before him.]

I solemnly swear that if I lose the argument I will plunge this sword
into my heart.

ANTICLEON [*prompting him*]: And if you fail to abide by the what-you-may-call it? The arbitrament?

PROCLEON: May I never drink neat pay again!

CHORUS:
> The orator who states our case, the champion of our school,
> If he would be advised by us, must keep this simple rule:
> Say something new, and say it well, and you will then
>   appear –

ANTICLEON:
> Go in and fetch my writing case, and quickly bring it here!
> [*A* SLAVE *departs on this errand.*]
> Yes, what will he appear, my friends, if he's advised by you?

CHORUS:
> To speak with more politeness than some younger people do.
> You see what you are up against: the contest will be tense,
> Such mighty matters are at stake; the issues are immense.
> If he should chance to beat you (which the gods forbid he
>   should) –
> [*The* SLAVE *returns with Anticleon's writing materials.*]

ANTICLEON:
> I'm going to write down every word: his speech had
>   best be good!

PROCLEON:
> Oh, please go on: if he should win – what were you
>   going to say?

CHORUS:
> Why, that would mean admitting that old men have had
>   their day.
> There'd be no further use for us, they'd mock us to our faces
> And call us affidavit-husks, the ghosts of parchment-cases.
> Be bold! Our sovereignty's at stake, and you must play
>   your part
> With every trick of rhetoric and glib persuasive art.

PROCLEON: Well, to get off to a flying start, I propose to prove to you that this power of ours amounts to nothing short of absolute sovereignty. Can you think of any living creature that is happier, more fortunate, more pampered, or more feared than a juror? No sooner have I crawled out of bed in the morning than I find great hulking fellows waiting for me at the bar of the court. As I pass, one of them slips his delicate hand into mine – the very hand he has dipped so deeply into the public funds; and they all bow down low, and plead with me in pitiful tones: 'Have pity, venerable sir,' they cry. 'Have you never made a bit on the side yourself? When you held some high office, perhaps, or went shopping for the corporal's mess?' That's how they talk to me – people who've never known of my existence till that moment, unless they've been tried before, *and* been acquitted.

ANTICLEON: Point one. Suppliants at bar of court. I'm noting that. [*He writes on his tablet.*]

PROCLEON: Then, after they've all crawled to me and tried to soften me up, I go behind the bar and take my seat, and forget all about any promises I may have made. I just listen to what they say – and there's nothing they won't say to flatter the jury in their efforts to get acquitted. Some of them bewail their poverty and pile on the agony: one will start quoting the legends, another comes out with funny stories from Aesop, or starts cracking jokes to make me laugh and put me in a good humour. And if he can't win me over that way, he drags his children out in front – all his little girls and boys: and I just sit and listen while they all grovel in a heap, bleating, and their father stands over them and pleads with me to ratify his accounts, for all the world as if I were a god. 'Master,' he cries, 'if thou delightest in the cry of the lamb, hear the cry of my son and have mercy. Or if thy tastes lie in other directions, let my daughter persuade thee.' And after that, perhaps I relax my severity a little. Isn't that power for you? Doesn't it make mere wealth look silly?

ANTICLEON [*writing*]: Makes – mere – wealth – look silly. And now tell me what advantages you gain from your dominion over Greece.

PROCLEON: Well, for one thing we see all the boys in the nude when they come up for inspection. And then – say we have Oeagrus up on a charge. He won't get off till we've heard him recite the big speech from *Niobe*. Or suppose we have a flute-player, and he wins his case, he'll show his gratitude by playing a nice tune for us on our way out. Suppose a man dies: he may have named a husband for his heiress, but what do we care for wills and solemn seals and signatures? We give her to the suitor who puts up the best show in court. And what's more, we can't be held to account afterwards, as the magistrates are. Theirs isn't real power: the real power belongs to us.

ANTICLEON [*making a further note*]: No, you're not held to account, and that's the first thing you've mentioned that I can really congratulate you on. But I'm not sure that I approve of tampering with the lady's seals.

PROCLEON: Then there's another thing: if the Council or the Assembly can't reach a decision on some big case, they hand the prisoner over to the jury courts. And then we have Evathlus and even the great shield-dropper himself[26] coming along to tell us that they'll never betray us, they'll fight for the people. And no one has ever had a motion carried in the Assembly unless they've arranged for the Courts to close down early so that we can attend. As for the Great Roarer, Cleon himself, we're the only people he never dares to nibble at: we lie safely in his arms and he keeps the flies off us. Which is a darn sight more than *you've* ever done for your old dad. Whereas a man like Theorus[27] – a man who ranks among the – a man who ranks – well, no lower than Euphemius – Theorus, I say, will come crawling to us with his jar and sponge to black our boots for us. You see? These are the kind of advantages you are trying to shut me away from; and you claim to be able to convince me that they amount to slavery and servitude!

ANTICLEON: Go on, have your say; you can't go on for ever, after all. And when you've finished, I'll tell you where you can put your precious power.

PROCLEON: I haven't yet mentioned the best thing of all: when I get home with my pay – ho, ho! they're all over me. Because of the money, you see. First my daughter comes to give me a wash and rub my feet with oil, and it's dear papa this and dear papa that, and she leans over to give me a kiss – and fish out those three obols with her tongue![28] And my little wife brings out a barley loaf to tickle my appetite and sits down beside me and presses me to eat: 'Do have some of this, do try one of these!' I enjoy all that – I don't want to have to depend on you and that steward of yours, and wait for him to bring me my lunch, muttering curses under his breath. As it is, if lunch is late, I've got this to stave off the pangs. [*He produces a squashed-looking cake from his wallet.*] And if *you* don't pour me any wine, I've got my donkey here. [*He brings out a vessel shaped like a donkey.*] Just tilt and pour. [*He demonstrates, pouring a jet of wine into his mouth. The wine comes out with a suggestive bubbling sound.*] You see what he thinks of you and your goblets! A fine martial bray!

[*He breaks into a dance, with the sword still erect in his right hand and the donkey-flask in his left.*]

[*Singing:*]

> The power of Zeus upon his throne
>   Is scarcely greater than my own.
> When people speak of me and Zeus,
>   The same expressions are in use:
> For when the court's assembled there
>   Our angry murmurs fill the air,
> And passers-by, in fear and wonder,
>   Exclaim, 'By heaven, how they thunder!'
> And when I flash, they cringe and cower
>   In dread of my almighty power,
> And, hoping that they won't be struck,
>   They click their tongues to bring good luck.
> The rich and powerful fear my frown
>   And tremble lest I bring them down;
> And *you* fear me, by heck you do –
>   I'm damned if *I'm* afraid of *you*!

[*The* CHORUS *burst into enthusiastic applause.*]

LEADER: A most sensible speech:
                    I enjoyed every word.
                 As frank an oration
                    As ever I heard.

PROCLEON: He thought he'd get by
                    Though his case *was* the weaker:
                 He never imagined
                    I'd shine as a speaker!

LEADER: A splendid performance,
                    Without any doubt.
                 He touched on each point,
                    And he left nothing out.

                 With pride and contentment
                    I felt myself swelling,
                 So fine were his words,
                    And his style so compelling.

60

> I honestly couldn't
> Have been more impressed
> If I'd been in a court
> In the Isles of the Blest.

[*The* CHORUS *applaud again.*]

PROCLEON:

You see the way he's fidgeting: he's clearly ill at ease.

ANTICLEON:

Before the day is over you'll be beaten to your knees.

CHORUS:

You'll have to weave a crafty web to make *that* boast come true.
The person who gets beaten is more likely to be you.
It takes a clever speaker to convert a hostile jury:
You'd better think of ways and means of countering our fury.
[ANTICLEON *clears his throat and takes up the posture of a professional orator.*]

ANTICLEON: It is a difficult undertaking, requiring a degree of skill and understanding far beyond the scope of the average – hm – comic poet, to cure the City of such an inveterate and deep-seated malady. [*He turns his eyes heavenward.*] But Thou, O Lord and Father –

PROCLEON [*thinking himself addressed*]: Now don't start Lord-and-fathering me: it won't get you anywhere. What you've got to do is to prove that I'm a slave, and you'd better hurry up about it. Otherwise I'll have to kill you. I suppose they'll debar me from the sacrificial feasts after that, but it can't be helped.

ANTICLEON: All right then, *Daddy.* Listen to me, and stop looking so stern. And for a start, just reckon up, roughly – on your fingers will do – how much tribute we get altogether from the subject cities. Add to that the revenue from taxes, percentages, deposits, the mines, market and harbour dues, rents, and confiscations. Add these up, and we get a total of nearly twelve million drachmas a year. Well, now work out how much of that annual sum goes to the jurors – six thousand of them, taking the maximum. And the total – am I right? – nine hundred thousand.

PROCLEON [*checking over the figures, in amazement*]: But that means – our pay doesn't even amount to ten per cent of the national income!

ANTICLEON: That's right.

PROCLEON: Then where does all the rest of the money go?

ANTICLEON: Why, it goes to those fellows you mentioned just now: 'I will never betray the Athenian – *riff-raff*! I will always fight for the – *rabble*!' The people you elect to rule over you, because you're taken in by their speeches. And on top of that there are the bribes they get from the subject cities: three hundred thousand drachmas at a time, extorted by threats and intimidation: 'If you don't pay up, I'll ruin your city with a single fulminating speech!' While you, apparently, are quite content to gnaw away at the left-overs: so much for your precious power. The subject states take one look at the scrawny rabble, feeding on scraps from the trough and greedily gobbling down nothing at all, and conclude that you aren't worth a tinker's damn, the whole lot of you. No, these others are the men they ply with gifts of pickle and wine and cheese and honey and sesame, rugs and cushions, cups and bowls, fancy cloaks and coronets and necklaces, and every conceivable luxury: and what do *you* get out of the empire you've sweated and fought for on land and sea? Not so much as a head of garlic to flavour your fish soup.

PROCLEON: That's true, I had to send out for three only yesterday. But when are you going to get to the point and prove that I'm a slave? I'm getting impatient.

ANTICLEON: Well, isn't it slavery when these men – and their stooges – all hold highly paid posts, while you sit back and croon with delight if you're given three obols? Obols which you yourself have toiled and rowed and battled and sieged into existence? And you're at their beck and call entirely. What infuriates me is to see some affected young pansy come mincing up to you, like this, and start ordering you around. 'You're to be in court first thing to-morrow morning. Anyone who isn't in his seat when the flag goes up will lose his three obols.' Huh! He'll get *his* fee as prosecutor all right – a whole drachma – however late he arrives. And they work together, too, do you know that? If a defendant comes up with a bribe, the two of them will share it, and then they'll play up to each other in good earnest, like two men with a saw – one gains a point, the other gives way. *You* never spot what they're up to, you're too busy gaping at the paymaster.

PROCLEON: No, no, it can't be true. They can't possibly do that sort

of thing to me. Now you really have shaken me, you know. I don't
know what to think.

ANTICLEON: Well now, think how rich you and everybody else
could be, if it wasn't for this gang of demagogues, keeping you tied
up just where they want you. Yes, I know you rule over scores of
cities, from the Black Sea to Sardinia: but what do you get out of it,
apart from this miserable pittance? Even that they squeeze out like
little drops of oil, just enough at a time to keep you alive. They
want you to be poor, and I'll tell you why: they're training you to
know the hand that feeds you. Then, when the time comes, they
can let you loose on some enemy or other: 'Go on! Good dog!
Bite him! That's the way!' If they really wanted to give the people
a decent standard of living, they could do it easily. At the moment
we have a thousand cities paying dues to Athens: give each of them
twenty men to feed, and you'd have twenty thousand of the
common folk feasting and banqueting on jugged hare and cream
cakes and beestings every day, with garlands on their heads, leading
a life worthy of the land they belong to, worthy of the victors of
Marathon. Instead of which you have to queue up for your pay
like a lot of olive-pickers.

PROCLEON: Here, here, what's coming over me? I've gone all limp,
I can't hold up the sword any longer. [*He lets his arm drop.*] All the
fight's gone out of me.

ANTICLEON: But if ever they get really scared – oh, then they'll
offer you the whole of Euboea, they'll promise you seventy-five
bushels of wheat all round. – But you never got it, did you? Five
bushels was all they dished out in the end, and barley at that: a pint
at a time, and then only if you could prove your ancestry. Do you
see now why I've been keeping you shut up? I want to look after
you properly, I don't want you made a mock of by these ranting
rhodomontaders. You've only to ask, and I'll give you anything
you like – except paymaster's milk.

[PROCLEON *remains silent. The* CHORUS *confer briefly, and then
announce their verdict.*]

CHORUS:
>   'You should never decide till both sides have been heard'
>   Is a saying that's ancient and true:
>   We are happy to state that you've won the debate
>   And converted us all to your view.

We freely admit we were hostile at first,
  But our anger has melted away;
So we'll lay down our staves (we don't *want* to be slaves)
  And agree to whatever you say.

LEADER:
  As for you, dear old friend, you must try to unbend,
    And confess that his argument's sound.
  If only *my* relatives talked such good sense
    I'd be keener to have them around.
  When the god of good fortune appears at your side,
    Such practical blessings bestowing,
  Don't choose to be stubborn, but hold out both hands
    For anything good that is going!

ANTICLEON:
  No pains I will spare: on appropriate fare
    I shall see that he's lavishly fed;
  A shawl he shall have, and a rug for his knees,
    And a woman to warm him in bed.

  But why is he silent? I don't like his looks;
    He ought to have spoken by now,
  If only to grumble: but no, not a word –
    And see, what a frown on his brow!

LEADER:
  I fancy he's feeling the pangs of remorse
    And his eyes have been opened at last;
  No doubt he's resolving to pay you more heed
    And make up for his faults in the past.

[PROCLEON *utters a piercing 'tragic wail', which must surely be audible throughout the length and breadth of Attica.*]

ANTICLEON [*who, like the Chorus, has completely forgotten Procleon's oath to kill himself if defeated in the debate*]: What on earth is the matter?

PROCLEON [*in the high tragic manner*]:
  Alas, what mean these promises to me,
    When all my heart lies yonder? How I yearn
  To sit once more among the things I love,
    And hear the chairman calling loud and clear:

64

'If any juror has not yet voted,
Will he please come to the urns immediately?'
And I would take my time – I always made
A point of voting last.

[*He raises the sword.*]

                              Speed, speed, my soul!

[*He strikes, but the sword becomes entangled in his clothing, and then in his beard.*]

Where *is* my soul? It must be under here.
Part, part, ye shady thickets, let me pass!²⁹
Yea, ten times rather die, by Heracles,
Than take my seat upon the bench again
And find my Cleon in the dock for theft!

[*He sinks to the ground, sobbing bitterly, as* ANTICLEON *gently relieves him of the sword.*]

SCENE 2: *The same*

ANTICLEON: Now, father, I beg you, listen to me and do as I ask.

PROCLEON: What is it you want me to do? One thing I'll never agree to.

ANTICLEON: And what's that?

PROCLEON: I won't give up jury work. On that point I shall stand firm to my dying day.

ANTICLEON: Yes, but if you're so set on trying cases, why bother to walk all the way down there to do it? Why not stay here and try your own household?

PROCLEON: Try them? For what? You're raving, boy.

ANTICLEON: You can do exactly what you do down there. Say one of the slave girls leaves the door on the latch – you can bend her over. I mean bind her over. That's the usual procedure, isn't it? And just think: if it's a fine sunny morning you can bask at your task; if it's snowing, you can sit by the fire; if it's wet, you don't have to go outside. And if you don't wake till midday, there'll be no court officer to lower the bar against you.

PROCLEON: I like the sound of that.

ANTICLEON: And what's more, if you get one of these speakers who just go on and on and on, you won't have to sit there starving, and then take it out on the defendant.

PROCLEON: Oh, but I'd never be able to judge so efficiently if I was chewing all the time.

ANTICLEON: Yes, you would – much more efficiently, in fact. Don't they always say, 'After chewing over the facts, the jury decided that the witnesses were lying?'

PROCLEON: You know, I'm beginning to like this idea. But there's one thing you haven't mentioned yet. Who's going to pay me?

ANTICLEON: I am.

PROCLEON: Good. That means I shall get the right change; I hate this sharing business. Do you know what that buffoon Lysistratus did to me once? They hadn't got change, so he and I were given a drachma between us, and we went to the fish market to change it. But what he put in my mouth[30] was three fish scales – I just stood there and let him do it, thinking they were obols. Ugh, the filthy-smelling things – disgusting! I had to spit them out, and then I went for him.

ANTICLEON: And what did he say?

PROCLEON: Oh, he laughed and said, 'Go on, you've got a stomach like a barnyard fowl: I bet it won't be long before you've digested the silver, anyway.'

ANTICLEON: Well now, you see what a lot you stand to gain by all this.

PROCLEON: Quite a lot, I agree. Very well, do as you wish.

ANTICLEON: Wait here, then, while I fetch the things.

[ANTICLEON *goes into the house.*]

PROCLEON: Well, look at that now, the oracles are coming true. I'd always heard that one day the Athenians would judge cases in their own homes; and that every man would build a tiny lawcourt in front of his house, like these little shrines of Hecate we have in the porch.

[ANTICLEON *returns with several* SLAVES, *laden with tables, benches, kitchen utensils, and other equipment, including a cock in a wooden cage. When the 'court' has been arranged to Anticleon's satisfaction, the* SLAVES *retire.*]

ANTICLEON: There, what more could you want? I've brought you everything I promised, and a lot more. Here's a jerry for you: let's hang it up here on the peg. Then it won't be far away when you need it.

PROCLEON: Now that I call a very sensible arrangement: just what an old man needs.

ANTICLEON: Right: now here's your fire [*he puts down a brazier*], and I've put a bowl of soup on to keep hot, in case you get hungry.

PROCLEON: That's a good idea too: now I can still get my pay even if I have a temperature. Just stay where I am and have my soup. But what have you brought that bird out here for?

ANTICLEON: To wake you up, of course, if someone makes a long speech for the defence and you go to sleep in the middle of it.

PROCLEON: There's only one thing missing now: everything else is fine.

ANTICLEON: What's that?

PROCLEON: No shrine of Lycus.

ANTICLEON: Yes, there is, I've got it here. [*He places an up-ended kneading trough at one side of the stage.*] And here's the hero in person. [*He produces the wolf image and sets it on the trough.*]

PROCLEON: Oh, Lycus, Lycus, how stern you look today!

ANTICLEON: Yes, he does look a bit like Cleonymus, doesn't he?

PROCLEON: Well, he's a hero without a shield, certainly.[31]

ANTICLEON: Now, the sooner you sit down, the sooner we can call the first case.

PROCLEON [*sitting down*]: I've been sitting down for ages. Call away, I'm ready.

ANTICLEON: Well now, what's the first case going to be? Has anyone in the house been misbehaving lately? Let's see – Thratta burnt the soup yesterday, didn't she?

PROCLEON: Hey, hey, wait a minute! What are you thinking of? You can't call a prisoner to the bar if you haven't got a bar! That's the most sacred thing of all.

ANTICLEON: You're right, we've forgotten that.

PROCLEON: I'll run inside and get one right away.

[*He leaps to his feet and runs into the house.*]

ANTICLEON: Now what's he up to? Dreadful the way homesickness takes some people!

[*Scuffling and shouting is heard from the kitchen, and a flustered* XANTHIAS *comes out of the house, brandishing a kitchen knife.*]

XANTHIAS: That ruddy dog! Beats me why we keep it at all.

ANTICLEON: What on earth is the matter?

XANTHIAS: Why, it's that dog Labes. Comes streaking into the kitchen, snatches up a fresh Sicilian cheese, and wolfs the lot.

ANTICLEON: Ha, that'll do nicely for the old man's first case. You'll have to attend as prosecutor.

XANTHIAS [*taking in the situation*]: Well, sir, actually the other dog has expressed a desire to open for the prosecution, if the case should come to court.

ANTICLEON: Very well then, bring them both here.

XANTHIAS: Very good, sir.

[*He goes into the house, almost colliding with* PROCLEON, *who is dragging a large wooden pig-pen through the door.*]

ANTICLEON: And what, may I ask, is that?

PROCLEON: It's the pig-pen from our inner sanctum.

ANTICLEON: Sacrilege, eh? What's the idea?

PROCLEON [*setting it up and taking his seat behind it*]: Nothing like starting from scratch, I always say. [*He rubs his back against the pen.*] Well, let's get on: I'm in a fining mood.

ANTICLEON: Wait while I get the notice-boards and the charge-sheets.

[ANTICLEON *goes into the house.*]

PROCLEON: You're driving me mad with all these delays. My nails are itching to plough through that wax again.

[ANTICLEON *returns with two wooden dishes, which he hangs up as notice-boards, and a bundle of documents. He sits down at a table.*]

ANTICLEON: There you are.

PROCLEON: Call on the case.

ANTICLEON: Right. – [*Calling out in an official voice*] Who appears before the Court?

PROCLEON: Damn and blast, what a fool I am. I forgot to bring out the urns. [*He starts to climb out of the pen.*]

ANTICLEON: Hey, where are you off to?

PROCLEON: To fetch the urns.

ANTICLEON [*picking up two large ladles and placing them on a table*]: No need to: that's what I brought these ladles out for.

PROCLEON [*resuming his seat*]: Ah, splendid. Now we really have got everything we need – oh no, we haven't a water-clock.

ANTICLEON [*indicating the jerry*]: What's that, then?

PROCLEON: My, you really have provided everything, haven't you? And all from local resources, as you might say.

ANTICLEON [*calling out*]: Bring me a taper, somebody – and we shall
    want some myrtle and incense. We must offer a prayer to the gods
    before we begin.

    [*One* SLAVE *brings out a taper, incense, and a libation-cup; another
    brings myrtle wreaths, which he places on the heads of all present.*]

CHORUS:

                We trust that by means
                    Of these prayers and oblations
                The seal may be set
                    On your friendly relations;
                And since you've decided
                    To cease being foemen,
                We'll gladly pronounce
                    A few words of good omen.

ANTICLEON: First let there be silence.

    [PROCLEON *and the* SLAVES *stand silent as* ANTICLEON *pours the
    libation and burns incense before the shrine of Apollo Aguieus in the
    porch. The* CHORUS *then chant their prayer.*]

CHORUS:

        Phoebus Apollo, grant that the transactions
        Soon to take place here, on thy very doorstep,
        May to thy servants, lately saved from error,
            Prove beneficial.

ANTICLEON:

        Master and neighbour, watcher of my doorway,
        Deign to accept the rite which now I bring you,
        Newly devised, worked out and cut to measure
            For my old father.

        Teach him to change his sharp and bitter nature,
        Soften his heart, and take away his sourness:
        Mix with his wrath a teeny drop of honey,
            Just as a sweetener.

        Oh, may he lose his nettle-sting of anger,
        Look upon men with eyes of loving kindness,
        So that his tears may flow for the defendant,
            Not the accuser!

CHORUS: Amen!

And now we'll gladly sing an Ode to start this novel session:
The chairman's opening words have made an excellent impression.
He seems to treat the People with a deep consideration
Not often found in members of the younger generation.

ANTICLEON [*calling out, as Court Officer*]: All jurors to take their places in the courtroom! No admittance after proceedings have begun!

[FIRST DOG *and* SECOND DOG, *as plaintiff and defendant respectively, enter from opposite sides, the latter escorted by two slaves in the capacity of guards.*]

PROCLEON: Which is the defendant?

ANTICLEON [*indicating Second Dog*]: This one.

PROCLEON [*rubbing his hands gleefully*]: Ha, wait till he hears his sentence!

ANTICLEON: Attention, please, for the indictment. Prosecution initiated by The Dog,[32] of Cydathenaeum, against Labes, of Aexone, on the ground that the said Labes did wilfully and feloniously wrong and injure one Sicilian cheese by eating it all himself. Penalty proposed: a figwood collar.

PROCLEON: No, no, a dog's death, if he's convicted.

ANTICLEON: The defendant, Labes, stands before the court.

[SECOND DOG *is led forward*].

PROCLEON: Oh, the brute! What a furtive look he has! Trying to get round me with that grin of his. Where's the plaintiff, the dog from Cydathenaeum?

[FIRST DOG *leaps forward and licks Procleon's face, wagging his hind-quarters ingratiatingly.* PROCLEON *pats him and gives him a plate of soup.*]

FIRST DOG: Bow-wow!

ANTICLEON [*as interpreter*]: Present!

PROCLEON: There, there now, quite a different kind of dog. Not like nasty Labes, eh? Knows how to bark and lick the plates, doesn't um?

ANTICLEON: Silence in court! Be seated! [*To First Dog*] Proceed with the charge.

PROCLEON [*ladling out some soup*]: I think I'll have some too, while this is going on.

FIRST DOG [*mounting the prosecutor's 'stand', an upturned pot*]: Gentlemen of the jury, you have heard the terms of the indictment filed by me against the defendant. He has committed the most atrocious offences, not only against me, but [*his voice rises to a scream*] against every single rating in the fleet – to wit and namely: ran away into a corner and *sicilicated* a large quantity of cheese and stuffed himself with it in the dark.

PROCLEON: The case is proved. A moment ago he belched in my direction. The odour of cheese was unmistakable. Disgusting creature!

FIRST DOG: On being asked by me for a share, he refused. I put it to you, gentlemen, how can anyone claim to be serving your interests if I, The Dog, am not given my proper share?

PROCLEON: Didn't he give you any at all?

FIRST DOG: No, not even to me, his own partner. He's hot and fiery –

PROCLEON [*taking a mouthful*]: Ow! So's this soup.

ANTICLEON: Now, father, I beg you, don't decide against him before you've even heard both sides.

PROCLEON: My dear boy, the thing's as plain as a pikestaff. It fairly shouts at you.

FIRST DOG [*confirming this by shouting at the top of his voice*]: Don't you acquit him, do you hear? He's a monophagist, that's what he is, an eat-it-all-your-self-ist. He's the most confirmed monophagist in the whole history of dogkind. Why, he cruised all round that island and gnawed all the plaster off the cities.[33]

PROCLEON: And here I am without enough to mend a pot with.

FIRST DOG: He must be punished for all this. There's no room for two thieves in one kitchen. And I don't see why I should go on barking for nothing. If you refuse to convict him, you'll not get another yap out of me. [*He stands down.*]

PROCLEON: Dear, dear, dear, what a lot of crimes you've accused him of. He must be a very dishonest sort of fellow. [*He appeals to the cock.*] Mustn't he, old cock-a-doodle? – Yes, look, he's winking at me, he agrees. – Officer! – Where's the man got to? – I want the chamber pot.

ANTICLEON: Take it down yourself. I have to call the witnesses.

[PROCLEON *takes down the pot and turns his back on the audience.*] Witnesses for the defendant's character, come forward!

[*As their names are called, the* WITNESSES *file out of the house, bow*

71

solemnly to Procleon's back, and take up their positions on the defendant's side of the court.]

Citizen Bowl! Citizen Pestle! Citizen Cheese-Grater! Citizen Brazier! Mistress Pot! And all the rest of you – come on, never mind if you *have* got burnt bottoms! [*To Procleon*] Ah, so you've run dry at last!

PROCLEON [*resuming his seat and pointing at Second Dog*]: I can tell you who's going to be *squeezed* dry very soon!

ANTICLEON: Must you always be so stern and severe, even with poor fellows who are up for trial? You've always got your knife into them. – Prisoner, stand up and make your defence.

[SECOND DOG *mounts another upturned pot, but remains tongue-tied.*]

ANTICLEON: Why don't you speak? Get on with it!

PROCLEON: He doesn't seem to have anything to say.

ANTICLEON: Thucydides[34] had the same trouble at *his* trial: sudden attack of paralysis of the jaw. [*To Second Dog*] All right, stand down: I'll conduct the defence myself.

[*He takes Second Dog's place on the 'stand'.*]

Gentlemen. Hr'm. It is a difficult undertaking to reply on behalf of a slandered dog, but nevertheless I will try. Hr'm. He is a good dog. He chases away the wolves.

PROCLEON: You mean he's a thief and a conspirator.

ANTICLEON: Not at all, he's the finest dog alive. Capable of guarding any number of sheep.

PROCLEON: What's the good of that, if he eats up all the cheese?

ANTICLEON: Why, he fights for you and guards the house, and he's a noble dog in every way. What if he did filch something? Can't you make allowances? After all, he was never taught to play the harp.

PROCLEON: Personally I think it's a pity he was even taught to read and write. Then he wouldn't have been capable of such disgraceful effrontery as to enter a defence.

ANTICLEON: Sir, will you please listen to my witnesses? Citizen Cheese-Grater, will you come up and testify? And speak up.

[CHEESE-GRATER *steps forward.*]

You were serving as quartermaster, I understand?

[CHEESE-GRATER *nods.*]

And what you grated was for the troops?

72

[CHEESE-GRATER *nods vigorously.*]

He says it was.

PROCLEON: He's lying.

[CHEESE-GRATER *and other witnesses leave the 'court', and* ANTI-
CLEON *braces himself for the final defence speech, which he delivers
with great emotion.*]

ANTICLEON: Kind sir, have pity on a creature in distress. While this
dog, Labes, slaves away untiringly, eating up the gristle, devouring
the fish-bones, always on active service, his opponent stays at home:
he's fit for nothing else. Stays at home – but demands his share of
anything that's brought in. And bites if he doesn't get it.

PROCLEON: This is dreadful: what's happening to me? I'm soften-
ing! I must be ill. You're beginning to convince me!

ANTICLEON: Come, father, I implore you, have pity on him, don't
send him to his ruin. Where are his children?

[*A* SLAVE *goes into the house and returns with a large family of puppies.*]

Unfortunate creatures, come up here and plead. Entreat him, pray
to him, with tears and whimpers!

[*The* PUPPIES *crowd round Anticleon's feet and set up a chorus of
lamentation.*]

PROCLEON [*in tears*]: Enough, enough! Stand down.

ANTICLEON [*in tears*]: I will. Though many a man has heard those
words in the past, and been deceived, yet, nevertheless, I will –
[*he sobs*] stand – down.

[*As soon as he can disentangle his feet from the puppies, he steps down
from the stand.*]

PROCLEON [*struggling to control his emotion*]: It's this confounded soup.
I knew it was a mistake. I'm quite sure I'd never have started
weeping like that if I hadn't been stuffed with soup.

ANTICLEON: You're going to acquit him, then?

PROCLEON [*hardening*]: It's hard to say.

ANTICLEON: Come, father dear, now's your chance to turn over a
new leaf. Take this pebble; screw up your courage and shut your
eyes, rush straight over to that second urn, and acquit him.

PROCLEON: No. *I* was never taught to play the harp, either.

ANTICLEON: Come on, I'll help you.

[PROCLEON, *still blinded by tears and in a state of great confusion,
allows* ANTICLEON *to help him out of his pen.*]

I'll take you the quickest way round.

[*He takes the old man's arm and leads him by a circuitous route so as to reach the 'acquittal' urn first. Here he pauses.*]

PROCLEON: Is this the first urn?

ANTICLEON: Yes.

PROCLEON: In she goes, then.

[*He drops the pebble into the urn, and* ANTICLEON *helps him back to his seat.*]

ANTICLEON [*to the audience*]: Foiled! He's acquitted him – unintentionally! [*To the slaves*] I'll empty them out now.

[*With great pomp and ceremony the* SLAVES *lift the two ladles and lay them before Anticleon.*]

PROCLEON: Well, how did it go?

ANTICLEON: We shall see in a minute.

[*Further rituals have to be carried out before the* SLAVES *empty out the ladles on to two dishes. One dish is empty, the other contains Procleon's pebble. The* SLAVES *hand the dishes to Anticleon, and retire.*]

ANTICLEON: Labes, you are acquitted.

[PROCLEON *falls in a dead faint as* SECOND DOG *joyfully embraces his puppies and leaves the court, a free dog.* FIRST DOG *sweeps out in disgust.* ANTICLEON *hurries across to his father.*]

ANTICLEON: Father, father! What's the matter? Holy gods, fetch some water, somebody.

[ANTICLEON *supports his father: a* SLAVE *brings water, which* ANTICLEON *dashes in the old man's face.*]

Sit up, that's the way.

PROCLEON [*faintly*]: Tell me – was he really acquitted?

ANTICLEON: Yes, he was indeed.

PROCLEON: May heaven forgive me!

ANTICLEON: Bear up now, don't take it to heart.

PROCLEON: How can I ever look myself in the face again? I have acquitted a prisoner! Oh, gods above, forgive me, it was an accident, it wasn't like me at all.

ANTICLEON: Now listen, there's nothing to get upset about. From now on I'm going to look after you properly: I'll take you out with me to all kinds of places, we'll go out to dinners and drinking parties and shows, and you'll be able to have a really good time now: and no Hyperbolus to trick you and laugh at you up his sleeve. Let's go in.

PROCLEON [*meekly*]: All right, if you say so.

[ANTICLEON *leads his father into the house, while the* SLAVES *clear away the 'courtroom' properties, leaving the Chorus in possession of the stage.*]

LEADER: In you go, then, and good luck to you.

CHORUS:

> Now, ye countless tens of thousands,
>   Seated on the benches round,
> Do not let our pearls of wisdom
>   Fall unheeded to the ground.
> Not that *you* would be so stupid,
>   So devoid of common sense –
> What it is to have enlightened
>   People for an audience!

[*The* LEADER *of the Chorus comes forward and addresses the audience.*]

LEADER:

> Now once again, spectators, if you love
> To hear plain speaking, pay attention, please!
> The author has a bone to pick with you
> For treating him unfairly, when, he says,
> You've had so many splendid things from him.
> Not always openly – in earlier days
> Full many a joke of his came from the lips
> Of other poets, while he lurked unseen
> And spoke through them, with ventriloquial art;[35]
> Till finally one day he ventured forth,
> Driving a team of Muses of his own,
> And won great honour, such as none before
> Had been accorded. Yet he did not rest
> Upon his laurels, suffer from swelled head
> Or flounce about the wrestling-schools, like some
> Successful poets we have known, nor yet
> Would he consent to prostitute the Muse
> And hold some simpering stripling up to scorn
> To satisfy a lover's jealous whim.
>
> No, when he first put on a play himself,
> He didn't bother to attack mere men!
> Scorning such petty fry, our Heracles

Took on the greatest monster in the land.[36]
Jag-toothed it was, and from its staring eyes
Shot rays more terrible than Cynna's smile;
And in a grisly circle round its head
Flickered the tongues of servile flatterers,
Foredoomed to groan; its voice was like the roar
Of mighty floods descending from the hills,
Bearing destruction: noisome was the stench
That issued from the brute as it slid forth,
With camel's rump and monstrous unwashed balls.[37]

Undaunted by the sight, he stood his ground
(In spite of all attempts to buy him off)
And fought on your behalf, and still fights on.
And then, last year, he says, he made assault[38]
On all those plagues and fevers, nightmare shapes
That came and hovered by your beds at night,
Smothering fathers, choking grandfathers,
And pinning lawsuits, summonses, and writs
On harmless, peaceful folk, till many leapt
In terror from their beds, and formed a queue
Outside the office of the Polemarch.[39]

So once again your Champion fought for you
And sought to purge the land of grievous ills.
And what did you do then? You let him down.
For when he tried last year[40] to sow a crop
Of new ideas, you failed to see the point,
And all was wasted; yet, with hand on heart,
He swears by Dionysus that in fact
There never was a better comedy.
The shame is yours for being so obtuse.
No man of sense will think the worse of him
If, driving so much better than the rest,
He passed them all – and overshot the goal.

> And if ever in future
>   A poet appears
> Who can give you a play
>   That is full of ideas,
> With a plot that is fresh

And a line that is new,
I advise you to give him
The praise that's his due.
If some of his phrases
Are cutting and keen,
Never mind if you don't
Understand what they mean:
Like quinces or apples,
When laid up in store
They will keep their fresh flavour
A twelvemonth or more.
So seize his fine notions,
Opinions, and views,
And pack them away
With your shirts and your shoes,
And next year, when again
On these benches you sit,
Why, even your clothes
Will be scented with wit.

CHORUS:

In the days when men were men
(And you should have seen us then)
We were noted for our vigour and agility;
We carried all before us
Both in battle and in chorus,
And no one could have questioned our virility.

Those days, alas, are gone,
And the feathers of the swan
Are no whiter than our hair, for we are old;
And yet, as you can see,
Feeble relics though we be,
In spirit we're still manly, young, and bold.

Yes, we may be poor old crocks,
But the whiteness of our locks
Does the City better credit, I would say,
Than the ringlets and the fashions
And the pederastic passions
Of the namby-pamby youngsters of today.

LEADER:

Should it strike you, dear spectators, as a somewhat curious thing
To find me thus embellished with a wasp-waist and a sting,
A word will be sufficient to complete your education
And elucidate the meaning of our garb and conformation.
Allow me, then, to mention that I feel a certain pride
In the handy little weapon that protrudes from my backside;
For the warriors who possess it are of native Attic birth,
As stubborn and as brave a breed as ever trod the earth.
'Twas we who served the City best when those barbarians came
And tried to smoke us from our nests, and filled the streets with flame.
Tight-lipped with rage, we ran straight out with warlike spear and
    shield;
Our hearts were set on battle, and we faced them in the field.[41]
All day we went on fighting, but Athena's owl had flown
Across our ranks that morning, and we knew we weren't alone:
So thick with arrows was the air, we couldn't see the sun,
But when the shades of evening fell we had them on the run.
We stung them in the eyebrows and we stung them in the cheeks;
We jabbed them in the buttocks through their baggy Persian breeks;
And among barbarian nations we're respected to this day –
'There is nothing so ferocious as an Attic wasp,' they say.

CHORUS:

Ay, we were dreaded in our day!
The Persians tried to get away,
    But that was not to be;
For, having beaten them on land
Our gallant three-tiered ships we manned
And, closing in on every hand,
    We walloped them at sea.[42]

Not one of us could make a speech,
Denounce, arraign, inform, impeach,
    Nor yearned such arts to master.
From these ambitions we forbore:
A question that concerned us more
Was how to ply a lusty oar
    And make the ship go faster.

78

This being so, we rowed with ease
To cities far across the seas
    And took them from the Persians;
And if the tribute-money still
Flows into the Imperial till
(From which the young now steal their fill)
    It's due to *our* exertions.

LEADER:

Now anyone who studies us from various points of view
Will find that we resemble wasps in everything we do.
No creature, to begin with, is more savage and irate,
When once provoked, than we are, or less easy to placate.
Observe our social structure and you'll see that it conforms
To that of wasps exactly – we are organized in swarms;
And according to the jury that we're privileged to be on
We buzz about the Archon's Court, or nest in the Odeon.
And some, like grublets in their cells, are packed around the wall:
They nod their heads, but otherwise they scarcely move at all.
Our economic system, too, is practical and neat:
By stinging all and sundry we contrive to make ends meet.
Of course we have our drones as well, dull stingless brutes who shirk
Their military duties, letting others do the work –
And sure enough they gobble up as much as they can get
Of the income *we* have earned them with no end of toil and sweat.
It makes us wild to think that those who've never raised a hand
Or risked a single blister to defend their native land
Can draw their pay with all the rest: I think the rule should be
That if you haven't got a sting you get no jury fee.

ACT TWO

SCENE I: *The same. Two couches have been placed outside the house*

[PROCLEON *comes out of the house, followed by* ANTICLEON *who is trying to pull the tattered brown juryman's cloak from his father's shoulders. In attendance is a* SLAVE, *carrying a heavy woollen gown and a pair of smart Laconian shoes.* PROCLEON *is protesting loudly.*]

PROCLEON: Nobody's going to strip me of this, I tell you. Not while there's breath in my body. We've stood shoulder to shoulder against many a cold north wind, my cloak and I.

ANTICLEON: Don't you *want* to be given a treat?

PROCLEON: No, I don't. Treats aren't good for me. Last time it was grilled sprats, and look what happened afterwards. The whole of my three obols went to pay the cleaner's bill.

ANTICLEON: Now, look – you've put yourself in my hands, for your own good: you might at least make an effort.

PROCLEON: What is it you want me to do?

ANTICLEON: Take off that shabby old cloak and throw this gown over your shoulders.

PROCLEON: Lot of good having sons and bringing them up, if all they can do is try and suffocate you!

ANTICLEON: Come along, get it on and don't talk so much.

    [*The* SLAVE *holds up the gown as* ANTICLEON *removes the old man's cloak.*]

PROCLEON [*wriggling away*]: In the name of all the gods, what *is* this horrible thing?

ANTICLEON: It's a Persian gown: some people call it a 'full-waister'.

PROCLEON: I thought it must be one of those goatskin things from the country.

ANTICLEON: You *would*. Now, if you'd ever been to Sardis,[43] you'd have known what it was; but it seems you don't.

PROCLEON: I most certainly don't. Looks to me like one of Mory-
chus' fancy wrappings.

ANTICLEON: No, these are woven in Ecbatana.

PROCLEON [*inspecting the sheepskin lining*]: What from? Tripe?

ANTICLEON: Really, you're hopeless! Don't you realize that this is
an extremely expensive Persian weave – why, at least sixty pounds
of wool must have gone to the making of this.

PROCLEON: In that case they ought to call it a *wool*-waster, not a *full*-
waister.

ANTICLEON: Now stand still and get it on, there's a good fellow.
[*Helped by the* SLAVE, ANTICLEON *succeeds in getting him half-way
into the gown.*]

PROCLEON [*wriggling away*]: Pouf, it's belching hot steam at me!

ANTICLEON: Come on, put it on.

PROCLEON: No! If I've got to be roasted, you might just as well
put me straight in the oven and have done with it.

ANTICLEON: Here, I'll help you myself. – All right, you can go.
[ANTICLEON *takes the gown from the slave and drapes it over
Procleon's shoulders. The* SLAVE *retires.*]

PROCLEON [*staggering under the weight*]: I hope you've got a fork
handy.

ANTICLEON: Whatever for?

PROCLEON: To fish me out before I'm stewed to pieces.

ANTICLEON: Now, undo those dreadful felt shoes and put on these
Spartans, quickly.

PROCLEON: Spartans? I wouldn't soil my sole with them. That's
enemy footwear, that is!

ANTICLEON: Come along, stick your foot in like a brave fellow.
[*He helps him on with one of the new shoes.*]

PROCLEON: I little thought I should ever set foot on enemy leather.

ANTICLEON: Now the other one.

PROCLEON: No, not that foot! The big toe's a rabid anti-Spartan.

ANTICLEON: Can't help that. On with it!
[PROCLEON, *with a show of reluctance, takes the second shoe. They
really are extremely smart and warm-looking.*]

PROCLEON: This is terrible! Now I shan't have a single chilblain to
comfort me in my old age.

ANTICLEON: Get it on quickly – that's right. And now let me see
you walk. No, no! Like this – with an elegant plutocratic swagger.

[PROCLEON, *having made his protest, is beginning to enjoy himself. The shoes are certainly very comfortable. He struts about happily.*]

PROCLEON: Just like one of your wealthy friends, eh? [*Adopting a mincing gait*] Which of them do I look like now?

ANTICLEON: You look like a boil with a garlic plaster on it.

PROCLEON: I shall have to practise this bottom-waggling business.

ANTICLEON: Well now, if you're going to mix with clever, educated men, will you be able to produce an impressive anecdote?

PROCLEON: Of course I will.

ANTICLEON: What will you tell them?

PROCLEON: Oh, I know lots. There's the one about that Vampire that farted when she got caught; or I could tell them what Cardopion did to his mother –

ANTICLEON: No, not that mythical stuff: something from real life – the kind of thing people usually talk about. Give it a domestic touch.

PROCLEON: Domestic, eh? Well, how about this? Once upon a time there was a cat and it met a mouse, and –

ANTICLEON: My dear fellow, where *were* you brought up? – as Theagenes said to the crossing-sweeper. You can't start talking about cats and mice to men of quality.

PROCLEON: What kind of thing do they want, then?

ANTICLEON: Something impressive. You know – 'Once when I was on a State mission with Androcles and Cleisthenes . . .'

PROCLEON: The only State mission I've ever been on was to Paros. They paid me two obols a day.⁴⁴

ANTICLEON: Well, then, tell them how you remember seeing Ephudion in his old age and how he wiped the floor with Ascondas; what a fine figure of a man he still was, for all his white hair: great strong hands, superb torso, good firm thighs – and how he passed out top of the whole list.

PROCLEON: Don't be silly! How could he win a wrestling match if he'd passed out?

ANTICLEON [*shrugging this off*]: That's the kind of conversation these bright sparks go in for. Now, here's another thing. If you're drinking with strangers, they'll want to know something about you. Could you tell them about some daring exploit of your younger days, perhaps?

PROCLEON: Like the time I pinched all the vine-props from old
Ergasion's vineyard!

ANTICLEON: You and your vine-props, you'll be the death of
me! No, you want to tell them how you went boar-hunting
or coursing, or ran in the torch race – some feat of sportsmanship.

PROCLEON: Sportsmanship, eh? Well, once, when I was little more
than a lad, I did take on Phayllus, the runner. And I beat him, too.
Yes, I sued him for slander, and won the case by two votes.

ANTICLEON: Well now, come and lie down over here. [*He indicates
the two couches.*] I'll show you how to behave at a fashionable
drinking party.

PROCLEON: Lie down? How am I supposed to lie?

ANTICLEON: Just recline, gracefully.

[PROCLEON *clambers on to one of the couches and lies down on his
back, with his knees up.*]

No, no, not like that, for heaven's sake!

PROCLEON: How, then? Show me.

ANTICLEON: You must straighten your knees – that's it – and sort of
pour yourself back into the cushions with a supple athletic grace.

[ANTICLEON *demonstrates, taking up a reclining position on the
other couch.* PROCLEON *practises 'pouring' himself into the cushions
until* ANTICLEON *is satisfied.*]

Good. But now you should say something complimentary about
the bronze ornaments – look up at the ceiling – admire the rugs on
the wall.

[PROCLEON *mimes all this as instructed.* ANTICLEON *now claps his
hands to summon the slaves, who have been briefed in advance. At each
stage of the imaginary party* ANTICLEON *demonstrates the correct
procedure and table manners.* PROCLEON *attempts to imitate his
gestures.*]

Bring the finger-bowls! [*The* SLAVES *do so.*]

Bring in the tables! [*The* SLAVES *do so.*]

Now we eat ... now wash hands again ... now the libation.

[*The* SLAVES *whisk away the tables.*]

PROCLEON: Was I dreaming, or were we supposed to be having
dinner?

ANTICLEON: Now, the flute-girl has played her piece, and you are
drinking with – let's say – Theorus, Aeschines,[45] Phanos, Cleon,

and that foreign fellow, the son of Acestor. He's at Cleon's head.
Can you take up a catch when it comes to your turn?

PROCLEON: Oh, yes, I'm good at that.

ANTICLEON: Well, we shall see. Now, I'm Cleon: suppose I start off
with 'Harmodius': and you have to cap it.

[Sings:]
Such a man was never seen in Athens . . .

PROCLEON [sings]:
Such a low-down, thieving little bastard . . .

ANTICLEON: If you sing that, you'll never survive the uproar: he'll
swear to have your blood, he'll threaten to ruin you and drive you
out of the city.

PROCLEON: If he threatens me, I've got another song for him:
[Sings:]
Take care, if too high in the city you rise,
You'll make her top-heavy and then she'll capsize!

ANTICLEON: And now supposing Theorus, lying next to Cleon,
takes his right hand and starts up this one:
[Sings:]
It's wise, as Admetus found out in the end
To choose a good man for your very best friend.
How are you going to cap that?

PROCLEON: Oh, I've got something very poetical for that.
[Sings:]
It isn't as easy, old boy, as it sounds
To run with the hare and to hunt with the hounds.

ANTICLEON: And now it's Aeschines's turn. He's a very learned,
cultured sort of fellow – he'll start off with [sings, rowdily]:

What a lot of money,
Power and propertee!
What a time we had of it,
Up in Thessalee![46]
Oh, we showed them what was what,
Clitagora and me –

PROCLEON [sings]:

I can boast to you, dear,
And you can boast to me.

ANTICLEON: Well, you seem to have got the idea pretty well. All
right, we'll go and have dinner at Philoctemon's. [He claps his

hands.] Boy! Pack up the food, we're going out on a binge for once in a while.[47]

PROCLEON: No, I don't approve of drinking, I know what wine leads to: breaches of the peace, assault and battery – and a fine to pay before you've got rid of the hangover.

ANTICLEON: Not if you're drinking with real gentlemen. They'll pacify the victim for you – or you can smooth him down yourself: just come out with a neat quotation from Aesop, or one of the stories about the Sybarites – something you heard at the party. Make a joke of the whole thing, and he'll just go away quietly.

PROCLEON: I see I shall have to learn a lot of those stories, if I want to avoid getting fined in future. Well, my boy, what are we waiting for? Let's go.

[XANTHIAS *brings out a basket of food.* PROCLEON *and* ANTI-CLEON *set out for the party, with* XANTHIAS *in attendance.*]

CHORUS:

> At last he has fallen on happier days,[48]
> And I envy his lot beyond measure:
> He's about to exchange his abstemious ways
> For a life of refinement and pleasure.
> It may not be easy at first, I dare say,
> A lifetime's opinions to smother;
> Yet many men find that they *can* change their mind
> When sincerely convinced by another.
> His son, as all right-thinking men will agree,
> Has displayed both good sense and devotion:
> His kindness and charm are so touching to see
> That I'm quite overcome with emotion.
> In preparing his sire for a life that is higher
> He has countered each single objection;
> The success he has had in defeating his dad
> Is a proof of his filial affection!

SCENE 2: *The same, a few hours later. It is now dark*

[XANTHIAS *re-enters from the street, rubbing his bruises and mutter-ing mutinously.*]

XANTHIAS: You want to be a ruddy tortoise in this job, with a shell to protect you. Clever, those tortoises are: roof yourself over with good strong tiles, and keep the blows off, I call that sensible. I'm black and blue from that stick.

LEADER: What's been going on, boy? – Boy, did I say? Well, I suppose that's right if you've just had a hiding, however old you are.

XANTHIAS: Well, the old man's been making the most frightful nuisance of himself: he's drunker than any of them. And that's saying something, considering who the others are: there's Hippyllus, Antiphon, Lycon, Lysistratus, Theophrastus, and Phrynichus with all his gang – but *he* got wilder than anybody. Once he'd got a bit of good food and drink inside him, he started leaping about like a young ass after a feed of barley: jumping up and down, laughing and farting – you should have seen him. Then he started knocking me about. 'Boy! Boy!' he kept shouting. And Lysistratus saw what was happening and started the comparison game. He told the old man he reminded him of a newly rich Phrygian, or a donkey that had got loose in a hayloft. 'Oh, I do, do I?' he shouted back. 'Well, *you* remind *me* of a locust when it's just shed its worn-out wings, or Sthenelus the actor shorn of his trimmings.' Well, everyone applauded – except Theophrastus, who looked down his nose. He fancies himself as a wit, you know. So the old man turns on Theophrastus: 'And who are you to give yourself airs and think yourself so smart, always sucking up to the man of the moment?' And that's how he went on, insulting them all one after the other, making crude jokes and telling very coarse stories, quite unsuitable to the occasion, I must say. Then, when he was quite drunk, he came away, knocking down everybody he met on the way home. Here he comes. Reeling drunk! I'm going to make myself scarce, before I get another pasting.

[*Angry shouting is heard offstage, and* XANTHIAS *hurries into the house as* PROCLEON, *still wearing his party garland, staggers into view. He has one arm round the shoulders of a* FLUTE GIRL *whom he has abducted from the party. In his free hand he carries a torch, with which he holds at bay an indignant crowd of fellow-revellers.*]

PROCLEON: Up and at 'em!

[*The* REVELLERS *scatter as he lunges at them with the torch.*]

Chase me, would they? Wait till I get at one of them: I'll make things hot for him all right. Clear off, you lousy scabs, or I'll serve you up grilled for breakfast.

REVELLER: All very fine and heroic, but you'll pay for this to-morrow, d'you hear? We'll be round in the morning, the whole lot of us, and you'll answer for this in court.

PROCLEON: In court? Yah! Boo! You're out of date, chums: I won't even hear the place mentioned. Yah! Yippee! To blazes with the voting urns: [*fondling the girl*] I prefer these. Are you going, or aren't you? Juryman? What juryman? Get out of my sight!

[*The* REVELLERS *withdraw, murmuring angrily.*]

Come on up here, my little ladybird. Hold on to this rope. Be careful, it's a bit old and worn: but you'd be surprised what it'll stand up to. That was a neat bit of work, getting you away from those fellows, you must admit. Just at the crucial moment, eh? Well, now you can show your gratitude, and be nice to *me*. But no, you won't, you'll let me down, you'll laugh at me. It won't be the first time you've left a man standing. But listen, you be nice to me, and when my son dies I'll buy you your freedom and have you for a concubine, how would you like that, eh? I've got the money, you see, but I'm not allowed to handle it myself just yet – not till I'm a bit older. It's my son, you know, he watches every move I make: he's a terrible old skinflint, and very strict. You see, I'm his only father. Sh! Here he comes. Looking for us, probably. Quick, take this torch and stand quite still: I'm going to pull his leg a bit – the way he used to make fun of me before I was – initiated.

[ANTICLEON *enters. He has been running.*]

ANTICLEON: Oh, there you are, you clot-pated old fornicator! What are you trying to do, screw yourself into your coffin? You'll never get away with this.

PROCLEON: Ah, how you'd love a nice court case, with vinegar dressing!

ANTICLEON: Is this a time for sauce? It's a serious matter, kidnapping a flute girl.

PROCLEON: Flute girl? What flute girl? Come to me with one foot in the grave and babble about flute girls?

ANTICLEON: Yes, this girl you've got here – Dardanis.

PROCLEON: Oh, you mean this torch. Yes, someone's burning it in honour of the gods, I suppose.

ANTICLEON [*prodding the girl*]: A torch, did you say?

PROCLEON: Surely. Pretty pattern it has on it, don't you think?

ANTICLEON: H'm. What's this dark patch in the middle?

PROCLEON: Oh, they get like that sometimes. It's the resin.

ANTICLEON: And what's this lump at the back? Feels uncommonly like a bottom to me.

[*The* GIRL *squeals.*]

PROCLEON: Oh, er – that's where there was a branch sticking out.

ANTICLEON: Branch my foot. [*To the girl*] You come with me.

PROCLEON: Here, here, what are you going to do?

ANTICLEON: Take her away from you. I don't believe you could have done anything about it anyway: you're too old for such things.

PROCLEON: Oh, indeed? Well, let me tell you something. Once when I was on a State mission to the Olympic Games, I saw Ephudion fight Ascondas, and the old man fought very well, let me tell you. I shall never forget the way he drew back his arm, like this – and then, with a smashing blow, he knocked the young man down.

[*He suits the action to the word. The* GIRL *escapes.*]

And the moral is: watch out, or you'll get a black eye.

ANTICLEON [*staggering to his feet*]: Well, you certainly seem to have learnt *that* lesson!

[*Enter a* BAKING-WOMAN, *with an empty tray.*]

BAKING-WOMAN [*to Anticleon*]: Oh, help me sir, please: that's the man! Pretty near did for me, he did, banging me with his torch like that. Ten obols' worth of loaves he knocked off this tray: ten obols' worth, and four over.

ANTICLEON: You see what you've done. More troubles, more fines to pay, all because of your drinking.

PROCLEON: No, no, these affairs can all be settled if you know how to tell a good story. Leave her to me, I'll soon straighten this out.

BAKING-WOMAN: No one's going to treat *me* like this and get away with it, I can tell you – I'm a respectable baking-woman, I am. Myrtia, daughter of Ancylion and Sostraté. You've destroyed my whole stock.

PROCLEON: Listen, my good woman, I – I wonder if you've heard this one. Very amusing.

BAKING-WOMAN: Now don't you start anything with me, old lad, it's not on.

PROCLEON [*clearing his throat like a professional raconteur*]: One night Aesop was walking home – he'd been dining out – when he was

88

barked at very rudely by an intoxicated bitch. 'Bitch,' said Aesop, 'bitch, instead of standing there yapping you'd be better advised to – go and buy some more flour!' [*He laughs immoderately at this.*]

BAKING-WOMAN: On top of everything, he laughs in my face. All right then, mister whoever-you-are, I'm summoning you before the Market Court for damage to my stock.

[*The philosopher* CHAEREPHON *is seen wandering along the street, deep in meditation.*]

Hi! Chaerephon! You'll act as my witness.[49]

[*She drags the bewildered* CHAEREPHON *into the middle of the stage, and points an accusing finger at Procleon.*]

PROCLEON: No, no, listen to this: I'm sure you'll see the point of this one. Once when Lasus found he was competing against Simonides,[50] he said – ha, ha, ha! – he said, 'What's that to me?'

BAKING-WOMAN: Oh, he did, did he?

PROCLEON: And as for you, Chaerephon, witnessing for a woman – you remind me of one of Euripides' heroines begging the author for a square deal.[51]

[*The* BAKING-WOMAN *storms out, dragging* CHAEREPHON *with her. The next visitor is a* CITIZEN *with a bandaged head. He has brought a friend with him to act as witness.*]

ANTICLEON: Here comes somebody else to summon you, by the look of it. He's brought a witness with him, I notice.

CITIZEN: I'm bringing an action against you for assault and battery.

ANTICLEON: Oh, no, for heaven's sake, that's a criminal charge.[52] I'll pay you compensation on his behalf – willingly. How much do you want?

PROCLEON: No, I'll be glad to settle this with him myself: I admit I knocked him about quite a bit. [*To the Citizen*] Come over here a minute. Will you leave it to me to decide how much I should pay you, so that we can be friends in future? Or would you rather name the sum yourself?

CITIZEN: Let's hear your offer. I don't really want all the fuss and bother of a court case.

PROCLEON: Reminds me of the story of the man from Sybaris who fell out of a chariot, and managed to injure his head pretty severely – he wasn't a very good driver. A friend of his came along, and said, 'A man should stick to his own trade.'

CITIZEN [*politely*]: Ha, ha.

PROCLEON [*suddenly changing his tone*]: Well, then, I'm not a doctor, am I? Get along to the hospital.

ANTICLEON: This is what I should have expected, the way you've been behaving.

CITIZEN [*to his friend*]: Take note of what he said.

[*The* CITIZEN *and his* FRIEND *prepare to go.*]

PROCLEON: Listen, don't go away. You know about the woman from Sybaris who broke a jug?

CITIZEN [*to his friend*]: I call you to witness.

PROCLEON: That's exactly what the jug did. It called a friend to witness. And the woman said, 'If you spent less time calling people to witness, and went out and bought a rivet, you'd be showing more sense.'

CITIZEN: Go on, insult me – till your case comes up in court!

[*The* CITIZEN *and his* FRIEND *depart in great indignation.*]

ANTICLEON: I'm not letting you stay here a moment longer, do you understand? I'm going to heave you over my shoulder – [*he does so*] – and carry you inside. Otherwise there won't be enough people left to act as witnesses for all these complainants.

PROCLEON [*kicking and struggling*]: When the – Delphians – accused Aesop –

ANTICLEON: Never mind about Aesop now.

PROCLEON: – of stealing a sacred cup, he told them the story of the beetle that –

ANTICLEON [*putting his hand over Procleon's mouth*]: One of these days I'll beetle *you*.

[*He carries Procleon indoors.*]

LEADER [*addressing the audience*]:[53]
　　I flatter myself I'm a bit of a lad,
　　　　And I've learnt all the tricks of the trade;
　　But there's one man I know – and he's in the front row –
　　　　Who can put even me in the shade.
　　Can you guess who I mean? He has upper-class hair
　　　　It's done up in a bun on the top:
　　And he gambles with dice, which is quite a nice vice
　　　　Provided you know when to stop.
　　But Amynias[54] didn't: you'd think, with no cash,

He would starve on an apple a day;
Yet he dines like the wealthy, and keeps very healthy –
Just how does he manage it, pray?
If you mention his recent Thessalian jaunt
He does get a little bit testy;
But it can't have been that – for a person so poor
Would only have met the *Penestae*.

Automenes, you happy man,
How proud you needs must be
To have three sons of such renown
And such ability!
The eldest is a friend to all
And plays upon the lyre;
The second plays upon the stage
With passion and with fire.
But young Ariphrades[55] is much
The brightest of the three:
In one respect, at least, he was
An infant prodigy.
They took him to a lady once
Who said that she could teach
Him twenty ways of making love
At half an obol each:
But when she'd taught him all she knew
(Or so his father swore),
He turned the lady upside down
And taught her twenty more.

[*The* LEADER *now masks himself to represent the* AUTHOR.]

Some people have been saying that since Cleon tanned my hide[56]
I've made a coward's peace with him and let my wrath subside.
They heard me scream blue murder when the dirty deed was done,
And rolled up in their hundreds – it was their idea of fun.
They didn't care a rap for me: they shouted 'Treat him rough!
'He may say something funny if you squeeze him hard enough.'
And so I bluffed them for a while, but now it's time to stop:
And won't the vine look foolish when I pull away the prop!

[XANTHIAS *comes out of the house, mopping his brow, and sits down.*
The LEADER *rejoins the Chorus.*]

XANTHIAS: Phew! You've no idea of the pandemonium that's broken loose in this house. The old man's not used to all that strong drink, and what with that and the music, he's so elated that we can't do anything with him. Looks as if he'll go on dancing all night, at this rate. He's been giving us 'Scenes from Thespis',[57] if you please: says the modern dancers are all old dotards, and threatens to come out and prove it by dancing a match with them.

[*Shouts, thumps, and flute-playing are heard within.*]

PROCLEON [*within*]: What ho! Who sitteth at the outer gate?

XANTHIAS: The curse has come upon us – what did I tell you?

PROCLEON [*within*]: Fling wide the portals, ho!

[*Nonchalantly,* XANTHIAS *crosses to the door and unbolts it.*
PROCLEON *flings it open dramatically and stands poised on the*
threshold, ludicrously dressed in the tights of a tragic dancer.]

         ... And let the dance begin!

     Tensed up to spring the dancer stands,
     With ribs stretched taut like metal bands;
     At last he takes a leap, and lands ...

XANTHIAS: In the madhouse.

[*In actual fact* PROCLEON'S *leap has landed him in the middle of the*
stage. He now demonstrates the type of dance that he admires.]

PROCLEON:

     With nostrils flared he snorts amain,
     His backbone creaks beneath the strain;
     Look out, he's going to leap again ...

XANTHIAS: What you need is a dose of hellebore.

PROCLEON: Now Phrynichus[58] admits defeat:
     See how he crouches at my feet!

XANTHIAS: You're mad: they'll stone you in the street.

PROCLEON: With soaring leg I touch the sky!
     Can modern dancers kick so high?

XANTHIAS: They'll split their arses if they try.

PROCLEON: And as the dancer leaps and whirls
     Each joint within its socket twirls.
     Now what d'you think of that? Not bad!

XANTHIAS: I've told you what I think – you're mad.

PROCLEON: Well, now for my challenge. If there is any tragic dancer present who claims to dance well, let him come forward and dance a match with me. No takers?

XANTHIAS: Only one: that fellow over there.

[*A* DANCER *costumed as a crab presents himself, using his hands as extra feet.*]

PROCLEON: That miserable creature? Who is he?

XANTHIAS: One of the sons of Carcinus the Crab.[59] The middle one.

PROCLEON: Pooh! I can swallow him at one gulp. I'll soon dispose of him with a knuckle dance. [*He beats out a rhythm on the crab-dancer's 'shell' with his knuckles. The* DANCER *wriggles away.*] Bah! He's got no sense of rhythm!

XANTHIAS: Here comes another tragic Crablet – his brother.

[*A larger* 'CRAB' *enters.*]

PROCLEON: I seem to be buying up the whole stall.

XANTHIAS: Crabs, crabs, and yet more crabs – here comes another of the tribe.

PROCLEON: This creeping creature? What is it? A shrimp, or a spider?

XANTHIAS: This is the tiniest of them all: the Little Nipper. He writes tragedies.

PROCLEON: Carcinus, I congratulate you on a fine brood of tomtits. Well, I must go down and take them on. And, Xanthias – you'd better start mixing the dressing, in case I win. I like them with plenty of salt.

CHORUS:
Make way, make way! The human tops are all wound up to spin;
Stand back and make a space for them, and let the show begin.

[*The* CHORUS *withdraw to the rear of the dancing area. While the* SONS OF CARCINUS *perform the Dance of the Crabs,* PROCLEON *executes a burlesque solo and the* CHORUS *sing the final lyric.*]

Ye sons of Him who rules the waves
 And brothers of the prawn,
Come where the salty ocean laves
 The sands where you were born.

Oh whirl and twirl upon the beach,
 Rotate with supple ease;
Then stand upright and try to reach
 Your stomachs with your knees.

Now kick straight upwards from the hips
   As Phrynichus might do,
And draw from each spectator's lips
   Admiring cries of 'Coo!'

Till crawling from the barren deep
   The proud Crustacean comes
To watch his offspring frisk and leap
   And spin like teetotums.

The time has come to end our play;
   But you can dance before us;
And this at least it's safe to say –
No comic poet till today
Has hit on such a clever way
   Of sending off his Chorus.

[*The* CHORUS *march out, preceded by the* SONS OF CARCINUS,
leaving PROCLEON *to finish his dance and receive the applause of the
audience.*]

The Poet and the Women
(Thesmophoriazusae)

Introductory Note to *The Poet and the Women*

The Festival of the Thesmophoria, from which the comedy took its Greek name, was celebrated every October (the time of the autumn sowing) by the women of Athens. On the first and third days of the festival they performed various religious rites; the second day was kept as a solemn fast. For the period of the festival the women took over the Pnyx (the hill upon which the Athenian Assembly held its meetings) and lived in tents. Men were strictly excluded from the celebrations, the nature of which was a strict religious secret. No doubt a good deal of humorous speculation was indulged in by husbands and sons on these occasions.

The *Thesmophoriazusae* (*The Women Celebrating the Thesmophoria*) was performed in 411 B.C. It contains some of Aristophanes' most brilliant parody as well as some of the funniest low comedy ever staged. It is full of gaiety and high spirits, and there is scarcely a word about politics or the war. Structurally it is of interest as illustrating the increasing freedom with which Aristophanes was adapting the traditional choral framework of *parodos – agon – parabasis* (see Introduction, p. 13) to his own dramatic requirements. The play as a whole is more closely knit than some of its predecessors, each episode having a direct bearing on the predicament of the protagonist, whose rescue is delayed till the very end of the play.

This comedy is not an attack on Euripides. The great tragedian had long been a favourite butt of comedy, and the conventional stage caricature of him was the embodiment of a well-established comic legend. Like many great men, the real Euripides was regarded with a mixture of admiration and distrust; and one method of defence against a man whose ideas are a little disturbing is to make a comic figure of him. Whatever Aristophanes may have thought of the real Euripides (and we come closer to finding out in *The Frogs*), in this comedy he is dealing with the legend, not the man. It is the old joke about the ingenuity of Euripides' plots. Let us put this ingenious fellow into a tight spot, says Aristophanes (the other old joke about his attitude to women will come in handy here), and see how many clever devices he can think up for our amusement. On the whole, Euripides comes out of it all rather well. And to Euripides the poet it cannot have been altogether unflattering to have practically a whole comedy devoted to parodies of his work.

CHARACTERS

EURIPIDES *the poet*
MNESILOCHUS *an old man, related by marriage to Euripides*
AGATHON *the poet*
CLEISTHENES *a notorious effeminate*
SERVANT *to Agathon (a slave)*
A MAGISTRATE
A SCYTHIAN CONSTABLE

FIRST WOMAN (MICCA, *wife of Cleonymus*)
SECOND WOMAN *a seller of myrtle in the Market*
THIRD WOMAN (CRITYLLA, *friend of First Woman*)
ECHO

Chorus of Athenian women

Silent Characters

MANYA *nursemaid to First Woman*
PHILISTA *another maid to First Woman* } *(slaves)*
A DANCING GIRL

ACT ONE

SCENE 1: *A Street in Athens*

[*Enter the poet* EURIPIDES.[60] *He enters briskly, apparently looking for a house; but keeps stopping to wait impatiently for his companion, who shuffles wearily behind him. This is* MNESILOCHUS, *an elderly relation by marriage, whose only desire at the moment is to sit down and rest.*]

MNESILOCHUS: They say the swallow brings fresh hope: I wish I could see one. – This man'll be the death of me: he's been lugging me about ever since dawn. Listen, Euripides: before I fall to pieces entirely, I should like to hear where you are taking me.

EURIPIDES: You can't talk about *hearing* things that you are going to *see*.

MNESILOCHUS: Eh? What? I can't hear . . . ?

EURIPIDES: Things that you're going to see.

MNESILOCHUS: And I suppose I can't see –

EURIPIDES: Things that are meant to be heard: exactly.

MNESILOCHUS: I don't follow, it's too clever for me. You mean I mustn't either hear *or* see?

EURIPIDES: The two concepts are, in the very nature of things, sharply differentiated.

MNESILOCHUS: You mean *not* hearing and *not* seeing?

EURIPIDES: Precisely.

MNESILOCHUS [*after a pause for thought*]: How do you mean, differentiated?

EURIPIDES: Let me explain how all these things were sorted out in the first place. When Ether first split herself up, and creatures capable of movement came into being within her, for purposes of visual perception she devised the eye – in imitation of the disc of the sun. For hearing, however, she provided a funnel, known as the ear.

MNESILOCHUS: Oh, I see. I mustn't hear or see, because of this funnel. Very kind of you to explain, I must say. What it is to have an intellectual in the family.

EURIPIDES: Oh, I can teach you any number of things like that.

MNESILOCHUS: Well, suppose we stop here and you can teach me how to be lame in both legs, like the fellow in your play.

[*He squats down in imitation of a lame beggar, and settles himself comfortably.* EURIPIDES *wanders off until he discovers the house he is looking for.*]

EURIPIDES: Come over here and give me your attention.

MNESILOCHUS [*getting up reluctantly and shuffling across*]: Well?

EURIPIDES: Do you see that door?

MNESILOCHUS [*peering at it; he suspects a verbal trap*]: Why, yes.

EURIPIDES [*with his finger to his lips*]: Keep quiet.

MNESILOCHUS [*copying his gesture*]: Keep quiet about the door?

EURIPIDES: Sh! Listen!

MNESILOCHUS [*putting his ear to the door*]: Not a word about the door, eh?

EURIPIDES: Listen to *me*, I mean. This is where the famous Agathon lives, the tragic poet.[61]

MNESILOCHUS: Agathon? What sort of a fellow would he be, now? I did know an Agathon once. Big, strong, dark fellow.

EURIPIDES: No, no, not that one.

MNESILOCHUS: Then I don't know him. – Oh! You mean that chap with the long bushy beard!

EURIPIDES: Come, come, you must have seen him.

MNESILOCHUS: No, I'm sure I haven't. Not so as to recognize him, anyway.

EURIPIDES: Ah, well, he meets most of his clients during the night-time, I suppose. Quick, come over here, out of sight! Here's a servant coming out with a brazier and myrtle twigs. He must be going to offer up a prayer for inspiration.

[*The* SERVANT *comes out of Agathon's house and sets up his paraphernalia. He begins to speak in high-pitched, priest-like tones.*]

SERVANT: Let all the people keep silence, and be ye closed, O ye mouths! Inasmuch as the Muses in mellifluous concourse do grace these lordly halls with their presence! Let not the air be moved with any commotion of breezes; and the blue wave of the sea, let it not roar.

MNESILOCHUS: Blah!

EURIPIDES: Sh! What's he saying?

SERVANT: Be still, ye tribes of birds, and lie down; neither let any foot of beast be heard in the forest.

MNESILOCHUS: Blah, blah!

SERVANT: For Agathon our champion, Agathon the fair of speech is about to –

MNESILOCHUS: What, in broad daylight?

SERVANT: Who said that?

MNESILOCHUS: A commotion of breezes.

SERVANT: – is about to lay the keel of a new drama, yea, with mighty crossbeams shall it be builded, with new arches of words shall it be constructed. For behold, he turneth the verses upon the lathe and sticketh them together; maxim and metaphor doth he hammer out, yea, in melted wax doth he mould his creation: he rolleth it till it be round; he casteth it –

MNESILOCHUS: And stuffeth it up his fanny.

SERVANT: Who is this ill-bred provincial who presumes to profane these private premises with his proximity?

MNESILOCHUS: Someone who'll take you and your precious poet and perforate your posteriors with his private protuberance.

SERVANT: You must have been a very rude little boy – when you *were* a little boy.

EURIPIDES [*to the Servant*]: Now, my good man, never mind about him. Call Agathon for me – you must get him out here at all costs.

SERVANT [*in a more natural voice*]: Nothing easier: he's coming out any minute now, to do some composing. It's this wintry weather, you know: very hard to bend the strophes into shape – has to bring them out into the sun.

[*The* SERVANT *goes into the house.*]

MNESILOCHUS: What about me, what am I supposed to do?

EURIPIDES: Stay where you are, he's coming out here. [*He begins to lament dramatically.*] Oh, Zeus, oh, Zeus, what shall I do this day?

MNESILOCHUS: I must say I should like to know what all this is in aid of. Why do you keep groaning like that? What's worrying you? Come on, you can tell me, I'm one of the family.

EURIPIDES: There's trouble brewing for me today.

MNESILOCHUS: What kind of trouble?

EURIPIDES: This day decides whether Euripides is to live or to die.

MNESILOCHUS: How can it? The juries aren't sitting today. Nor is the Council. Why, it's the second day of the Thesmophoria.

EURIPIDES: That's just it! And I fear it'll be my last. The women have been plotting against me. And today, at the Thesmophoria, they're going to discuss my liquidation.

MNESILOCHUS: But why on earth . . .?

EURIPIDES: They say I slander them in my tragedies.

MNESILOCHUS: Well, so you do. Serve you right if they did get you. – How do you plan to escape them?

EURIPIDES: I thought of persuading Agathon to go to the Thesmophoria.

MNESILOCHUS: What do you want him to do there? Tell me more.

EURIPIDES: He could sit in the assembly with all the women, and speak in my defence, if necessary.

MNESILOCHUS: What, openly? Or in disguise?

EURIPIDES: Disguised. Dressed up in women's clothes.

MNESILOCHUS: What a magnificent idea! That's really up to your best standard. For downright cunning, we take the cake,[62] I must say.

EURIPIDES: Sh!

MNESILOCHUS: What is it?

EURIPIDES: Agathon's coming out.

[*The front of the house swings open, revealing* AGATHON, *cleanshaven and bewigged, wearing female attire and seated at a dressingtable.*]

MNESILOCHUS: Where? I can't see him.

EURIPIDES: There he is, don't you see? Coming round on that revolving affair.

MNESILOCHUS: I must be going blind. I can't see a man there at all. Only someone who looks like Sinful Cyrene in person.

EURIPIDES: Be quiet, he's getting ready to sing.

[AGATHON *rises, clears his throat, and utters a few practice trills and arpeggios in a fruity falsetto.*]

MNESILOCHUS: He's got ants in his larynx.

[AGATHON *sings, taking the part of Chorus Leader and Chorus of Maidens alternately. An invisible chorus joins in the singing of the choral stanzas. The music is skilful and attractive, but over-florid, with a touch of parody about it.*]

AGATHON

[*As Leader:*]

> Come, ye maids, receive the torches
> Sacred to the twain infernal!
> Dance, your voices freely raising
> In the fashion of your homeland.

[*As Chorus:*]

> Which God shall we celebrate, then?
> We are only too delighted
> Any of the gods to worship
> On the slightest provocation.

[*As Leader:*]

> Sing, for lo! the archer Phoebus
> With his bow of gold appeareth,
> By his presence sanctifying
> All the glades of fair Simois.

[*As Chorus:*]

> With our fairest songs we greet thee,
> Phoebus, on thy throne of glory
> O'er all graceful arts presiding
> And the sacred prize bestowing.

[*As Leader:*]

> Praise ye now the virgin huntress,
> Ranger of the tree-clad mountains.

[*As Chorus:*]

> Child of Leto, maid untainted,
> Artemis, we glorify thee.

[*As Leader:*]

> It is time to mention Leto
> And the lyre that sets us dancing
> To the subtle Phrygian rhythm
> When the strings go twingle twangle.

[*As Chorus:*]

> We have not forgotten Leto
> Or the twangling harp of Asia,
> Mother of our songs and dances:
> Loudly let us sing their praises!

[*As Leader*:]
> Now with eyes divinely flashing,
> Voices raised in sudden outcry,
> Sing the praise of lordly Phoebus.

[*As Chorus*:]
> Hail to thee, O son of Leto!

MNESILOCHUS: Ah, what soft seductive strains! How feminine, how deliciously voluptuous! What titillation of the senses! Sexy stuff, it does things to you. – And as for you, my young friend, I can only ask, in the words of Aeschylus: 'Whence art thou, womanish creature? What is thy costume, what thy fatherland?' Tell me, why this perturbation of nature? A lute, a yellow gown? A lyre and a hair-net, a woman's girdle and a wrestler's oil flask? A sword and a hand-mirror? It doesn't make sense. What are you – a man? Then where's your cloak? Where are your shoes? And what have you done with your tool? But if you're a woman, what's happened to your bosom? Well, speak up! If you won't tell me, I shall have to judge by your singing.

AGATHON: Come, come, my aged friend, do I detect a note of envy in your criticism? I refuse to be riled. I wear my clothes to suit my inspiration. A dramatic writer has to merge his whole personality into what he is describing. If he is describing a woman's actions, he has to participate in her experience, body and soul.

MNESILOCHUS: What an exhausting time you must have when you are writing about Phaedra!

AGATHON: If he's writing about a man, he's got all the bits and pieces already, as it were; but what nature hasn't provided, art can imitate.

MNESILOCHUS: Let me know if you are writing a satyr play, and I'll come and help with the rude bits.

AGATHON: Anyway, it's terribly uncultured for a poet to go round looking all wild and hairy. Look at Ibycus, and Anacreon of Teos, and Alcaeus, with those exquisitely tempered harmonies of theirs – they all wore the proper minstrel's sash, and their movements were graceful, like mine. [*He demonstrates.*] And Phrynichus, you actually went to his recitals perhaps:[63] what a handsome fellow and how beautifully dressed – and that's why his dramas were so beautiful too: what you write depends so much on what you *are*, you know.

MNESILOCHUS: Ah, that explains why that shocking fellow Philocles writes such shocking verse. And why Xenocles writes so *badly*, and Theognis so *frigidly*.[64]

AGATHON: Of course it does. And knowing this, I gave myself the full treatment.

MNESILOCHUS: How did you manage that, for goodness' sake?

EURIPIDES: Don't bark at him like that! I was just the same myself at his age, when I first began writing.

MNESILOCHUS: Then I don't envy you your training.

EURIPIDES: Now, if you don't mind, I should like to get down to business.

AGATHON: What's on your mind?

EURIPIDES: Agathon, I – well, a wise man keeps his speeches short. I'm in trouble again and I want you to help me.

AGATHON: And what can I do for you?

EURIPIDES: The women are meeting up at the Thesmophoria today, and [*he sobs*] they're going to condemn me to death for slandering them.

AGATHON: And what help do you imagine *I* can give you?

EURIPIDES: All the help in the world. If you would only go up there secretly and take your seat with the women, just as if you were one of them, you could speak up for me and save my life. Only you could do it – but *you* could make a speech that would really be worthy of me.

AGATHON: Why don't you go there yourself and conduct your own defence?

EURIPIDES: Well, obviously, in the first place I'm well known by sight. Secondly, I'm old and white-haired and bearded; whereas you are good-looking, fresh-complexioned, clean-shaven, you have a woman's voice and a dainty manner, you'd be quite pretty to look at.

AGATHON: Euripides!

EURIPIDES: Yes?

AGATHON: In one of your plays, a character says: 'You love your life: your father loves his too.'[65]

EURIPIDES: That's right.

AGATHON: Then why do you expect me to bear your misfortunes for you? I should be crazy to do it. Your troubles are your own, and you must cope with them yourself. Calamities are not meant to be wriggled out of, they have to be endured.

EURIPIDES: H'm. – And now tell me honestly why you're afraid to go.

AGATHON: Why, it would be even worse for me than for you.

EURIPIDES: How so?

AGATHON: They consider I steal their business.

MNESILOCHUS [*greatly amused*]: Steal their business! That's good! I see their point – and his too, I must say.

EURIPIDES: Well, will you do it?

AGATHON: Not on your life! [*He settles down to his writing.*]

EURIPIDES: Oh, dear, how very unfortunate! I'm done for, done for.

MNESILOCHUS: My poor dear fellow. But uncle's here, don't give up like this.

EURIPIDES: But what can I do?

MNESILOCHUS: Tell him to go to blazes. Now, can't you use *me* somehow? I'll do *anything*.

EURIPIDES [*with new hope*]: Well, in that case – off with that cloak!

MNESILOCHUS [*taking it off*]: There! Here, what are you going to do to me?

EURIPIDES [*indicating Mnesilochus' beard*]: Shave all this off.
    [*He peers under Mnesilochus' tunic.*]
The rest we'll have to singe.

MNESILOCHUS [*with an effort*]: All right, if you have to. It's my own fault for offering.

EURIPIDES: Agathon, you're always armed with a razor – lend us one, will you?

AGATHON: Take one out of the razor case there.

EURIPIDES [*selecting one*]: That's kind of you. – [*To Mnesilochus*] Now, sit down. Puff out your right cheek. [*He starts to shave him.*]

MNESILOCHUS: Hey, that hurts!
    [MNESILOCHUS *continues to scream and groan.*]

EURIPIDES: What are you making all this fuss about? I'll have to gag you if you don't pipe down.
    [MNESILOCHUS *utters a wild howl and makes off.*]

EURIPIDES: Hey, where are you off to?

MNESILOCHUS: To the holy altar. I'm not going to stay here to be hacked to pieces.

EURIPIDES: Won't you look a little odd with only one cheek shaved?

MNESILOCHUS: I don't care.

EURIPIDES: Now don't let me down, I implore you. Come back here.

MNESILOCHUS [*returning reluctantly*]: Oh dear, oh dear!

EURIPIDES [*resuming the operation*]: Sit still, can't you, and keep your chin up. And stop twisting yourself into knots.

[*He takes hold of Mnesilochus' nose, so as to shave his moustache.*]

MNESILOCHUS: Mh, mh!

EURIPIDES: Stop mooing, it's all over now.

MNESILOCHUS: Oh, deary me. [*Feeling his chin*] I feel like a raw recruit.

EURIPIDES: Don't worry, you look really handsome. [*He picks up one of Agathon's mirrors.*] Like to take a look at yourself?

MNESILOCHUS: All right, give me the mirror.

[EURIPIDES *hands the mirror to* MNESILOCHUS, *who takes one look and thrusts it away in horror.*]

EURIPIDES: Well?

MNESILOCHUS [*brokenly*]: It's not me, it's Cleisthenes!

EURIPIDES: Now stand up and bend over, I've got to singe you.

MNESILOCHUS: No, no, help, help! I shall be grilled like a sucking-pig.

EURIPIDES [*calling into the house*]: Will someone bring me out a torch or a lamp, please?

[*A* SLAVE *comes out with a blazing torch.*]

Bend over!

[*He takes the torch and begins the singeing operation.*]

Keep that tail of yours out of the way, can't you?

MNESILOCHUS: That's what I'm trying to do, but I'm on fire. Help! Water, water, quickly, before my backside catches fire too!

EURIPIDES: Cheer up, it's all over now.

MNESILOCHUS: Cheer up, when I'm burnt to a frazzle?

EURIPIDES: Nothing more to worry about, the worst part's over.

MNESILOCHUS: Phew, what a stink of soot! You've carbonized my crutch!

EURIPIDES: Don't worry, some satyr will wipe it for you.

MNESILOCHUS: If anyone tries to wipe *my* bottom, I'll wipe *him*!

EURIPIDES: Agathon, if you're not prepared to help personally, could you at least lend me a dress and headband for my friend here? You can't pretend that you don't possess such things.

AGATHON: Yes, yes, help yourself, use anything you like.

MNESILOCHUS [*surveying Agathon's wardrobe*]: Hm! Now which one shall I take?

EURIPIDES: Here you are, take this yellow gown and put it on.

MNESILOCHUS [*burying his nose in it*]: Ah, what a delicious perfume! [*Sniffing again, with distaste*] Intimate, you might say.

EURIPIDES: Come on, get it round you.

[MNESILOCHUS *puts on the gown.*]

MNESILOCHUS: Pass me the girdle.

EURIPIDES: Here you are.

MNESILOCHUS: Help me, will you, I can't get this bit round the legs right.

[*Between them they make a thorough mess of things, but eventually they achieve a result which appears to satisfy them.*]

EURIPIDES: Now we shall want a hair-net and a head-dress.

AGATHON: You can borrow this wig if you like. I wear it at night.

EURIPIDES: Oh, yes, that's exactly what we need.

[MNESILOCHUS *puts the wig on.*]

MNESILOCHUS: Does it suit me?

EURIPIDES: You look superb. Now you want a wrap.

AGATHON: You can have that one on the couch there.

EURIPIDES: And shoes?

AGATHON: Here you are, here's a pair of mine.

MNESILOCHUS: Will they fit me, I wonder? – You probably prefer a loose fit yourself.

AGATHON: Well, now that you've got everything you need, I'll leave you to it. Perhaps someone would kindly wheel me in again.

[EURIPIDES *and* MNESILOCHUS *bow their farewells to Agathon as a* SLAVE *pushes the front of the house back into position.* EURIPIDES *and* MNESILOCHUS *are now alone.*]

EURIPIDES: Well, you certainly look like a woman now. But when you speak, mind you put on a real feminine voice.

MNESILOCHUS: I'll do my best.

EURIPIDES: Right: off you go.

MNESILOCHUS: Not unless you swear me a solemn oath.

EURIPIDES: What oath?

MNESILOCHUS: That if anything happens to me you'll come to the rescue, without fail.

EURIPIDES: I swear to you by Ether, the dwelling-place of Zeus –

MNESILOCHUS: No, that won't do. Might as well swear by a block of flats.[66]

EURIPIDES: Then I'll swear it by the gods. The whole lot of them.

MNESILOCHUS: And remember it was your heart that swore, not just your tongue. And I didn't force it on you.[67]

[*A babble of feminine voices is heard, as the* WOMEN *flock to the temple.*]

EURIPIDES: Hurry along now, I can see the flag going up over the temple for the assembly. And I think *I'd* better be getting along.

[EURIPIDES *departs as the* WOMEN *begin to arrive. Scene 2 follows without a break.*]

SCENE 2: *The Forecourt of the Temple of Demeter Thesmophoros*

The background now represents the façade of the temple. WOMEN *pour into the forecourt and gather round about the altar to deposit their offerings. In addition to the members of the* CHORUS *and their* LEADER, *the crowd includes* FIRST WOMAN, *a formidable figure — one feels sorry for her husband — and* SECOND WOMAN, *a haggard, worried-looking type.* FIRST WOMAN *is accompanied by two* MAIDS, *one of whom carries a baby. Conspicuous in his yellow gown,* MNESILOCHUS *mingles with the chattering throng and addresses an imaginary slave-girl of his own.*]

MNESILOCHUS: Come along, Thratta, this way. Oh, Thratta, look, look at all the smoke! What a lot of torches!

[*He approaches the altar, where numerous women are performing obeisances and uttering short prayers.*]

Oh, beauteous Twain, receive me now, and may I be blessed with good fortune – both coming and going.

[*He suddenly realizes that the women are placing offerings before the altar.*]

Oh, yes, er, Thratta, just put the basket down and take out the sacrificial cake – that's right. [*Skilfully purloining somebody else's cake*] Thank you, dear. – Beloved mistress Demeter, divine Persephone, grant that I may sacrifice to you often and often – or at least get away with it this time. Show favour to my little ones. May my little daughter, Vagina, find the right sort of husband – rich and stupid; and my little son Erektos, give him lots of brains, amen![68] Now where shall I sit, I wonder, so as to hear the speakers? All right, Thratta, you can go now; slaves aren't allowed to listen to the speeches.

[*The* CHORUS *and the other* WOMEN *take their seats, and* MNESI-
LOCHUS *places himself among them.*]

LEADER: Silence, silence! Pray ye now to Demeter and the Divine
Maiden, the Holy Twain; pray ye to Pluto, and to the mother of all
beauty, the fruitful nourishing Earth! Pray ye to Hermes and the
Graces! That this present assembly and congregation may in fair
and seemly debate bring blessing to the City of the Athenians and
haply to ourselves as well; and she who in act and speech best
serves the people of Athens and the interests of women, let her
word prevail. Pray ye for these things, and for blessing upon your-
selves. Lift up your hearts!

CHORUS:

> And may the gods rejoice also,
> Appearing gladly among us,
> And sanctify our prayers.
> Come, mighty Zeus:
> For great is Thy name.
> Come, Apollo, Lord of holy Delos,
> Bearing the golden lyre.
> Come, bright-eyed Pallas, all-conquering Maid,
> For Thy spear is of gold
> And Thy City envied and desired of gods and men.
> Come, child of golden Leto, huntress of beasts:
> Many are Thy names.
> Come, dread Poseidon, ruler of the salty oceans:
> Forsake Thy deep hiding-places
> In the fish-filled, frenzied sea.
> Come from your streams and rivers, O Nereids:
> And descend, ye roaming Nymphs of the mountains.
> May the strings of the golden lyre echo our prayers,
> And our ceremonies be acceptable:
> Hear the free-born women of Athens, O ye gods.

LEADER:

Now raise your voices and invoke the great Olympian gods
And goddesses, and call upon the mighty Delian gods
(And goddesses), and supplicate the noble Pythian gods
(And goddesses), and pray to all the other, lesser gods
(And all the lesser goddesses) – to take this opportunity
Of castigating those who harm our Feminine Community.

A curse upon the man who plans our enemies to please,
The man who parleys with the Mede[69] or with Euripides,
Aspires to be a tyrant or to set one on the throne,
Or tells a woman's husband that the baby's not her own;[70]
The maid who 'knows the very man' when Mistress wants some fun,
But spills the beans to Master when the long night's work is done;
The messenger who bears false tales; the lover who seduces
With talk of all the gifts he'll bring – and then no gift produces;
The girl who takes his presents when he goes to her instead,
The hag who presses gifts on *him* to lure him to her bed;
And, worst of all the characters who meet with our displeasure,
The tapster or the tapster-ess who dares to serve short measure.
On these and on their houses may the wrath of heaven fall,
But otherwise we pray the gods to guard and bless us all.

CHORUS:

> We pray then for blessing
> On people and State,
> And on all that is said
> In our solemn debate:
> That she who speaks wisely
> May carry the day,
> And none play us false
> Or our secrets betray.
> On all who from motives
> Of malice or greed
> Dishonour the City,
> Conspire with the Mede,
> Or basely endeavour
> The laws to reverse,
> We hereby pronounce
> An appropriate curse;
> And to Zeus our most humble
> Petition we tender,
> That our prayers may be valid
> In spite of our gender.

LEADER: Attention, please. [*Reading.*] 'At a meeting of the Women's
Council, held under the chairmanship of Timoclea, it was proposed
by Sostraté that an assembly be held on the morning of the second
day of the Thesmophoria, this being the least busy time, to decide

what steps should be taken for the punishment of Euripides, who is unanimously agreed to be guilty. Signed: Lysilla, secretary.' – Who wishes to speak?

FIRST WOMAN [*rising*]: I do.

LEADER [*handing her the speaker's garland*]: Put this on first. Silence, attention, everyone. She's clearing her throat just like a professional orator. I can see we're in for a long speech.

FIRST WOMAN: I assure you, ladies, my getting up to speak like this isn't from any desire to push myself forward, it's just that I can no longer bear to sit by and see us women besmirched with mud from head to foot by this cabbage-woman's son Euripides.[71] The things he says about us! Is there any crime he hasn't tried to smear us with? Give him a stage and a theatre full of people, and does he ever fail to come out with his slanders? Calling us intriguers, strumpets, tipplers, deceivers, gossips, rotten to the core and a curse to man-kind. And naturally the men all come home after the play and give us that nasty suspicious look, and start hunting in all the cupboards for concealed lovers. A woman can't do any of the things she used to do in the old days, he's filled our husbands' minds with such awful ideas – why, if you just sit plaiting a wreath your husband thinks you must be in love with someone; and suppose you acci-dentally drop something about the house, 'Oh,' he says, 'breaking the crockery – that's bad,' he says: 'she must have her eye on the lodger' – remember that guest from Corinth?[72] Or perhaps a girl isn't feeling too well: in comes her brother and says, 'Whence come these guilty flushes to thy cheek?' And then, another thing. Supposing a woman finds she can't bear her husband a child – she's got to produce one from somewhere, hasn't she? But what chance has she got, with her husband sitting watching her the whole time? And what's happened to all the rich old men who used to marry young girls? Euripides has put them off completely: 'An old man weds a tyrant, not a wife,' he says.[73] It's all because of him that they've started putting bolts and seals on the doors of the women's quarters, and keeping those great Molossian dogs to scare off the boy-friends. One might forgive him all that, but now we're not even allowed a free hand on our own side of the house any more, we can't even get at the flour or the oil or the wine: our husbands carry the keys around with them – horrid complicated Laconian things with three teeth. Ugh! In the old days you could get a ring made for three obols that'd reseal any larder door in Athens, but now this slave Euripides has got them all wearing seals that look like pieces of worm-eaten wood. – In conclusion, ladies, I feel that somehow or other we have got to devise a nice sticky end for him: perhaps poison might be a suitable method. Anyway, that's all I intend to say in public: I propose to draw up a more detailed indictment with the help of the secretary.

[*She returns the garland to the Leader and sits down, amid applause.*]

CHORUS:

> I've never heard a woman speak
> With such assurance, such technique:
> Such fine felicity of phrase
> Is worthy of the highest praise.
> It was no negligible feat
> To think of arguments so neat;
> She said exactly what was fitting,
> No aspect of the case omitting.
> If, after winged words like these,
> We had a speech by Xenocles,[74]
> Even this audience, I'm sure,
> Would find the man a crashing bore.

[SECOND WOMAN *rises to speak, is handed the garland, and puts it on.*]

SECOND WOMAN: I wouldn't be wanting to say more than a few words, this lady's covered everything very well, I think, except I should just like to tell you what I've been through myself, you see my husband died in Cyprus and left me with five young children to look after, it was as much as I could do to keep them half alive, selling myrtle in the market. And then *he* comes along and starts writing his tragedies and persuading people there aren't any gods, my trade's gone down to half what it was.[75] I tell you ladies one and all, that man ought to be punished and no mistake; he's that rough, the way he treats us. Comes of being brought up on the *vegetable* stall, I suppose – no class. Well, I must be getting back to the market myself, I've got some gentlemen waiting for twenty wreaths – specially ordered.[76]

[*She returns the garland, gathers up her things, and departs, amid applause.*]

CHORUS:

> Bravo! Did you ever
> Hear phrases so clever,
> A style so well polished and neat?
> Every word that she said
> Hit the nail on the head:
> A real oratorical treat!
> In sensible terms
> She amply confirms
> What we've hinted a number of times;
> And now that his guilt
> Is proved up to the hilt,
> The rascal must pay for his crimes.

[MNESILOCHUS *now rises and assumes the garland.*]

MNESILOCHUS: Well, I'm not surprised, my dears, that you're all feeling very cross with Euripides, after hearing all this about him. I expect you're all quite boiling with indignation. Personally I can't stand the man: [*feelingly*] I've got reason enough to hate him, heaven knows. But listen, as this is all just between ourselves – after all we're all girls together here, and no one's going to tell tales on us – why are we attacking him and getting so worked up, just because he's found out two or three of our little tricks and let the cat out of the bag? There are thousands of little things he *doesn't* know about, aren't there? [*He giggles.*] Take me, for instance, I'm terrible. . . . I think the most *awful* thing I ever did was when we'd been married just three days. There was my hubby sound asleep beside me, and – well, I had a friend. Just a boy-and-girl affair, you know. Seduced me when I was seven. Well, the boy-friend *wanted* me – you know? – and came and tapped ever so lightly on the door, I knew who it was at once!

[*As* MNESILOCHUS *warms to his theme, the* CHORUS *listen in fascinated silence. But they are beginning to have misgivings.*]

– So I started to creep downstairs, and suddenly my hubby called out, 'Hey, where are you going?' 'It's me stomach,' I said, 'I've got such a pain, fair twisting me up, it is,' I said, 'I'm just going down to the jakes.' 'All right,' he said, and started pounding up dill and sage and juniper to cure my stomach-ache, while I got some water to stop the door squeaking and went out to my loving boy.

Oh, what a lover! – up against the bay tree, with my other arm round the statue of Apollo. Ahhh! – now, you see, Euripides never said anything about that! And what about that trick of chewing a bit of garlic in the morning, when you've had a bit of fun? Dad comes home from duty on the Wall, takes one sniff and says, 'Well, she's not been up to mischief this time, anyway.' You see? Euripides has never mentioned that. If he wants to go off the deep end about Phaedra, let him get on with it, I say. He's never said a word about the woman who spread her skirt out wide, to show her husband how nice it looked in the light. Her boy-friend was underneath. I know another woman who said her pains had come on, and she had to keep it up for ten days, because she couldn't get hold of a baby. Her husband went all round the town buying medicines to speed things up. In the end the old midwife managed to find a baby and brought it home in a jar, with its mouth bunged up with beeswax to stop it yelling; and when the old woman gives her the wink, my friend calls out to her husband, 'Go away, go away, it's starting!' Husband trots off delighted; they pull out the baby, unbung its mouth – baby cries. And the old midwife runs off to the husband, beaming all over her wicked old face: 'It's a boy,' she says, 'a real lion of a boy and the image of his Dad, even down to his precious little wiggle-waggle – the very same kink about half-way along.' I ask you, ladies, do we do these things or don't we? Very well, then. Why pick on Euripides? He's done nothing worse than we have.

[*The* CHORUS *remain silent as* MNESILOCHUS *hands back the garland and resumes his seat. A murmur of indignation then breaks out.*]

CHORUS:

> Where can the creature come from?
> I'm shocked, amazed, distressed.
> I little thought I'd ever hear
> Such sentiments expressed.
>
> To say such things in public –
> I don't know how she dared!
> Well, there it is – it goes to show
> You have to be prepared.

What says the ancient proverb?
'Be careful where you tread;
Where'er you walk an *orator*
May raise his ugly head.'

LEADER [*aside, to the audience*]: Nothing can be worse than a shameless woman – except another woman.

[*There is an awkward silence. Everybody glares at Mnesilochus. Eventually* FIRST WOMAN *springs to her feet.*]

FIRST WOMAN: Women, women, what are you thinking of? What has come over you, are you bewitched, or what? Are you going to let this outrageous woman stand up here and insult us all? – All right, if no one else will help, I and my maids will have to deal with her ourselves. She must be plucked and singed. Into the breach, my friends!

[*The three advance menacingly*.]

MNESILOCHUS: Oh, not my breach – not that, I beg you, no! Listen to me, ladies: every woman here has the right of free speech. Just because I tell you the truth about Euripides, do I have to be plucked and singed like an adulteress?

FIRST WOMAN: Do you expect to get away scot-free, when you have the nerve to stand up for that man? A man who goes out of his way to choose plots with bad women in them? It's always Melanippe or Phaedra – he never writes a play about a respectable woman like Penelope.

MNESILOCHUS: Of course not. There aren't any women like Penelope nowadays, they're Phaedras to a woman.

FIRST WOMAN: There she goes again, the shameless hussy! Do you hear what she's saying about us all?

MNESILOCHUS: I haven't finished yet, not by a long chalk. Would you like me to tell you what else I know?

FIRST WOMAN: You've spilt quite enough already; there can't be anything left to tell.

MNESILOCHUS: Oh, yes, there is! You haven't heard the thousandth part of it yet. The things we women get up to! Did Euripides ever mention our latest dodge for tapping the wine jar? Well, you know those long-handled things you have in the bath, to scratch your back with . . .?

FIRST WOMAN: Scandalous!

MNESILOCHUS: Or how we give the meat from the Apaturia[77] to our pimps, and then say the cat's taken it?

FIRST WOMAN: Outrageous!

MNESILOCHUS: He never let on about the woman who did her old man in with an axe; or the one who gave her husband a drug that sent him mad; or the woman from Acharnae who buried her father under the hot-water tank in the kitchen.

FIRST WOMAN: Shame on you!

MNESILOCHUS [*rising to his feet and pointing at her*]: Ha, ha, and he never let on about *you*, did he? How you had a girl and your maid had a boy, and you changed them round and passed the boy off as yours?

FIRST WOMAN: How *dare* you say such things to me – I'll tweak your tufts, I'll –

MNESILOCHUS: Keep your hands off me!

FIRST WOMAN [*stamping her foot*]: Yah!

MNESILOCHUS [*doing the same*]: And yah to you!

FIRST WOMAN [*stripping off her cloak and flinging it to one of her maids*]: Hold this, Philista.

MNESILOCHUS: Just you lay a finger on me, and by Artemis I'll –

FIRST WOMAN: Well?

MNESILOCHUS: You'd better be careful, that's all – you know what seedcake does to you. I saw you!

LEADER: Now stop this squabbling, there's a woman on her way up here, in a great hurry by the look of it. If everyone will kindly settle down quietly before she gets here, we can receive her in an orderly fashion and find out what she has to say.

[*The newcomer, on closer inspection, turns out to be* CLEISTHENES, *who now hurries in, ambiguously dressed and breathless with excitement.*]

CLEISTHENES: My dears, I come as a friend. I do assure you – look at my cheeks! I adore you all – you do resemble me so very very closely, I often think – and I always try to protect your interests. The thing is, I've just heard a most terribly important piece of news, they were all talking about it down in the market place, and I've come *straight* up here to warn you, you must keep your eyes open and look about you, otherwise something *awful* might happen.

LEADER: Now, what's the matter, sonny? [*Realizing her mistake*]

I mean – I'm so sorry, but you do look so like a little boy, with those smooth cheeks.

CLEISTHENES: They're saying that Euripides has sent an old man up here, a relative of his.

LEADER: With what object?

CLEISTHENES: To spy on you. To listen to what you say and find out what you intend to do.

LEADER: Do you really think we wouldn't have noticed him, if he'd been here? A man among all these women?

CLEISTHENES: Euripides has singed him and plucked him and dressed him up as a woman.

MNESILOCHUS: What a preposterous story! I ask you – what man would be so stupid as to allow himself to be singed? I don't believe a word of it, by – [remembering, just in time, to make it a feminine oath] – by the Holy Twain.

CLEISTHENES: Then you're mistaken. Do you think I'd have come all the way up here to tell you about it, if I hadn't had it on the very best authority?

LEADER: Ladies, this is a most disturbing piece of news. There's not a moment to be lost. He must have been sitting here among us the whole time. We must find out at once where he is. And if you, kind protector, can help us to identify him, we shall be even more deeply indebted to you.

CLEISTHENES [looking searchingly at the assembled women]: Well, let me see, now. [Picking on First Woman] Who are you?

MNESILOCHUS [aside]: How am I going to get out of this?

CLEISTHENES [still to First Woman]: I'm afraid you'll all have to be questioned.

MNESILOCHUS [aside]: Oh, help!

FIRST WOMAN: I'm the wife of Cleonymus, if you want to know.

CLEISTHENES [to the Chorus]: Do you know this woman?

LEADER: Yes, yes, we know her. Go on to the others.

CLEISTHENES: Well now, who's this with the baby?

FIRST WOMAN: She's my nursemaid.

[It is now the turn of Mnesilochus.]

MNESILOCHUS [aside]: This is it! [He starts to scurry away.]

CLEISTHENES: Hey, where are you off to? You stay here! What's the matter?

MNESILOCHUS [*with tremendous dignity*]: Kindly allow me to pass. I wish to make water. Impertinent creature!

CLEISTHENES: All right, you can do that. I'll wait here.

[MNESILOCHUS *retires out of sight.*]

LEADER: Yes, wait there, and see that she comes back. She's the only one we really don't know.

CLEISTHENES [*calling to Mnesilochus*]: You're making rather a *lot* of water, aren't you?

MNESILOCHUS [*off*]: No, dear, it's that cress I had yesterday. Holds it back something dreadful.

CLEISTHENES [*hauling Mnesilochus back into view*]: Stop gibbering about cress, and come back here.

MNESILOCHUS: I'll thank you not to maul me about like that. Can't you see I'm not well?

CLEISTHENES: Well now, who is your husband?

MNESILOCHUS: Ah, my husband. Yes, ah-ha-ha-ha-ha. [*He is seized with a fit of coughing, during which* CLEISTHENES *waits patiently.*] Oh, yes! You want to know who my husband is? Yes, yes, of course. He's – you know, old Thing-o'-me-bob, up at Cothocidae.

CLEISTHENES: Thing-o'-me-bob? [*Considering seriously*] Oh, you mean old Thing-o'-me-bob who used to –

MNESILOCHUS [*ecstatically*]: Yes! That's right! Old Thing-o'-me-bob, son of What's-his-name!

CLEISTHENES: I believe you're bluffing. Tell me, have you been here before?

MNESILOCHUS: Oh, been coming here for years.

CLEISTHENES: Who's your tent-mate?

MNESILOCHUS: Oh – er, What's-her-name, *you* know. [*Aside*] That's torn it!

CLEISTHENES: You haven't answered my question.

FIRST WOMAN: All right, Cleisthenes, leave her to me. I'll question her about the rites we performed last year. So if you would kindly withdraw out of earshot, being – h'm – a man . . . Thank you. – [*To Mnesilochus*] Now, tell me: what holy ceremony came first?

MNESILOCHUS: Let me see now, what did we do first? [*He has a sudden inspiration.*] Why, we drank.

FIRST WOMAN: Right, and what did we do after that?

MNESILOCHUS [*after a pause for thought*]: We drank some more.

FIRST WOMAN: Someone's been telling you! – And what happened after that?

MNESILOCHUS: Xenylla asked for a basin: there wasn't a jerry.

FIRST WOMAN [*triumphantly*]: Wrong! There was. Cleisthenes, come here, I've found him!

[CLEISTHENES *hurries back.*]

CLEISTHENES: What would you like me to do with him?

FIRST WOMAN: Strip him. He's been saying the most dreadful things.

MNESILOCHUS: Strip me? You'd never strip a mother of nine!

CLEISTHENES: Off with that girdle, quick!

MNESILOCHUS: Oh, what a – you ought to be ashamed of yourself!

[*He continues to squawk as* CLEISTHENES *and* FIRST WOMAN *undo the girdle. The upper half of his robe falls open, but he continues to clutch the lower half. They inspect his chest carefully.*]

FIRST WOMAN: If this is a woman, it's a mighty tough specimen. [*Pointing triumphantly*] There you are, you see? No tits like ours at all.

MNESILOCHUS: That's because I'm barren. [*Pathetically*] I never had a child.

FIRST WOMAN: A moment ago you were the mother of nine.

[*Despite* MNESILOCHUS' *feverish clutching,* CLEISTHENES *now manages to fling open the lower half of the robe. In desperation,* MNESILOCHUS *bends down as if to do up his shoe.*]

CLEISTHENES: Stand up straight!

[MNESILOCHUS *does so, adopting a statuesque feminine pose. There is no sign of what one might have expected to see, and* MNESILOCHUS' *face bears a complacent smirk.*]

What have you done with it?

FIRST WOMAN [*lifting the robe from behind, and screaming*]: Oooh! He's pushed it through to the back. [*She hastily lets the robe fall again.*] A beauty, too – such a pretty colour.

[*The* CHORUS *shriek and titter at the revelation.*]

CLEISTHENES [*lifting the robe in his turn*]: Where? I can't see it.

FIRST WOMAN: It's back in front again.

CLEISTHENES [*running round to the front*]: No it isn't.

FIRST WOMAN [*from behind*]: No, here it is again.

CLEISTHENES: What is all this, a shuttle service across the Isthmus?[78]

FIRST WOMAN: Oh, the scoundrel! And to think that he was standing up there, abusing us and defending Euripides!

MNESILOCHUS [*aside*]: Well, this is a fine mess I've got myself into.

FIRST WOMAN: What shall we do with him?

CLEISTHENES: Keep him guarded, and see that he doesn't escape. I'll go and inform the Council right away.

[CLEISTHENES *departs.*

FIRST WOMAN *and her maids stand guard over Mnesilochus, as the* CHORUS *prepare for the Torch Dance.*]

LEADER:

> Come and light your torches,
>> Quickly, don't delay!
> Hitch your skirts up boldly,
>> Cast your cloaks away.
> Run and search the hillside!
>> Flit without a sound
> Through the tents and gangways,
>> In between and round.
> Prying, peeping, peering
>> Everywhere you can:
> Any little cranny
>> May conceal a man!

Hurry now, and form a circle: cover every inch of ground;
If another male is lurking, track him down, he must be found!

[*The* CHORUS, *having lit their torches at the altar, form a circle, and the dance begins.*]

CHORUS:

> If any other man has dared
>> To desecrate our Mystery,
> His punishment, when once he's found,
>> Will be the worst in history.
> The story of his gruesome fate
>> Will serve to teach Society
> The perils that attend upon
>> The practice of impiety.
> The man who fails to lead a life
>> Of strict religiosity,
> Neglects his pious duties or
>> Commits some mad atrocity,

Is apt to find himself held up
Before the whole community
To prove that gods are gods and none
Can slight them with impunity.

[*While his guards are busy applauding the dancers,* MNESILOCHUS *snatches First Woman's baby and runs to the altar.*][79]

FIRST WOMAN: Hey, hey, where are you going? Hey, you, stop! – Oh! He's taken my baby! Snatched it from my very breast!

MNESILOCHUS: Scream away! You'll never feed it again, unless you let me go. [*He picks up the sacrificial knife from the altar.*] I shall sever its limbs with this knife, and the altar will run with its blood.

FIRST WOMAN: Oh, no, for pity's sake! You women, can't you help? Shout, or set up a trophy, or something.[80] Don't stand by and see me robbed of my only child!

CHORUS: Mercy on us, what an outrage!
Gracious goodness, did you see?
Friends, I ask you, have you ever
Heard of such audacity?

Wickedness could go no further.

MNESILOCHUS: I'll soon stop your little game!

FIRST WOMAN: He has snatched my precious baby !

CHORUS: Has the man no sense of shame?

MNESILOCHUS: Madam, I will stick at nothing.

CHORUS: But you will not get away!
You'll not live to tell the story
Of the things you've done today.

MNESILOCHUS: There I hope you are mistaken!

CHORUS: Foolish man, your hopes are vain.
Do you think the gods would help you?

FIRST WOMAN: Give that baby back again!

MNESILOCHUS: No, I never will release her.

CHORUS: We shall get our own back soon:
For your insults we'll requite you
And you'll have to change your tune.

LEADER: Seize your torches, build a bonfire,
Pile the brushwood round his feet!

CHORUS: He shall be incinerated,
Our revenge shall be complete.

FIRST WOMAN [*to the nursemaid*]: Come along, Manya, we'll collect some brushwood. [*To Mnesilochus*] I'm going to have you burnt to a cinder.

[FIRST WOMAN *and her* NURSEMAID *go off.*]

MNESILOCHUS [*calling after them*]: That's right, roast me alive, carbonize me! – Now, baby dear, off with these Cretan creations and we'll have a look at you. [*He starts to unwrap the baby.*] You're going to die, you know that? And it's all your own mother's fault – hullo! what have we here? It isn't a baby at all, it's a skin full of wine! [*He shows it to the audience.*] Ah, doesn't it look sweet in its little Persian booties? Oh, women, women, women! [*He declaims, as if quoting :*][81]

> One passion rules a woman's heart,
>   One thought with ardour fires her;
> And ah, to what ingenious schemes
>   That raging thirst inspires her!
> No guile a woman's guile excels,
>   No cunning can be deeper:
> She is the bane of all mankind
>   Except the tavern-keeper.

[FIRST WOMAN *and the* NURSEMAID *return with their arms full of brushwood.* MNESILOCHUS *partially re-wraps the 'baby'.*]

FIRST WOMAN [*dumping her load*]: Pile it up, Manya, we need lots and lots.

MNESILOCHUS: Yes, pile it up, pile it up. But tell me something. You say this is your child?

FIRST WOMAN: I should know, I carried her nine months.

MNESILOCHUS: You – carried – *this*?

FIRST WOMAN: By Artemis, I certainly did.

MNESILOCHUS: Well, I've heard of people who could carry quite a skinful, but really . . .

FIRST WOMAN [*with a scream*]: Oh, what have you done? You dreadful man, you've undressed my baby! The poor wee mite!

MNESILOCHUS [*holding up the skin*]: Poor wee mite! Why, she must be getting on for three! Gallons, that is.

FIRST WOMAN [*weeping*]: Four, last Dionysia. – Give her back to me!

MNESILOCHUS: Never.

FIRST WOMAN: Then you must be burnt.

MNESILOCHUS: All right, burn me. But meanwhile I propose to slaughter the victim.

FIRST WOMAN: No, no, I implore you, no! Do what you like to me, I'll take her place.

MNESILOCHUS: Could a mother's love go further? All the same, I'm going to slay the victim. [*He plunges the knife into the skin and directs a jet of wine into his mouth.*]

FIRST WOMAN: My child, my child! Quick, Manya, the bowl – at least I'll catch my baby's blood.

[*By now* MNESILOCHUS *is squirting wine all over the place.*]

MNESILOCHUS: Hold it out, then, I won't grudge you that.

[*She holds out the bowl and* MNESILOCHUS *directs a powerful jet into it. Some of it splashes into her face, the rest is spilt.*]

FIRST WOMAN: You mean, selfish, spiteful thing! There's none left for the priestess!

MNESILOCHUS: She can have this. Catch! [*He tosses her the empty wineskin.*]

[*Enter* THIRD WOMAN. *Seeing First Woman holding the empty skin, she hurries over to her, exclaiming in horror.*]

THIRD WOMAN: Oh, Micca, my poor dear, you've had a puncture! Your darling daughter, quite, quite drained – who did it?

FIRST WOMAN: This scoundrel here. – Look, since you're here, would you stay and keep an eye on him? I must go and catch Cleisthenes: the Council must be informed of this.

[FIRST WOMAN *and her* MAIDS *go off.*]

MNESILOCHUS [*aside*]: Now, how am I going to escape, I wonder. I'll have to think up some daring scheme, something really brilliant. But where's Euripides? It's all his fault, he got me into this; and there's no sign of him yet. How can I get a message to him? – I know! A trick out of one of his own plays: the *Palamedes*, you remember? Chap wrote a message on oar-blades. [*He looks round hopefully.*] Don't seem to *be* any oar-blades.[82] Where can I find some? Let me think – oar-blades, oar-blades . . . I've got it! These votive tablets, they're made of wood: the very thing!

[*He takes a number of the tablets from the temple wall and goes through the motions of carving letters on them with the sacrificial knife, which is much too big. He sings to himself as he works.*][83]

My hands, assist me if you can
To execute this daring plan:

Upon these slabs of wood we'll send
An urgent message to a friend.

Sweet tablets, on your backs allow
My knife its furrowed track to plough.
E, U, then R – another nick –
It's easy once you get the trick.

And now, dear tablets, if you please,
Fly quickly to Euripides:
[*He flings them out among the audience.*]
Fly you, and you! Fly left, fly right!
Inform him of my hopeless plight.

[MNESILOCHUS *sits down forlornly to await the arrival of Euripides.*
THIRD WOMAN *settles down to guard him. The* LEADER *of the
Chorus now steps forward and addresses the audience.*]

LEADER:
It's time we women stood up for ourselves,
                    and glorified the name
Of a sex that nobody praises much,
                    and everyone seems to blame.
According to you we're a plague and a curse,
                    the source of trouble and strife
And grief and war and sorrow and pain
                    and everything evil in life.
That's all very well, but tell me this:
                    if what you say is right,
What makes you so anxious to marry a plague,
                    and saddle yourselves with a blight?
You won't allow us to leave the house,
                    or even peep out of the door,
And if ever you find your wife is out,
                    you bellow, you rage, and you roar,
When what you should do if your taunts are true,
                    and women are all that you say,
Is go down on your knees and give thanks to the gods
                    for taking your burden away.
She may have been paying a neighbourly call
                    on a woman who's just had a son,[84]

126

And be sleeping it off in an innocent way
>> when the games and the dancing are done:
But what do you do? Can you leave well alone?
>> No, you come with a growl and a grouse
To retrieve your affliction, your 'source of all friction',
>> and haul her back into your house!
If a woman is seen when she happens to lean
>> from her window to look at the view,
Do you shrink from the sight of this horrible blight,
>> as you might be expected to do?
No, you peep and you peer, you snigger and leer,
>> and when she draws back in disdain
You don't go away, you wait there all day
>> till she comes to the window again.
I think I have shown, by examples alone,
>> that the feminine sex is the best;
But if you're unmoved, well, the thing can be proved
>> by a simple comparative test.
Just mention a man: think as hard as you can,
>> we'll surpass him, whatever his fame;
We'll produce, I repeat, a woman to beat
>> any man that you're willing to name.

[*Members of the* CHORUS *impersonate the various characters as they
are mentioned.*]

Charminus,[85] you say? Why, his fleet ran away!
>> We don't have to look very far:
Here's Nausimachē, 'Victorious at Sea',
>> to show you what cowards you are.
Oh, here's Salabaccho, the queen of the drabs:
>> can anyone viler be found?
Why yes, she's a model of virtue and grace
>> if Cleophon's knocking around!
Strătŏnikē my dear, come and stand over here!
>> (Her name means 'Unbeaten in War'.)
I'd like to see any man taking *her* on:
>> your Marathon days are no more.
And as for Eubūlē, 'Good Counsel', well, truly –
>> can any ex-Councillor claim,

After handing his job to another last year,
                    to have earned such a glorious name?
Have you heard of a woman who'd steal from the State
                    to the tune of a million or so,
And drive it away in a whacking great dray,
                    like one politician I know?
You won't catch a woman behaving like that;
                    it's not good, it's not clean, it's not right!
What she takes from the bin when her husband's not in,
                    she pays back in kind the same night![86]

CHORUS:
                    Well, you must admit it's true
                    That it's chiefly among you
          That gluttons, thieves, and criminals abound.
                    Have you heard of banditesses,
                    Let alone kidnapperesses?
          Are there any female pirates to be found?

                    And then there's your omission
                    To keep up your old tradition
          As the women of our race have always done:
                    We maintain our ancient craft
                    With the shuttle and the shaft
          And a canopy to shield us from the sun;

                    But the shafts of war are dusty
                    And the points have all gone rusty,
          And though, like us, you ought to have a shield,
                    We dare not ask a fella
                    What he's done with *his* umbrella,[87]
          In case it's been abandoned on the field!

LEADER:
If ever it came to a case in court,
                    we'd have charges by the score
To bring against men, but I'll tell you the thing
                    that really makes us sore:
If one of us women should bear a son
                    who does big things for the State,
An admiral or a general, say,
                    or anyone brave and great,

She ought to be treated with great respect
                     and given an honoured seat
At the various games and festivals
                     where the women are wont to meet;
But the mother whose son is a low poltroon,
                     a creature depraved and base,
Should come with her hair cropped short, and sit
                     in a less conspicuous place.
When Lamachus' mother attends the games,
                     do you citizens think it right
For Hyperbolus' mother to sit there too,
                     in a robe of spotless white,
And lend out money?[88] I know one thing –
                     if she tried to make *me* pay
At the rate of something per cent per month,
                     I'd grab the money and say:
We endured your son, do you want us to bear
                     your rates of interest too?
Begone, begone! We have borne enough –
                     and so, by heaven, have you!

ACT TWO

SCENE: *The same. There is no break in the action*

[MNESILOCHUS *is seated on the steps of the altar.* THIRD WOMAN *is still watching him conscientiously.*]

MNESILOCHUS: I'm going cross-eyed with all this watching and waiting. And still no sign of him. What's holding him up, I wonder? Perhaps he's embarrassed at having to be Palamedes – not virile enough. Now, which of his plays will really fetch him? I know! I'll be his new-style Helen:[89] I'm certainly dressed for the part.

[*He adopts a suitable pose and expression, partially veiling his face with his robe.*]

THIRD WOMAN: Now what mischief are you up to? What's the matter with you, rolling your eyes like that? I'll Helen you where you least expect it, if you don't behave yourself. Just sit there quietly till the Magistrate comes.

MNESILOCHUS [*as Helen*]:

> Here flows the Naiad-haunted stream of Nile,
> Whose waters, spreading o'er the shining plain,
> Do duty for the showers, and bring relief
> To Egypt's constipated citizens.

THIRD WOMAN: You're up to no good, I can see that all right.

MNESILOCHUS:

> Great Sparta was my home, and great the fame
> Of Tyndareus my father.

THIRD WOMAN: Well, if your father was famous, I can tell you what he was famous *for*.

MNESILOCHUS:

>   Yes, my name
> Is Helen.

THIRD WOMAN: At it again – pretending to be a woman! Before you've ever been punished for your first little game!

MNESILOCHUS:

> And many lost their lives
> On grim Scamander's banks, because of me.

THIRD WOMAN: A pity you didn't lose yours, I'm thinking.

MNESILOCHUS:

> And here I sit: but of my darling spouse,
> The wretched Menelaos, there's no sign.
> Why am I still alive?

THIRD WOMAN: Don't ask me, ask the crows.

MNESILOCHUS:

> And yet, and yet, there flickers in my heart
> A ray of hope – O Zeus, may it prove true!

[*Enter* EURIPIDES, *dressed for the part of the shipwrecked Menelaos in the 'Helen': he is dripping wet and festooned with seaweed.*]

EURIPIDES:

> What lord within these rugged halls doth dwell?
> Will he give shelter to a shipwrecked crew
> That lately struggled in the stormy sea?

MNESILOCHUS:

> These are the halls of Proteus.

EURIPIDES: Who is he?

THIRD WOMAN [*to Euripides*]: Don't take any notice, he's having you on. Why, it's ten years and more since old Proteas died.

EURIPIDES:

> What country, friend, is this?

MNESILOCHUS:

> Why, this is Egypt.

EURIPIDES: What a place to land!

> We've drifted miles and miles away from home.

THIRD WOMAN: You mustn't believe a word he says: I tell you he's talking nonsense. This is the Thesmophorion – you're in Athens!

EURIPIDES:

> Is Proteus now at home, or is he out?

THIRD WOMAN: You must still be suffering from seasickness. I keep telling you, Proteas is *dead*. Is he at home, indeed!

EURIPIDES:

> What, dead? How sad! And where would he be buried?

MNESILOCHUS:

> Here is his tomb: I'm sitting on it now.

THIRD WOMAN: You'll come to a bad end, you know, really you will. The sacred altar a tomb – what an idea!

EURIPIDES:

What makes thee sit all day upon a tomb,
Shrouded from head to foot?

MNESILOCHUS:

They'll have me wed,
Whether I will or no, the son of Proteus.

THIRD WOMAN: Why do you keep telling the gentleman such lies? [*To Euripides*] This fellow's up to no good, I tell you, sir: he just sneaked in among the women, to steal their jewellery.

MNESILOCHUS:

Ay, scold away! Pile insults on my head!

EURIPIDES:

Who is this dame that doth abuse thee so?

MNESILOCHUS:

Why, she is Proteus' child, Theonoé.

THIRD WOMAN: I beg your pardon, but I'm nothing of the kind. My name is Critylla, daughter of Antitheos, from Gargettos. The cheek!

MNESILOCHUS:

Talk on, I'll pay no heed:
For never, never will I wed thy brother
Or be unfaithful to my Menelaos
Who's gone away to fight the Trojan War.

EURIPIDES:

What didst thou say? Come, let me see thy face.

MNESILOCHUS [*in his natural voice*]:

I hardly like to, with my cheeks like this.

EURIPIDES:

Alack, what ails me? I can hardly speak.
Oh, gods, what do I see? Who art thou, woman?

MNESILOCHUS:

Who art thou, man? Ha, strange coincidence!
Thou took'st the very words out of my mouth!

EURIPIDES:

Art thou a Greek, or native to this place?

MNESILOCHUS:

Oh, I am Greek, but tell me, what art thou?

132

EURIPIDES:
>   Thou hast a look of Helen – art thou she?

MNESILOCHUS:
>   Thou look'st like Menelaos – thou art he!
>   I know thee by the greenstuff thou dost bear![90]

EURIPIDES:
>   Thou art correct: I am that wretched man.

MNESILOCHUS:
>   Oh, husband, husband, to thy loving arms
>   Take me at last! (How long you took to come!)
>   Let me embrace thee! Lift me in thy arms!
>   (And for heaven's sake get me out of here, quickly!)

THIRD WOMAN: If anyone tries to take you away from here, he'll get this torch in his face, and he won't like it, I can tell you.

EURIPIDES:
>   Alas, my wife, the child of Tyndareus!
>   Wilt thou not let me take her home to Sparta?

THIRD WOMAN: It's my belief you're in this together, the two of you. You can't fool me by talking Egyptian. – Well, this one's going to be punished now, at any rate: here comes the Magistrate with a constable.

EURIPIDES: Oh, that's bad. Well, I think I'd better be getting along.

MNESILOCHUS [aside to Euripides]: Yes, but what about me? What am I to do?

EURIPIDES [aside to Mnesilochus]: Don't worry, I won't let you down, as long as there's breath in my body. I know hundreds of other tricks.

[EURIPIDES hurries off.]

THIRD WOMAN [chuckling]: He didn't get much on his hook with that bit of bait!

[Enter a MAGISTRATE[91] and a SCYTHIAN 'ARCHER' or constable.]

MAGISTRATE: We've had a report from Cleisthenes. Is this the culprit? [To Mnesilochus] Stand up straight there! [To the Scythian] Take him off and tie him to the plank,[92] and then stand him up out here and keep your eye on him. Don't let anyone come near him: if anyone tries, use your whip.

THIRD WOMAN: That's right, there was a fellow here just now, one of these Egyptian yarn-spinners, and nearly got him away from me.

MNESILOCHUS: Oh, sir, I beg you, by your right hand – the one you hold out so readily – grant me one small favour before I die.

MAGISTRATE: What is your request?

MNESILOCHUS: Tell the constable to strip me before he ties me to the plank. I'm an old man, sir; please don't leave me dressed up in these feminine fripperies! I don't want to give the crows a good laugh as well as a good dinner.

MAGISTRATE: The Council's decision is that you are to be exposed with all this on, so that the passers-by can see what a villain you are.

MNESILOCHUS: O yellow dress, O yellow dress, what have you done to me? There's no hope of rescue now.

[MNESILOCHUS *is led into the temple by the* SCYTHIAN. *The* MAGISTRATE *and the* THIRD WOMAN *also depart, leaving the* CHORUS *in possession of the stage.*]

CHORUS:

> The day of the dancing has come round again,
> The day when we fast for the Goddesses 'Twain
> And pray them to free us from sorrow and pain
>   And crown us with joy everlasting.
> And Pauson[93] is with us in spirit today:
> For year after year he joins in when we pray
> For many returns of the wonderful day
>   When he isn't the only one fasting.

[*The tune of the round-dance is struck up. At the* LEADER'S *summons the* CHORUS *form a circle.*]

LEADER:

Come forward with a tripping step and listen as I sing:
Take hands as quickly as you can and get into a ring.
Pick up the rhythm as you go, and cast a circling glance
To check on your position for the merry whirling dance.

[*The round-dance proper begins.*]

And as we dance in ecstasy, let each one raise her voice
In praise of the Olympian gods!

CHORUS: We praise them, and rejoice!

[*As the dance proceeds, they utter ecstatic cries. During the last repetition of the tune, however, their words are addressed to the audience.*]

If any of you gentlemen expect us to abuse
The audience, we'd have you know it's not the time to choose.[94]

   A woman in a temple court should never soil her lips
     With satire and buffoonery, coarse jokes and dirty quips.

LEADER:
But now the measure must be changed, the merry whirl must end:
Step forward now, and pray the gods our revels to attend.

   [*The* CHORUS *take up positions for the second dance.*]

CHORUS:
      Let us praise the Far-Darter; the Lord of the Lyre,[95]
        And Artemis, Queen of the Bow;
      And pray that Apollo will grant to our choir
        The prize that is his to bestow.
      Be with us, sweet Hera, great Goddess and Queen,
        Take part in our dancing today!
      Defender of marriage, Protectress serene,
        Lend grace to our revels and play!
      On the gods of the countryside, Hermes, and Pan,
        And the nymphs of the woodland we call:
      We have fasted all day, let us do what we can
        With our dances to gladden them all.

   [*The* CHORUS *now partake of the ceremonial wine. The final dance, to
Bacchus, is wild and maenadic in character.*]

          Come, leap and jump
          With rhythmic thump
       In Bacchic frenzy prancing!
          The God of Joy,
          The Madcap Boy,
     Shall lead us in our dancing!
          Evi, evoi!
          The God of Joy
     Shall lead us in our dancing.

          He loves to leap
          On hillside steep
     And dance across the mountains,
          While nymphs in praise
          Do sing their lays
     Beside Cithaeron's fountains.
          Evi, evoi!
          The Madcap Boy,
     Who loves the wooded mountains!

The hills around
In joy resound
Whene'er the god advances;
The ivy weaves
Its pretty leaves
About him as he dances.
Evi, evoi!
The God of Joy
Has come to lead our dances!

[*Shouts and screams are heard from within the temple. The* SCYTHIAN *comes out, carrying* MNESILOCHUS, *whom he has now bound to the 'plank'. This he props up, with its complaining occupant, against one of the columns of the temple portico.*]

SCYTHIAN: You want to make-a da noise, you make-a da noise out here, in da open air.

MNESILOCHUS: Oh, constable, constable, I beg you –

SCYTHIAN: You not-a beg-a me, no good.

MNESILOCHUS: *Please* loosen the peg a bit!

SCYTHIAN: Lik-a dis, yes? [*He tightens the peg.*]

MNESILOCHUS: Stop, you're making it tighter!

SCYTHIAN: Ah, you want I screw him tighter? [*He does so.*]

MNESILOCHUS: Yow! What are you doing, damn you?

SCYTHIAN: You keep-a da mouth shut! I go fetcha da mat, den I lie down and keep-a da eye on you.

[*The* SCYTHIAN *goes off to fetch his mat.*]

MNESILOCHUS: Well, this is a fine mess Euripides has got me into, I must say.

[*At this moment* EURIPIDES *sails into view at one side of the stage, attired as Perseus. He is taking a trial run on the device normally used for spectacular descents by gods or goddesses in tragedy. His passage across the stage is slow and jerky at first, but suddenly his speed increases and he is whisked right across the stage, over the head of Mnesilochus, and out of sight. He just has time to make an agitated sign to Mnesilochus.*]

MNESILOCHUS: Thank heavens! There's still hope! He's not going to let me down after all. Perseus! And he was signalling to me: he wants me to be Andromeda, I suppose.[96] Well, I'm certainly tied up all right, should look the part. He *must* be coming to save me: he wouldn't have flown by just to pass the time of day.

[*As Andromeda:*]

> Say, ye gentle virgins, say,
> How am I to get away?
> How can I to safety flee
> With that Scythian watching me?
> Echo in thy rocky grot,
> Dost thou hear, or dost thou not?
> Hush thy voice and save my life:

[*In his own voice:*]

> I must get back to my wife.

[*Wailing dramatically:*]

> Pitiless, ah me,
> Was the hand that bound me.
>
> > [*Wailing from the* CHORUS.]
>
> Bad enough to be alone
> With that dreadful toothless crone:
> Now my state is worse by far –
> Lord, how rough these Scythians are!
> Here my mournful moan I make,
> Tied to this confounded stake,
> Waiting till I end my woes
> As a titbit for the crows.

[*Wailing:*]

> Was ever maiden
> So forlorn, so forlorn?
>
> > [*Wailing from the* CHORUS.]
>
> Not for me the jocund dance,
> While the young men round me prance;
> Not for me the bridal choir,
> Joyful chords of lute and lyre.
> Cords I have, but far from sweet:
> How they hurt my hands and feet!
> And my tender limbs shall please
> None but whales – or Glaucetes.

[*Conversationally:*]

> They say *he'll* eat anything.
>
> > [*Wailing from the* CHORUS.]
>
> Ah, bewail my horrid fate,

Weep and groan as I relate
How a kinsman stern and harsh
Shaved my whiskers and moustache:
Dressed me up in frills and lace,
Sent me to this awful place,
Full of females fierce and grim,
Keen to tear me limb from limb.

[*Snarling from the* CHORUS.]

[*Wailing*:]

O cruel demon of Fate,
Accursed, accursed am I.

[*Wailing from the* CHORUS.]

Who can look upon my plight
And not shudder at the sight?
Thunder-god, thy lightning send,
Bring my anguish to an end!
Little boots it now to gaze
On the sun's immortal rays:
It would suit me just as well
Down among the shades to dwell.

[*The last four lines of the Lament are accompanied by dismal echoes, in
which the words 'little boots' take on a strange significance.* ECHO,
*in the form of a coy and spinsterish female of indeterminate age, now
enters in person.*][97]

ECHO: Hail, dearest daughter! May the gods destroy thy father
Cepheus, for leaving thee exposed like this!

MNESILOCHUS: Who art thou, that tak'st pity on my plight?

ECHO: Echo, the mocking singer-back of words. – [*In an ordinary
voice*] Don't you remember? I was here last year[98] with Euripides
for the drama festival. We work together. – But now, my child,
you must play your part, uttering piteous lamentations.

MNESILOCHUS: Aha, and then you lament after me.

ECHO: Yes, yes, leave all that to me. [*She conceals herself behind a
column of the temple portico.*] All right, you can start now.

MNESILOCHUS [*in a mournful wail*]:

O holy night,
Long, long is the journey
You take in your chariot,

Crossing the ridges of the starry sky
Over proud Olympus.

ECHO [*nearly missing her cue*]: Proud Olympus.

MNESILOCHUS:

Why should I, Andromeda,
Of all maidens, have so great
A share of woe?

ECHO: Share of woe.

MNESILOCHUS:

Ah, wretched me!

ECHO: Ah, wretched me!

MNESILOCHUS: Oh, come off it!

ECHO: Oh, come off it.

MNESILOCHUS: Stop it, you're coming in too often.

ECHO: Too often.

MNESILOCHUS: I should be greatly obliged if you would kindly let me get on with my monologue. Shut up!

ECHO: Shut up!

MNESILOCHUS [*losing his temper*]: Go to hell!

ECHO: Go to hell!

[ECHO *now sounds equally angry, and the scene degenerates into a shouting match.*]

MNESILOCHUS and ECHO [*almost simultaneously*]:

What's the matter with you?
Just you wait!
You want a good hiding!

[*The noise is at its height as the* SCYTHIAN *hurries back with his mat.*]

SCYTHIAN: You call-a me, yes?

ECHO: You call-a me, yes?

SCYTHIAN: I fetcha da magistrato.

ECHO: I fetcha da magistrato.

SCYTHIAN: You dare-a spick-a like dat!

ECHO: You dare-a spick-a like dat!

SCYTHIAN [*perplexed*]: Where dis voice-a come from?

ECHO: Where dis voice-a come from?

SCYTHIAN [*to Mnesilochus*]: You spick-a to me?

ECHO: You spick-a to me?

SCYTHIAN: You want I punch-a da nose?

ECHO: You want I punch-a da nose?

SCYTHIAN: You mock-a me, yes?

ECHO: You mock-a me, yes?

MNESILOCHUS [*in terror, as the* SCYTHIAN *raises his fist*]: It's not me, it's this woman here.

ECHO [*from somewhere quite different*]: This woman *here*.

SCYTHIAN [*hunting up and down the portico, as* ECHO *dodges from pillar to pillar*]: Da saucy bitch-a, where she go, ha? She done-a da bunk. Now where you go? I give-a you what for.

ECHO [*with a well-aimed kick from behind*]: I give-a *you* what for.

SCYTHIAN: You still make-a da mock?

ECHO: You still make-a da mock?

SCYTHIAN [*making a grab*]: Now I catch-a da trollop!

ECHO [*from somewhere else*]: Now I catch-a da trollop!

[ECHO *makes her escape.*]

SCYTHIAN: Oh, da bloody woman, she talk-a too much.

[*Enter* EURIPIDES, *once again by air. He is still disguised as Perseus, complete with winged sandals and Gorgon's head. This time he makes a perfect landing, just by Mnesilochus and the Scythian.*]

EURIPIDES:

> Gods, to what barbarous country have I come
> On my swift sandal, cleaving through the sky
> My winged path? For Argos am I bound,
> And in my hand the Gorgon's head I bear.

SCYTHIAN: Gorgias da philosoph? You gotta his head? Hooray!

EURIPIDES: The Gorgon's head, I said.

SCYTHIAN: Da Gorgias' head, yeah. Hooray!

EURIPIDES:

> But soft, what rock is here? And what is this?
> A beauteous virgin tied up like a ship?

MNESILOCHUS:

> Have pity, stranger, on my wretched fate,
> And loose me from my bonds!

SCYTHIAN: You keep-a da mouth shut! You goin' to bloody die, and you no keep-a da mouth shut?

EURIPIDES:

> Fair virgin, how my heart with pity fills
> To see thee hanging there.

SCYTHIAN: No, no, he not any virgin, he just a dirty ol' man.

EURIPIDES:

> Oh, Scythian, thou art wrong:
> This is Andromeda, the child of Cepheus.

SCYTHIAN: You no believe-a me? I show you. [*He lifts Mnesilochus' skirt.*] Is big enough, yes?

EURIPIDES:

> Lend me thy hand, that I may reach the maid.
> Come, Scythian, help me up! For men are prone
> To every kind of ill, and in my case
> Love for this maid hath smit me at first sight.

SCYTHIAN: Then you got-a da verra peculiar taste. If he was tied up da oder way round, yes, den I undertand.

EURIPIDES:

> O Scythian, let me but her bonds untie,
> And I will bear her to the bridal bed.

SCYTHIAN: You want-a verra much make-a love to da ol' gentleman, you gotta go round-a da backside, yes. Bore-a da hole through da wood, ha ha!

EURIPIDES: Nay, I will free her!

SCYTHIAN: No, I beat-a you.

EURIPIDES: I will, I say!

SCYTHIAN: You touch him, I cutta your head off, so – wid da knife, slisha-di-slash.

EURIPIDES [*aside*]:

> Alas, what can I do? What can I say?
> He doesn't understand, his barbarous mind
> Is much too dim to waste my wisdom on.
> I'll have to think of something less abstruse.

[EURIPIDES *takes wing once more, and is wafted away.*]

SCYTHIAN: Da dirty fox, he make-a da monkey of me!

MNESILOCHUS:

> Farewell then, Perseus, but forget me not:
> Never was maiden left in tighter spot.

SCYTHIAN: You still want-a da whip?

[*He glares at Mnesilochus for a while, and then spreads out his mat and settles down to sleep.*]

CHORUS: [*the Hymn to Pallas*]:

> Who but we should call her,
> Who but we, the dancers?

Pallas, Girl and Goddess!
Pallas, the unwedded!
Pallas of Athens!
For she takes delight
In song and in the dance,
And the keys in her hand
Are the keys of our City.
Hers is the power,
And she is our Goddess.
Who but we should call her?
Who but we, the Chorus?

Come to us, Pallas,
Enemy of tyranny!
Come to the call
Of the women of Athens!
Come, and bring peace,
For then we shall have feasting!

[*The Hymn to Demeter and Persephone:*]
And you, Immortal Pair,
Come, come joyfully
To your sacred grove
And the rites no man may look upon.
Show us the holy vision
In the dazzle of the torches.
Hear us, O hear!
If ever you have come at our call,
Come to us now!
Come to us, O come!

[*The* SCYTHIAN *is still asleep. Enter* EURIPIDES, *carrying a lyre and the mask and costume of an old woman. He approaches the Chorus conspiratorially.*]

EURIPIDES: Ladies, if you would care for us to come to terms once and for all, now is your chance. I would promise solemnly never again to say anything bad about you, ever, anywhere. There, that's a serious offer.

LEADER: And what do you want of us, that you come forward with such a proposal?

EURIPIDES: Well, as a matter of fact, the gentleman on the plank there is a relative of mine. And if I can only get him away, you'll never hear another bad word from me. But if you refuse to help, I'll – when your husbands come back from the war, I'll tell them everything that's been going on at home.

LEADER [*after a quick glance round the Chorus*]: As far as we're concerned, it's a deal. But [*indicating the Scythian*] you'll have to tackle *him* yourself.

EURIPIDES: Leave that to me. [*He puts on the disguise, and calls out in an old woman's voice*] Come, Twinkletoes!

[*A young* DANCING-GIRL *enters.*]

And remember what I told you on the way along. Now, we'll just run through it – and don't forget to hold your skirts up. [*To a piper in the orchestra*] Give us a Persian dance, will you, Teredon?

[*The* PIPER *begins to play, and the* SCYTHIAN *wakes up.*]

SCYTHIAN: Oh, da buzzing and da droning, she wake-a me up. [*Seeing the girl*] Ah, da revels!

EURIPIDES: She just wants to rehearse her dance, officer. She's got to go and dance for some gentlemen.

SCYTHIAN: Oho, rehearse-a da dance! Verra nice! I no stoppa her.

[*The* GIRL *begins her dance.*]

Ah, pretty, pretty! So light! Like-a da flea on da sheep's back.

EURIPIDES [*as the dance ends*]: Now put your cloak down here, dear, and sit down a moment – here you are, on the Scythian gentleman's knee – and give me your foot, now, while I loosen your shoes.

SCYTHIAN: Thassa right, thassa right, si' down li'l girlie. Oh, da nice firm titties, like-a da turnip.

EURIPIDES [*to the piper*]: Make it lively, now. [*To the girl*] You're not afraid of the nice Scythian any more, are you?

[*The* GIRL *dances again, with fewer clothes on.*]

SCYTHIAN: Oh, da nice round bottie. An' you stay inside, you ol' rascal. Oh, da beautiful shape, all round da fanny.

EURIPIDES: Very good. Well, on with your cloak again: time we were off.

SCYTHIAN: Oh, you no let-a me kiss her first?

EURIPIDES: Give the gentleman a kiss, dear.

[*The* GIRL *does so.*]

SCYTHIAN: Oh, la, la, mmmph! Oh, da sweet tongue, like-a da best Attic honey. You sleep-a wid me, yes?

EURIPIDES: Now, constable, really! She couldn't do that, you know.

SCYTHIAN: Yes, yes, ol' woman – you fix it for me, yes?

EURIPIDES: One drachma.

SCYTHIAN: Yes, yes, I give-a da drachma.

EURIPIDES: Hand it over, then.

SCYTHIAN: Oh, dear, I no gotta da drachma. I know: I give-a da quiver – you give-a da girl, yes? [*He hands his quiver to Euripides.*] Come on, li'l girlie, you come-a dis way. [*To Euripides*] You watch-a da prisoner – what you called?

EURIPIDES: Artemisia.

SCYTHIAN: I no forgetta da name. Am-nesia.

[*The* GIRL *runs off and disappears.*]

EURIPIDES: Oh, Hermes, god of trickery, nice work, nice work! [*To the Scythian, who has already set off in pursuit*] Run quickly and catch her!

[*The* SCYTHIAN *is by now out of sight.*]

And now to free the prisoner. [*To Mnesilochus*] As soon as you're free, run for it, hard – straight back home to your wife and children.

MNESILOCHUS: Don't you worry, I'll do that all right – if ever I get out of this contraption.

[EURIPIDES *works quickly to release him.*]

EURIPIDES: There, you're free. Now, off with you, quickly, before he comes back and catches you.

MNESILOCHUS: I'm off, don't worry.

[MNESILOCHUS *hurries off, followed by* EURIPIDES. *The* DANCING-GIRL *runs across the stage once more, pursued by the panting* SCYTHIAN.]

SCYTHIAN [*pausing for breath, and chuckling*]: She like-a da fun, your daughter. She no say no, she understand. – Hey! Where da ol' woman gone? Hah? I tink-a she do da dirty. What, da ol' man gone too? Hey! Ol' woman! Ol' woman! Now I no like-a da ol' woman. Hey! Amnesia! – I give-a da quiver, she give-a da slip!

LEADER: Are you by any chance looking for the old woman with the harp?

SCYTHIAN: You see her, yes?

LEADER [*pointing in the wrong direction*]: She went that way. She had an old man with her.

SCYTHIAN: Ol' man is having da yellow frock, yes?

CHORUS [*all speaking at once, and pointing in different directions*]: That's right. You can still catch them, if you go that way.

SCYTHIAN: Hah? Which way she go? Oh, da dirty ol' woman! [*Calling*] Amnesia!

CHORUS [*severally*]: Straight up there. – No, no, where are you going? – Come back! – This way, that's right! – No, you're going the wrong way!

> [*The* SCYTHIAN *runs wildly about, trying to follow their instructions, and eventually runs off stage.*]

SCYTHIAN [*as he disappears*]: Amnesia! Amnesia! I lost da Amnesia!

CHORUS:

> Run along, run along; you can run straight to Hell
>   If you like, and good riddance, I say.
> But it's time we were all moving off, truth to tell,
>   For we've had enough fun for one day.
> May the Goddesses bless us, and praise us as well,
>   If they're pleased with our work – and our play.

The Frogs

Introductory Note to *The Frogs*

'A poet should teach a lesson, make people into better citizens.'
'And if he has failed to do this?'

'Schoolboys have a master to teach them, grown-ups have the poets.'

'From the very earliest times the really great poet has been the one who had a useful lesson to teach.'

> 'Grant that when we dance and play
> As benefits your holy day,
> Part in earnest, part in jest,
> We may shine above the rest.'

> 'We chorus folk two privileges prize:
> To amuse you, citizens, and to advise.'

'What do you want a poet for?'
'To save the City, of course.'

In no other play did Aristophanes insist so firmly on his conception of the poet's proper function in society; in no other play did he endeavour so earnestly to fulfil it.

In January 405 B.C. Athens was not a cheerful city. At Decelea, only a few miles away, the Spartans lay encamped: not many months before, they had marched right up to the city walls, 30,000 strong, and the Athenians had only just managed to man the defences in time. And now Lysander, the Spartan admiral, supported by Cyrus the Persian, was preparing for the spring offensive in which he hoped to inflict the final blow on the Athenian fleet. Last summer, admittedly, the Athenians had scored a considerable naval victory at Arginusae, sinking seventy-five enemy ships. But the Athenian casualties had been heavy, and in the storm that blew up after the battle everything had gone wrong: survivors had not been picked up, fifty enemy ships had been allowed to get away, and twelve disabled Athenian ships had been left to their fate. Angry and confused, a depleted Assembly had agreed to the execution of six of the eight commanders (the other two had escaped). The vote was illegal: repentance followed at once. The Athenians were shocked and horrified by what they had done. Never had the shortcomings of the democratic system been brought home to them with such force.

During the years that followed the writing of *The Wasps*, opposition to the 'rule of the people' had steadily gained strength among the upper and middle classes, many of whom favoured a moderate form of oligarchy which would give them more say in the conduct of affairs, while others were more extreme in their views and were even prepared to collaborate with the enemy in order to gain power. In 411 a group of oligarchs, led by Antiphon, Phrynichus, Peisander, and Theramenes, carried out a *coup d'état* and set up a 'Council of Four Hundred' to administer the State. It was planned to draw up a list of 5,000 citizens of substance, who would form the new electorate and replace the Assembly as the sovereign body. Naturally a good many of those who stood a chance of inclusion were drawn into supporting the new régime; and when democracy was restored in 410 many of these were deprived of their citizenship. Quite apart from the personal hardships which it involved, this measure had the effect of reducing the moderate vote in the Assembly; and the power of the extreme democrats was subsequently increased still further by the enfranchisement of a large number of slaves who had rowed in the fleet at Arginusae.

After Arginusae, the Spartans had offered to evacuate Decelea and make peace on the basis of the *status quo*. Under the influence of Cleophon and the other extreme democrats, the Athenians had turned down the offer. Many of the 'allied' cities which had been contributing to the cost of the war were now in enemy hands. Funds were running out: the gold and silver objects in the temples had already been melted down to provide an emergency coinage (which had at once been pounced upon by eager hoarders), and Athenians were now reduced to using 'shoddy silver-plated coppers'; the upper classes were being taxed almost beyond the limits of endurance; there was no one who could even afford to provide a Chorus for *The Frogs* – the job had to be shared.

There was one man who might yet be able to extricate Athens from her difficulties; one man who had the necessary skill in strategy and diplomacy to take over the conduct of the war and bring it to a speedy but honourable conclusion. But he was not there: Alcibiades, like Orestes (p. 198), 'didn't trust the people in power'. He sat on, a voluntary exile, in his castle on the Hellespont, reading the war reports from both sides. And indeed he had little reason to trust the Athenian democracy. True, the Assembly had revoked the sentence of death and the solemn curse they had laid upon him for impiety. True, he had returned to Athens as a hero in 407 and been given supreme command of the Athenian forces. But when a subordinate, acting against his orders, had involved the Athenians in a humiliating naval defeat at Notium, Alcibiades had at once been relieved of his command; and he had known better than to return to Athens. If he distrusted the democracy, the democracy distrusted him. He was an aristocrat, an intellectual, a playboy, an atheist, a traitor, a potential tyrant. He had helped the Spartans, he had played with the Persians, he had backed the oligarchs in their revolutionary schemes (never mind that he had also saved Athens from civil war). No, the Athenians would never recall Alcibiades. And yet . . .

Such was the atmosphere in which Aristophanes produced his comic masterpiece. It has sometimes been suggested that *The Frogs* is a splendid piece of escape literature: a flight from the grim controversies of the day into the safe, neutral world of literary criticism; a gentle intellectual frolic on the slopes of Parnassus. Nothing could be farther from the truth.

In the first place, Aristophanes is so far from shirking the painful realities of the day that he takes every possible opportunity of mentioning them – whether in brief, pointed asides like his 'Better to have been an Athenian commander at Arginusae!' or in the long, reasoned appeal of the *parabasis*. The whole comic sequence of the slave who changes places with his master is a political allegory, as the Chorus later reveals.

In the second place – and this is where the modern reader can so easily go astray – the concept of literary criticism as a purely intellectual activity, a sort of school subject, simply did not exist in Aristophanes' day. Questions of poetical technique were doubtless discussed, and there were teachers of poetical composition just as there were teachers of rhetoric. But to judge a work of art on its technical merits alone, without reference to its *moral* value, would have been regarded by every Athenian, whether he happened to be an expert or not, as the height of absurdity.

Apart from politicians, orators, and sophists, whom nobody trusted, only one kind of man was in a position to influence the ideas and attitudes of the public – the poet. For two hours or more at every dramatic festival, each competing poet had the undivided attention of his fellow-citizens of all classes – possibly in greater numbers than could ever be roped in to attend even the Assembly on a single day. And the role of the poet – though perhaps not of the comic poet – as teacher, preacher, and wise counsellor was universally recognized. Instead of the Bible, people quoted Homer or Hesiod: everybody knew passages from the great poets by heart and had themselves been taught morality by their aid. And now, it seemed, most of the great poets were dead. Sophocles had died only a few months ago, soon after the news of Euripides' death had reached them from Macedonia.

Aristophanes, then, is not saying to his audience 'Let us forget all about war and politics for a brief space and indulge in a harmless literary jest.' What he is saying is something more like this: 'The City is in great danger. Unless we can find advisers who are both wise and good, we shall perish. We have listened to our orators and our politicians, but their advice has been neither wise nor good, and we have been led to the brink of disaster. Is it not time that we turned to our other advisers, the poets? Admittedly the living ones are not much to write home about, but Dionysus, the patron of this festival, is a god of great power. Can he not be persuaded to bring us back one of our great poets, even if only for a few brief minutes, so that we can hear what he has to say?'

Euripides at first seems the obvious choice: a teacher and adviser if ever there was one. For fifty years his plays, his ideas, his original way of looking at things, his fresh approach to morality and religion, his clever use of words, have held the attention of the public, shocked them out of their old traditional attitudes, helped to create the modern outlook.

But it is not Euripides whom Dionysus brings back in the end – it is Aeschylus: Aeschylus, who fought at Marathon and died fifty years ago: Aeschylus, that dry old 'classic', with his slow-moving plots and his ponderous, majestic language that so cries out to be parodied. As the great debate proceeds – and it is conducted with the utmost fairness, thrust for thrust – we perceive that on the *moral* issues the points are steadily mounting up in Aeschylus' favour. True wisdom, we begin to see, is not the same thing as cleverness. Wisdom is bound up with moral qualities, such as courage, integrity, justice, and moderation – old-fashioned virtues perhaps, but of more value to Athens than the ability to talk them out of existence. 'In my heart of hearts,' Dionysus confesses as he proclaims Aeschylus the winner, 'I have known all along.'

Into this parable Aristophanes, sometimes discreetly, sometimes openly and eloquently, inserts his own advice to the Athenians: 'Stop listening to Cleophon and his friends, and choose your leaders from the better-educated, more responsible classes; re-enfranchise the citizens who were misled into supporting the oligarchs; above all, end the war quickly and honourably – even if it means recalling Alcibiades, it will be worth the risk.'

Viewed in this way, the play is seen to possess a remarkable unity of theme and purpose. In writing *The Frogs*, Aristophanes was more than usually conscious of his responsibilities as a poet; and little though we may care about Cleophon or Cleigenes today, the seriousness that underlies this brilliantly funny play may be one factor in its greatness.

CHARACTERS

DIONYSUS *patron god of drama*
XANTHIAS *his slave*
HERACLES (*Hercules*)
A CORPSE
CHARON *ferryman of the dead*
AEACUS *doorkeeper of Hades*
MAID *to Persephone*
Two LANDLADIES
AN ELDERLY SLAVE *servant to Pluto*
EURIPIDES *the dramatist*
AESCHYLUS *the dramatist*
PLUTO

THE CHORUS: *a band of Initiates, old and young*[99]
CHORUS OF FROGS

A CASTANET GIRL
CORPSE-BEARERS, SLAVES, DANCING-GIRLS, DISTIN-
GUISHED RESIDENTS OF HADES, *etc.*

ACT ONE

SCENE 1: *The action begins on the outskirts of Athens, and ends in Hades. A building in the background represents, first, the house of* HERACLES, *and later, the palace of* PLUTO

[*Enter* DIONYSUS *and his slave* XANTHIAS. *The god, here represented as a paunchy but still handsome middle-aged man-about-town, is dressed in the yellow robe appropriate to a Dionysiac festival, which resembles a woman's garment, and in the buskins or high laced-up boots of a tragic actor – these also have a somewhat feminine look. Over the robe he wears a lion-skin, and in his hand is an enormous club: he has attempted to disguise himself as* HERACLES. *He is on foot, but his slave is riding a donkey. The slave is laden with bundles of bedding and other packages, many of which are suspended from a stout pole which rests across his shoulder.*]

XANTHIAS [*surveying the audience unenthusiastically*] : What about one of the old gags, sir? I can always get a laugh with those.

DIONYSUS: All right, Xanthias, but don't just keep saying 'Cor, what a load!' I've got enough to put up with as it is.

XANTHIAS: Something a bit wittier, eh, sir?

DIONYSUS: Yes, but don't start off with 'Oh, my poor neck!'

XANTHIAS: Oh. Pity. What *can* I give them, then? – Oh, you mean something really *funny*?

DIONYSUS: Yes. And I don't mean just shifting that pole about and saying you want to *ease yourself* of a –

XANTHIAS: Well, how about this:

'If nobody will take away my pack
I'll let a fart and blow it off my back.'

DIONYSUS: Keep that one till I really need an emetic.

XANTHIAS: Do you mean to say I've been lugging all these props around and now I'm not even allowed to get a laugh out of them? It's the regular thing, I tell you. Phrynichus, Lysis, Ameipsias, all the popular writers do it. Comic porter scene. There's one in every comedy.

DIONYSUS: Well, there's not going to be one in this one. Every time I go to a show and have to sit through one of these scintillating comic routines, I come away more than a year older.[100]

XANTHIAS: Oh, my poor neck, and all for nothing.

DIONYSUS: Anyway, things have come to a pretty pass, I'm not sure that it isn't sacrilege or something, when I, Dionysus, son of Jug, have to struggle along on foot, while this pampered creature is allowed to ride, so that he won't tire himself out carrying the luggage.

XANTHIAS: I like that. I *am* carrying the luggage, aren't I?

DIONYSUS: Of course not, you're riding.

XANTHIAS: Never mind, I'm carrying the luggage just the same.

DIONYSUS: I don't get that.

XANTHIAS: No, I've got it. And I'm telling you, it weighs a packet.

DIONYSUS: But the donkey's carrying all that.

XANTHIAS: Oh, is he? You ask my shoulders!

DIONYSUS: Ah, well, in that case the donkey's not being much use to you, is he? You'd better change places with him.

XANTHIAS: Oh, for heaven's sake! If only I'd been in that sea-battle,[101] I'd be a free man now. And if I got my hands on you . . .

DIONYSUS: Come on, get down off that moke. Here we are, if I'm not mistaken. This is where we pay our first call. You see, I've walked the whole way.

[*While* XANTHIAS *disentangles himself and his burdens from the donkey,* DIONYSUS *approaches the front door and knocks cautiously. There is no response.*]

Hallo there!

[*There is still no response. Remembering his disguise, he swings his club, hitting the door with a resounding crash.*]

Hallo, there! Slave! Open up!

HERACLES [*within*]: Ho, ho, who smites my door? Some Centaur, doubtless.

[*The door opens, and* HERACLES *himself appears. He stares in amazement at Dionysus.*]

What . . . who . . . ?

[*In a convulsion of mirth and amazement he collapses to the ground.*]

DIONYSUS: There, did you notice?

XANTHIAS: Notice what?

DIONYSUS: How I frightened him.

XANTHIAS: Mistook you for a madman, I expect, sir.

HERACLES: Oh, by Demeter, I can't stop laughing. [*He struggles to his feet and retires into the house.*]

DIONYSUS: Come back a minute, old boy, there's something I want to ask you.

HERACLES [*returning*]: Sorry, old man, but really I can't help it. A lion-skin over a yellow nightdress! What's the idea? Why the buskins? Why the club? What's your regiment?

DIONYSUS: Well, it's like this, you see. I was on Cleisthenes' ship –

HERACLES: Clei –! [*He splutters.*] Saw a good bit of action, I expect, one way or another?

DIONYSUS: Oh, yes, we sank twelve enemy ships. Or was it thirteen?

HERACLES: What, just the two of you?

DIONYSUS: Yes, by Apollo.

XANTHIAS: And then I woke up.

DIONYSUS: Well, as I was saying, I was on the ship and one day – I was reading the *Andromeda* at the time – do you know, I suddenly felt the most passionate longing – you can't imagine how I longed –

HERACLES: For a woman.

DIONYSUS: Not a bit of it.

HERACLES: A boy? [DIONYSUS *shakes his head.*] A man, then?

DIONYSUS: Oh, come, come, really!

HERACLES: You did say Cleisthenes was a friend of yours?

DIONYSUS: Don't laugh at me, old man, this is deadly serious. I'm in a terrible state. *Consumed* with desire.

HERACLES: Yes, but what sort of desire, my dear fellow?

DIONYSUS: Ah, you wouldn't understand. Let me put it this way. Have you ever felt a sudden craving for – let's say – pea soup?

HERACLES: Ah, now you're talking! When do I *not* have a craving for pea soup?

DIONYSUS: Are you with me, or would you care for another illustration?

HERACLES: No, no, pea soup will do nicely. I understand perfectly. [*He smacks his lips.*]

DIONYSUS: Well, that is the kind of desire that I feel for – Euripides.

HERACLES: But he's – a corpse! I mean to say!

DIONYSUS: No one on earth can stop me from going to seek him out.

HERACLES: What, down to Hades?

DIONYSUS [*dramatically*]: And deeper still, if need be.

HERACLES: With what object, may I ask?

DIONYSUS: I need a poet who can *write*. There are only two kinds of poet nowadays, the slick and the dead.

HERACLES: Oh, come! What about Sophocles' son, young Iophon?

DIONYSUS: He's the only one left that's any good, and even then I'm not sure.

HERACLES: Why not fetch back Sophocles, if you must have one of them back? He was much better than Euripides.

DIONYSUS: Not till I've seen how Iophon manages without his father to help him. Besides, Euripides will be readier to sneak away with me, he's a much more slippery customer; whereas Sophocles, well, he always took life as it came – he's probably taking death as it comes too.

HERACLES: And what's happened to Agathon?

DIONYSUS: Gone, gone; he too has left me. [*He sighs.*] A good poet; his friends will miss him.

HERACLES: Where has he gone, poor fellow?

DIONYSUS: To the Banquet of the Blessèd. Specially laid on by the King of Macedon.

HERACLES: And what about Xenocles?

DIONYSUS: Oh, Xenocles be hanged.

HERACLES: And Pythangelus?

XANTHIAS: Never a word about little me. And look at my poor shoulder, it'll never be the same again.

HERACLES: But surely there are dozens of these young whipper-snappers churning out tragedies these days: for sheer verbiage, if that's what you want, they leave Euripides standing.

DIONYSUS: Small fry, I assure you, insignificant squeakers and twitterers, like a lot of swallows. A disgrace to their art. If ever they *are* granted a chorus, what does their offering at the shrine of Tragedy amount to? One cock of the hind leg and they've pissed themselves dry. You never hear of them again. I defy you to find a really seminal poet among the whole crowd of them: someone who can coin a fine resounding phrase.

HERACLES: What do you mean, seminal?

DIONYSUS: A poet who can produce something really audacious, like 'Ether, the residence of Zeus', or 'the foot of Time', or that business about the tongue being able to perjure itself and the heart not being committed, you remember?[102]

HERACLES: You like that sort of thing?

DIONYSUS: I'm crazy about it.

HERACLES: But that stuff's all eyewash, you must see that.

DIONYSUS: 'Seek not within my mind to dwell,' as the poet says. You've got a house of your own.

HERACLES: What's more, it's downright immoral.

DIONYSUS: When I want advice about *food*, old man, I'll come to you. Meanwhile –

XANTHIAS: Never a word about little me.

DIONYSUS: But to come to the point – I see you're looking at my lion-skin. Well, I took the liberty, seeing that you travelled in those parts when you went down after Cerberus – well, I wondered if perhaps you could give me a few tips: any useful contacts down there, where you get the boat, which are the best eating-houses, bread shops, wine shops, knocking shops . . . And which places have the fewest bugs.

XANTHIAS: I might as well not exist.

HERACLES: You don't seriously intend to go down there? You're crazy!

DIONYSUS: Never mind that, just give me a simple answer: which is the quickest way to Hades? I want a route that's not too warm and not too cold.

HERACLES: Let me see now. You could go via Rope and Gibbet: that's a very quick way, if you don't mind hanging around for a bit, to begin with.

DIONYSUS: Don't give me a pain in the neck!

HERACLES: Well, there's a good short way of executing the journey, via Pestle and Mortar. That's used a lot these days – you can just *pound* along.

DIONYSUS: Hemlock?

HERACLES: That's right.

DIONYSUS: Now you're giving me cold feet![103]

HERACLES: You want a way that just goes straight down?

DIONYSUS: Exactly. You see, I'm not much of a walker.

HERACLES: Oh, a *runner*! Well – you know the tower in the Potters' Quarter? Well, just go and hang on to the top of that tower, and watch the start of the torch race. And when they shout 'One, two, three, *off*!' – well, off you go.

DIONYSUS: Where to?

HERACLES: To the bottom.

DIONYSUS: Oh, no, just think – all those lovely brains. I'm not going that way.

HERACLES: Which way *do* you want to go, then?

DIONYSUS: The way you went.

HERACLES: Ah, but that's a long trip. The first thing you come to is a great big bottomless lake.

DIONYSUS: How do I get across?

HERACLES: There's an old ferryman who'll take you across in a tiny boat, about so big, for two obols.

DIONYSUS: Amazing what you can do with two obols these days![104]

HERACLES: Ah, yes, it was Theseus who introduced the idea down there: an Athenian, you see. Well, after that you come to the snakes and the wild beasts – thousands of 'em.

DIONYSUS: Now, it's no good trying to scare me off.

HERACLES: And then you come to the Great Muck Marsh and the Eternal River of Dung – you'll find some pretty unsavoury characters floundering about in that: people who have wronged a guest, or had a pretty boy and failed to pay him, or knocked their mothers about, or punched their fathers on the jaw, or committed perjury –

DIONYSUS: Or learnt to dance the jelly-wobble, like Cinesias, or published a play by Morsimus, or –[105]

HERACLES: After that you'll hear the sound of flute-playing and you'll come out into brilliant daylight, just like it is up here. Farther on you'll see plantations of myrtle, and happy bands of revellers, men and women, tripping around and clapping their hands and so on.

DIONYSUS: What on earth for?

HERACLES: Oh, those are the Initiates[106] – been through the mystic rites and all that.

XANTHIAS: I'm going to stand up for *my* mystic rights, and have a sit down. [*He starts to divest himself of his numerous burdens.*]

HERACLES: They'll tell you anything you want to know; they're right on the road to Pluto's palace. Well, good-bye, old man, and the best of luck.

DIONYSUS: Don't worry, I'll be all right. Bye-bye, keep well!

[HERACLES *waves good-bye and goes indoors.*]

Now, you! Pick up all that baggage, and we'll get going.

XANTHIAS: I haven't even got it off yet.

[*He looks round for the donkey, but it has wandered off and is not seen again.*]

DIONYSUS: Come on, look sharp.

XANTHIAS: Now look, guvnor, have a heart! Look at all these stiffs they're carrying out. Might have been ordered specially.

[*Several corpses are carried in slow procession across the stage. Mournful music.*]

Go on, hire one of them to take your things down with him.

DIONYSUS: Supposing they won't?

XANTHIAS: Then I'll do it.

DIONYSUS: Well, all right. – Ah, here comes one, I'll ask him. Er – hullo, excuse me! Yes, you there! Stiff!

[*The* BEARERS *of the last litter come to a halt. The* CORPSE *sits up with a jerk.*]

Ah, would you do me a favour and take my baggage to blazes?

CORPSE: How many pieces?

DIONYSUS: Just these.

CORPSE: That'll be two drachmas.

DIONYSUS: Too much.

CORPSE: Bearers, proceed!

DIONYSUS: Hi, wait a minute! Can't we come to some arrangement?

CORPSE: Two drachmas, cash down, or nothing.

DIONYSUS [*counting out his small change*]: I can pay you nine obols.[107]

CORPSE: I'd sooner live!

[*The* CORPSE *lies down again with a jerk, and is carried off.*]

XANTHIAS: Well, of all the stuck-up blighters. He'll come to a bad end. [*Resignedly*] All right, guvnor. Load me up again.

[DIONYSUS *helps him load up, and they begin to move on.*]

DIONYSUS: That's a good lad. Now, where's this ferry boat?

CHARON [*off*]: Yo, heave, ho! Yo, heave, ho!

[*The stage grows darker and more eerie.*]

XANTHIAS: Where are we?

DIONYSUS: This must be the lake he was talking about, and – ah! here comes the boat.

[CHARON *comes into view, propelling a small boat on wheels.*]

XANTHIAS: And *that* must be Charon.

DIONYSUS: Charon! [*No response.*] Charon!! Charon!!! [*No response.*] Well, he's not Charon much about *us*, is he?[108]

CHARON: Any more for Lethe, Blazes, Perdition, or the Dogs? Come along now, any more for a nice restful trip to Eternity? No more worries, no more cares, makes a lovely break! [*To Dionysus*] Well, come along then, if you're coming.

DIONYSUS [*climbing in warily*]: Er – can I go to Hell?

CHARON: You can as far as I'm concerned.

DIONYSUS: Ah, splendid. Two, please.

CHARON: Sorry, sir, no slaves allowed. Not unless they fought in the sea-battle.[109]

XANTHIAS: Exempted on medical grounds, I was. Weak sight.

CHARON: Well, you'll have to walk round.

XANTHIAS: Where shall I find you?

CHARON: Just past the Withering Stone, you'll find an inn. 'The Last Resting Place', they call it.

DIONYSUS: Got that?

XANTHIAS: I've got the creeps, that's what I've got. It's not my lucky day. [*He staggers off into the shadows.*]

CHARON: Sit to the oar. Any more for Lethe, Blazes – Here, what are you doing?

DIONYSUS: Sitting on the oar, like you said. But –

CHARON: I didn't say *on* the oar, you pot-bellied loon. This is where you sit, here on the cross-bench.

DIONYSUS: Like this?

CHARON: Yes. Now stretch your arms forward and take hold of the oar – that's right.

DIONYSUS: Like this?

CHARON: Don't talk so much: shove her off.

  [CHARON *settles down comfortably in the stern, while* DIONYSUS *makes clumsy efforts to get the boat moving.*]

DIONYSUS: How do you expect me to drive this thing? I'm not a sea-going type.

CHARON: It's easy. Come on, man, get forward. Just a couple of strokes, and then you'll have the singing to help you. Lovely, it is.

DIONYSUS: Singing?

CHARON: Yes, the Frogswans. It's a treat.

DIONYSUS: Right: you start me off, then.

CHARON: I-i-i-n, OUT! I-i-i-n, OUT!

[*As soon as* DIONYSUS *has got his stroke adjusted to the tempo set by* CHARON, *the voices of the* FROG CHORUS *are heard off-stage, singing in an entirely different rhythm.*]

FROGS: Brekeke-kex, ko–ax, ko–ax,
        Ko–ax, ko–ax, ko–ax!
    Oh we are the musical Frogs!
    We live in the marshes and bogs!
    Sweet, sweet is the hymn
    That we sing as we swim,
    And our voices are known
    For their beautiful tone
    When on festival days[110]
    We sing to the praise
    Of the genial god –
    And we don't think it odd
    When the worshipping throng,
    To the sound of our song,
    ROLLS HOME through the marshes and bogs,
        Brekekex!
    Rolls home through the marshes and bogs.

DIONYSUS:
    I don't want to row any more,
FROGS: Brekekex!
DIONYSUS:
    For my bottom is getting so sore.
FROGS: Brekekex!
DIONYSUS:
    And what do you care?
    You are nothing but air,
    And I find you a bit of a bore.

FROGS: Brekeke-kex, ko–ax, ko–ax,
        Ko–ax, ko–ax, ko–ax!
    Your remarks are offensive in tone,
    And we'd like to make some of our own.
    Our plantation of reeds
    For all musical needs
    In the very best circles is known.
    Should Apollo require

A new bridge for his lyre,
He comes to the Frogs
Of the marshes and bogs;
We've exactly the type
That Pan needs for his pipe
When he plays for our chorus;
The Muses adore us!
We're the rage on Parnassus,
For none can surpass us
In harmony, sweetness, and tone,
     Brekekex!
In harmony, sweetness, and tone.

DIONYSUS:

What a sweat! I'm all wet! What a bore!
I'm so raw! I'm so sore! and what's more,
     The blisters have come
     On my delicate bum,
Where I've never had blisters before.

–Any minute now and it'll join in the chorus.

FROGS: Brekeke-kex, ko-ax, ko-ax –
DIONYSUS: Listen, my melodious friends, put a sock in it, can't you?

FROGS: Ko-ax, ko-ax, ko-ax!
What, silence our chorus? Ah, no!
Let us sing as we sang long ago,
When we splashed in the sun
(Oh, wasn't it fun)
'Mid the weeds and the sedge
At the pond's muddy edge.
If it came on to rain
We'd dive under again
(To avoid getting soaked)
And still harder we croaked,
Till from under the slime
Our subaqueous rhyme

Bubbled out loud and clear
For all men to hear,
And burst with a plop at the top,
    Brepeplep!
And burst with a plop at the top.

DIONYSUS:
    It's all this exertion, no doubt,
    But I fancy that I am about
        To take over from you!
FROGS: We'll be sunk if you do!
DIONYSUS:
    I shall burst if I don't, so look out!

FROGS: Brekeke-kex-ko-ax, ko-ax –
DIONYSUS: Ko-ax, ko-ax, ko-ax!
    Now listen, you musical twerps,
    I don't give a damn for your burps!
FROGS: Then we'll burp all the more,
    Twice as loud as before,
    Till our cavernous throats
    Cannot hold all the notes
    Of the ear-splitting song
    That we'll chant all day long:
DIONYSUS [*getting in first*]:
    Brekekex! Brekekex! Brekekex!
    It's hopeless, you see:
    You can never beat me!
FROGS: We shall see about that.
DIONYSUS:
    You won't, and that's flat:
    I'll go on till I bust –
    Yes, all day if I must;
    But I know I shall win in the end,
        BREKEKEX!
    [*He pauses: the Frogs are silent.*]
    Yes, I *knew* I should win in the end.

CHARON: Whoa there, land ahoy! Ship your oars!
    [*The boat grounds with a crash.*]

Well, here we are, sir; don't forget the ferryman.

DIONYSUS [*staggering ashore*]: Ah, yes, those two obols.

　　[*He pays the fare, and the boat moves off.*]

　　Xanthias! Where are you? Xanthias!

　　[*It is now quite dark. Ghostly shadows flit across the stage. An owl hoots.*]

XANTHIAS: Coo-ee!

DIONYSUS: Come here!

XANTHIAS [*emerging from the shadows*]: You called, sir?

DIONYSUS: What's it like over here?

XANTHIAS: Very dark, sir. And very muddy, sir.

DIONYSUS: Any sign of those murderers and perjurers he told us about?

XANTHIAS: Use your eyes, sir.

DIONYSUS [*seeing the audience*]: By Jove, yes, I see them now. Well, what are we going to do?

XANTHIAS: We'd better be pushing on, guvnor. The place is full of 'orrible monsters, or so the gentleman said.

DIONYSUS: Yes, the old scoundrel – he was just piling on the horrors, to scare me off. Jealous, you know – a chap like me with a military record. . . . Terribly sensitive about his exploits, old Heracles. I must say I rather hope we do meet something. One ought to slay a dragon or two on a trip like this, what?

XANTHIAS: Tsh! What's that noise?

DIONYSUS [*in a panic*]: Where's it coming from?

XANTHIAS: It's somewhere behind us.

DIONYSUS: Here, let me go in front.

XANTHIAS: No, it's in front of us!

DIONYSUS: On second thoughts, old man, you'd better go first.

XANTHIAS: There it is! Oh, what a dreadful monster!

DIONYSUS: W-what sort of a monster?

XANTHIAS: Horrible – it keeps on changing. It's sort of like a bull – no, now it's a mule! Wait a minute, it's changing again. [*He whistles.*] Oh, my, what a beautiful girl!

DIONYSUS: Here, let me past, quickly!

XANTHIAS: Oh, what a shame – it's stopped being a woman, it's turned into a dog.

DIONYSUS [*with a shudder*]: It must be the Empusa.[111]

XANTHIAS: Her face is all lit up.

DIONYSUS: Has she got a copper leg?

XANTHIAS: Yes, I do believe you're right, sir. And the other one's made of cow dung.

DIONYSUS: Oh, where can I go?

XANTHIAS: Where can *I* go, come to that?

DIONYSUS [*appealing to the priest of Dionysus, who is sitting in the front row*]: Oh, mister priest, oh, protect me – oh, oh, help, help! Remember that drink we're going to have after the show!

XANTHIAS: Heracles, old man, we've had it.

DIONYSUS: Sh! Don't call me that, for heaven's sake: don't breathe that name down here.

XANTHIAS: Well, Dionysus, then.

DIONYSUS: No, no, that's even worse.

XANTHIAS [*to the spectre*]: Over that way! That's right! Now keep straight on!

[DIONYSUS, *thinking these remarks are addressed to him, flees blindly through the auditorium.*]

No, no, not you! Come back! This way, guvnor!

DIONYSUS [*returning*]: What's happened?

XANTHIAS: It's all right now. We've weathered the storm. Or, as Hegelochus would say, the pillows heave no more.[112] In other words, she's gone.

DIONYSUS: You're not kidding?

XANTHIAS: I swear it.

DIONYSUS: Swear it again.

XANTHIAS: Cross my heart.

DIONYSUS: You're quite sure?

XANTHIAS: She's gone, I tell you.

DIONYSUS [*airily*]: I must say she had me quite worried for a moment, Xanthias. Which of the gods do we have to thank for that little spot of bother, I wonder? Ether, the residence of Zeus? Or the Foot of Time? [*He laughs heartily at his own joke.*]

XANTHIAS: Tsh!

DIONYSUS [*in a panic again*]: What is it?

XANTHIAS: Listen, can't you hear it?

DIONYSUS: What?

XANTHIAS: Music. Flute-playing.

DIONYSUS: So it is. [*He sniffs the air.*] And a most mystical whiff of torches. Keep quiet, let's crouch down here and listen.

[They conceal themselves. The sound of music comes nearer, and the CHORUS *is heard chanting 'Iacchos, Iacchos!']*

XANTHIAS: These must be the happy bands of Initiates he told us about. Yes, they're singing the hymn to Iacchos, by that fellow Diagoras.[113]

DIONYSUS: Yes, I think you're right. Let's keep quiet and make sure.

[Enter, by torchlight, the CHORUS OF INITIATES,[114] *the men and the women entering in separate groups, each with a male leader.]*

CHORUS:

Come, Iacchos, leave your temple,
    Join your celebrants devout!
Come and dance across the meadows,
    Lead us in the mystic rout!

Toss your head and swing the berries
    On your myrtle crown so gay;
Stamp and prance with feet delirious,
    Whirling every qualm away.

Here with dancing, songs, and laughter –
    All the best of all the arts –
We your worshippers await you:
    Come, oh come! The revel starts!

[They dance, with suitable abandon, as the sacrificial meal is prepared and the wine cups filled.]

XANTHIAS *[mocking them]*: Oh, Persephone, Paragon of Perfection, oh, Divine Daughter of Demeter – what a wonderful smell of pork!

DIONYSUS: You'd better keep quiet, or you won't get so much as a sausage.

[The CHORUS *resume their hymn. At the cue in the second line, the torches are raised and flare up, and a strange and beautiful light fills the stage.]*

CHORUS:

Call upon him, call Iacchos!
    Raise the torches, wake the flame!
See, at once the darkness scatters
    As we shout the sacred name.

See, the meadows blaze! Iacchos,
Day-star of our secret rite,
Comes to wake the mystic knowledge
Born in us at dead of night,

Turning all to dance and movement,
Setting souls and bodies free;
Aged knees shake off their stiffness
In the rhythmic ecstasy.

Shine for us, and we will follow!
Lead us on, our strength renew:
Young and old shall dance together
'Mid the flowers, drenched with dew.

[*They dance again, and then sit down to partake of the sacrificial meat and wine. Meanwhile the two* LEADERS *pronounce the traditional warning to the uninitiated.*]

MEN'S LEADER:

Now all you bystanders, keep silent, we pray!
The holy procession proceeds on its way.
And all you outsiders who know not our rite,
Stay away from our revels and keep out of sight.

CHORUS: Stand away there, outsiders, you're not wanted here.

WOMEN'S LEADER:

We've no use for bounders who don't understand
The traditions of Comedy noble and grand;
Who snigger and leer till the festival's ended,
And find dirty meanings where none are intended.

CHORUS: Stand away there, outsiders, you're not wanted here.

MEN'S LEADER:

We don't want the leaders who fan party strife
When what we all need is a peaceable life;
Or the customs inspector from somewhere near by[115]
Who's been smuggling out naval supplies on the sly.

CHORUS: Stand away there, outsiders, you're not wanted here.

WOMEN'S LEADER:

Oh we don't want the traitor who sides with the foe,
We don't want the soldier who lets the fort go;
The greedy official who's even prepared
To betray his own City, if suitably squared.

CHORUS: Stand away there, outsiders, you're not wanted here.
MEN'S LEADER:

> Some people there are who, when guyed in a play,
> Take it out on the poet by cutting his pay.[116]
> We've no use for them, nor for poets who bore us
> And who get taken short in the middle of the chorus.[117]

CHORUS: Stand away there, outsiders, you're not wanted here.

[*The feasting over, the* CHORUS *group themselves for the ceremony, which consists of songs and dances in honour of Persephone, Demeter, and Iacchos.*]

MEN'S LEADER [*solemnly*]: Sing now, and let the festival begin.
CHORUS:

> Now we're well fortified,
> Let's get into our stride;
> To the sweet flow'ry meadow let's march off in pride;
> At distinguished bystanders
> We'll jest and we'll jeer;
> It's the feast of the Goddess, we've nothing to fear.
>
> The praises we'll sing
> Of the Princess of Spring,
> Who returns at this season salvation to bring;
> Though traitors[118] endeavour
> Her plan to frustrate,
> We know she will save us before it's too late.

WOMEN'S LEADER: And now, in a different strain, let us honour our Queen and Goddess Demeter, Bringer of Plenty, with a holy hymn.

CHORUS:

> Queen Demeter, stand before us,
> Smile upon your favourite Chorus!
> Grant that when we dance and play
> As befits your holy day,
> Part in earnest, part in jest,
> We may shine above the rest,
> And our play in all men's eyes
> Favour find, and win the prize.

MEN'S LEADER: Now with your songs call forth the youthful god, to join us in our dancing.

MEN:

> Iacchos, Iacchos, lead on to the shrine! [119]
> Our hearts are on fire with your music divine!
> Come, teach us to dance over hedgerows and stiles –
> And to keep up the tempo for twelve blooming miles.

ALL:

> Iacchos, Iacchos, dance on and we'll follow.

WOMEN:

> Last night as we revelled from twilight to dawn
> My clothes and my sandals to ribbons were torn.
> It's the fault of the god, but perhaps his defence is
> That it raises a laugh and cuts down the expenses. [120]

ALL:

> Iacchos, Iacchos, dance on and we'll follow.

MEN:

> A girl I did spy as we sported and played:
> A really remarkably pretty young maid.
> She winked and she giggled, but what I liked best
> Was the little pink titty that peeped from her vest.

ALL:

> Iacchos, Iacchos, dance on and we'll follow.

XANTHIAS: Come to that, I wouldn't mind sporting with her myself. Being a sociable sort of fellow, and all that.

DIONYSUS: Come along, then, what are we waiting for?

> [*They join in the ensuing dance, after which the* CHORUS *halts, facing the audience, with* DIONYSUS *and* XANTHIAS *now in the centre, and proceeds to 'jest and jeer' at notable members of the audience, as promised in the hymn to Persephone.*]

CHORUS:

You've heard of Archedemus? [121] Well, he's not renowned for looks;
His parentage is doubtful, and he isn't on the books;
Yet up among the dead men he's the prince of all the crooks –
It's the way they do things now.

Oh what's come over Cleisthenes? [122] He looks so full of care;
He's lost his lovely boy-friend and his sad cries rend the air
As he wields a pair of tweezers on his last superfluous hair –
It's the way they do things now.

Now Callias[123] the naval man is at his best ashore,
Where he can show his seamanship in actions by the score:
And when they see his lion-skin the girls cry out for more –
  It's the way they do things now.

DIONYSUS:
Excuse me interrupting, but we're strangers here in Hell:
Can some kind person tell us, where does Master Pluto dwell?

CHORUS:
His house is not so distant, you can find it very well –
  It's just behind you now.

DIONYSUS:
Pick up the luggage, Xanthias, let's knock and take a chance.

XANTHIAS:
I'm tired of all this portering, I'd rather stay and dance.
Another time I hope you'll send your luggage in advance –
  It's the way they do things now.

  [DIONYSUS and XANTHIAS *return to their luggage as the* CHORUS
  prepare for the procession.]

MEN'S LEADER: Dance on then merrily through the flowery grove;
  let all that have part in our festival tread the sacred precinct of the
  Goddess.

WOMEN'S LEADER: And I will bear the holy torch for the girls and
  the women; let them dance to the glory of the Goddess, the whole
  night long.

  [*The* WOMEN *and their* LEADER *dance off.*]

MEN:
  Let us hasten to the meadow, where the roses are so sweet,
  And the little flowers grow in profusion at our feet;
  With the blessèd Fates to lead us we will laugh and sing and play,
  And dance the choral dances in our own traditional way.

  Oh, to us alone is given, when our earthly days are done,
  To gaze upon the splendour of a never-setting sun;
  For we saw the holy Mysteries and heard the god's behest,
  And were mindful of our duty both to kinsman and to guest.[124]

SCENE 2: DIONYSUS *and* XANTHIAS *stand before the palace of*
PLUTO

[*The* CHORUS *are present, but stand well apart from the action.*]

DIONYSUS [*approaching the door*]: What sort of a knock should one give, I wonder? [*He raises his hand to knock, but thinks better of it.*] Must conform to local customs, you know.

XANTHIAS: Now come on, don't shilly-shally! Don't forget you're supposed to be Heracles!

DIONYSUS [*knocking timidly*]: Hallo there! Slave!

[*The door is opened by* AEACUS, *the doorkeeper of Hades, a formidable figure.*]

AEACUS: Who's there?

DIONYSUS: Heracles the b-b-bold.

AEACUS: Ah, so it's you, foul, shameless, desperate, good-for-nothing villain that you are. Ought to be ashamed of yourself, you ought! Coming down here, trying to throttle a poor little dog! Poor old Cerberus! I was responsible for that there animal, let me tell you. Well, you're caught now, see? Hah! I'll have you flung over the cliff, down to the black-hearted Stygian rocks, and you'll be chased by the prowling hounds of Hell and the hundred-headed viper will tear your guts out and the Tartessian lamprey shall devour your lungs and the Tithrasian Gorgons can have your kidneys and – just wait there a moment while I go and fetch them.

[AEACUS *goes back into the palace.* DIONYSUS *collapses in terror.*]

XANTHIAS: Here, what are you doing down there?

DIONYSUS: Dear me, an involuntary libation! Invoke the god.[125]

XANTHIAS: Stand up, sir, do: somebody might see you.

DIONYSUS: I feel a little faint, Xanthias – I don't feel very well, really. Here, give me a sponge.

[XANTHIAS *extracts one from the luggage.*]

Press it on my heart, there's a good lad.

XANTHIAS: There you are.

DIONYSUS: No, here. That's it.

XANTHIAS: Heart's slipped a bit, hasn't it, sir?

DIONYSUS: What? Oh, yes, it does that sometimes, you know. Sudden shock. Gets mixed up with the lower intestine.

XANTHIAS: Looks like a common case of blue funk to me.

DIONYSUS: Xanthias, how can you say such a thing? After I've had the presence of mind to ask you for a sponge.

XANTHIAS: Very courageous of you, sir.

DIONYSUS: Yes, I think it was, rather. Most people would have been frightened by all those threats and long words. Confess, now, weren't you a weeny bit scared yourself?

XANTHIAS: Didn't turn a hair.

DIONYSUS: Well, if you're feeling so brave and resolute, how about taking my place? Here you are, you take the club and lion-skin. Chance to show your courage. And I'll carry the luggage for you. There!

XANTHIAS: Anything you say, guvnor; you're the boss.
    [*They make the exchange.*]
There, how do I look? Reckon the part suits me better than it does you, you old coward!

DIONYSUS: Hm! A very good imitation of a slave dressed up as Heracles. Come on, let me have those bundles.
    [*Persephone's* MAID *comes out of the palace.*]

MAID [*to Xanthias*]: Oh, Heracles, dear, how sweet of you to come and see us again! As soon as my mistress heard you were coming she started baking – and there's several cauldrons full of pea soup, and we're roasting a whole ox for you, and she's been making cakes and biscuits – but come along in!

XANTHIAS: Well, thank you very much, but I –

MAID: Nonsense, in you come: the birds are done to a turn, and you should just see the dessert! She's mixed the drinks herself, they're very special. [*She tries to drag him inside.*] Come along, there's a dear.

XANTHIAS: Well, as a matter of fact. I've had breakfast already.

MAID: Don't be ridiculous. I'm not going to let you get away like that. There's such a pretty flute-girl waiting for you inside, and some other girls to dance for you.

XANTHIAS [*rubbing his hands*]: Dancing-girls, eh?

MAID: Hand-plucked, and all in the freshest bloom of middle age. Come in and see for yourself. The cook's just ready with the fish, and the table's laid.

XANTHIAS: Just tell those dancing-girls I'll be with them directly. [*To Dionysus*] Boy, bring the luggage in, will you?
    [*The* MAID *goes in.*]

DIONYSUS: Here, wait a minute! Can it be that you are taking my little joke seriously? Just give me back my things and get back to your luggage!

XANTHIAS: *Can it be* that you are thinking of taking back this beautiful lion-skin, after you gave it me and all?

DIONYSUS: I'm not *thinking* of doing so, I *am* doing so. Hand it over, sharp!

XANTHIAS: Well, I'll be – ! Ye gods!

DIONYSUS: Gods my foot. Don't you forget that I'm a god and you're not, my boy. You didn't really expect to get away with it as Heracles, did you? Why, you're only a puny mortal!

XANTHIAS: All right, all right, take them. [*Viciously*] If there's ever any other little services I can render . . .

CHORUS:
> The moral is plain as plain can be;
> As everyone knows who has served at sea,
> If you want to be comfy just roll with the ship!
> Don't stand like a fool with a stiff upper lip,
> But learn from Theramenes, that shrewd politician,[126]
> To move with the times and improve your position.

DIONYSUS:
> You can hardly expect me to watch my own man
> Getting down to the job on a handsome divan
> And giving me orders, as likely as not:
> 'Boy, straighten these covers and bring me the pot!
> And take that lascivious grin off your face,
> Or I'll teach you a slave should remember his place!'

[*No sooner has* DIONYSUS *resumed the lion-skin than two* LANDLADIES *enter.*]

FIRST LANDLADY: Come here quick, here's that scoundrel who came to our inn once and ate up sixteen loaves.

SECOND LANDLADY: Why, so it is.

XANTHIAS: This isn't going to be nice for somebody.

FIRST LANDLADY: And twenty portions of roast lamb at half an obol each.

XANTHIAS: Who's going to get it in the neck now?

SECOND LANDLADY: And all those onions.

DIONYSUS: Nonsense, madam, you don't know what you are talking about.

FIRST LANDLADY: Thought I wouldn't recognize him, in his lady's boots! – And what about all that salt fish you had?

SECOND LANDLADY: Yes, and the cheese, fresh that day it was. Wolfed the lot, he did, baskets and all.

FIRST LANDLADY: And when I asked him for the money, oh, you should have seen the look he gave me. Started roaring like a lion.

XANTHIAS: That's him all right. He goes round doing that.

FIRST LANDLADY: Then he comes at me with his sword – I thought he'd gone off his head.

SECOND LANDLADY: Don't blame you, dearie.

FIRST LANDLADY.: Oh, he did give us a turn, didn't he, ducks? Had to run upstairs and lock ourselves in. Then, of course, off he went like a streak of lightning. *And* took the best doormat with him.

XANTHIAS: That's right. He never can resist a doormat.

FIRST LANDLADY: Well, we must do something. I know: what about Cleon,[127] he's down here now, isn't he? He'll help us. Run and see if you can find him, will you, dear?

SECOND LANDLADY: Yes, or Hyperbolus – he's passed over too.

FIRST LANDLADY: We'll fix him – look at that great greedy mouth of his – I'd like to knock his teeth down his throat for him, eating us out of house and home!

SECOND LANDLADY: Over the cliff with him!

FIRST LANDLADY: Slit his throat with a billhook!

SECOND LANDLADY: I'll go and find Cleon: he'll have him up in court this very day as ever is.

[*The* LANDLADIES *shake their fists at Dionysus and go out.*]

DIONYSUS: You know, Xanthias, I've grown very fond of you.

XANTHIAS: Ah, no, you don't! I know what you're getting at. I am *not* going to be Heracles again.

DIONYSUS: Dear Xanthias! *Nice* Xanthias!

XANTHIAS: How could I possibly get away with it as Heracles? I'm only a puny mortal.

DIONYSUS: Yes, yes, I know I've offended you, and you've every right to be cross. Look, you take this lovely lion-skin, it suits you beautifully. And if ever I ask for it back, may I rot in hell, and my wife and children too – and bleary old Archedemus[128] as well, while we're about it.

XANTHIAS: Right! On those terms, I'll do it.

[*He takes the lion-skin and club, and loads* DIONYSUS *once again with the baggage.*]

CHORUS:

Well, now you're dressed up just the same as before,
    And a sight to make everyone tremble,
You must roll your eyes and swagger and roar
    Like the god you're supposed to resemble.

If you flinch or boggle or muff your part
    And don't talk as brave as you oughter,
You'll be back with the baggage and breaking your heart
    'Cos you're only a perishing porter.

XANTHIAS:

I'm sure you are right: I've been thinking a lot –
    I know my own master, and if he
Considers there's anything good to be got,
    He'll have all these things back in a jiffy.

Meanwhile I must practise my vinegar face,
    And throw out my chest and stand steady.
How's this for a truly horrific grimace?
    (Just in time – someone's coming already!)

[AEACUS *returns, with numerous* SLAVES *carrying whips, ropes, fetters, and instruments of torture.*]

AEACUS: Quick, tie up this dog-stealing bastard and let me give him what he deserves. Get cracking!

[*Two stalwart* SLAVES *bear down on* XANTHIAS.]

DIONYSUS: This isn't going to be nice for somebody!

XANTHIAS [*as Heracles*]: Hands off, ye dastardly varlets!

AEACUS: Tough, eh? Ditylas! Skobylas! Pardokas! Come here! The gentleman wants a fight.

[*Three more* SLAVES *come forward.*]

DIONYSUS: Ought to be ashamed of himself. Taking other people's things, and then resisting arrest!

AEACUS: Unheard-of effrontery.

DIONYSUS: A hardened criminal.

XANTHIAS: Listen, I've never been here before and I've not stolen so much as a bean belonging to you, strike me dead if I have. I'll tell you what I'll do: I'll let you torture this slave of mine.[129] And if I'm proved guilty, take me off and kill me.

AEACUS [*with relish, and a sharp change of attitude*]: What kind of torture do you suggest, sir?

XANTHIAS: Oh, give him the whole works. Rack, thumbscrew, gallows, cat-o'-nine-tails: pour vinegar up his nostrils, pile bricks on his chest – anything you like. Only don't hit him with a leek or a fresh spring onion. I won't stand for that – brings tears to my eyes.

AEACUS: Fair enough. But if he gets damaged in the process, I suppose you'll be wanting compensation.

XANTHIAS: No, no, don't worry about that. Just take him away and do your stuff.

AEACUS: We might as well do it here, under his master's eye. [*To Dionysus*] Come on, put down those traps, and mind you tell the truth.

DIONYSUS: No, no, look here, you can't – I mean to say – you can't torture *me*! I'm an immortal. I – I – I forbid it! If you do, I shall hold you responsible.

AEACUS: I beg your pardon?

DIONYSUS: I'm immortal, I say. I'm a god. Dionysus, Son of Zeus. And this fellow's a slave.

AEACUS: You hear that?

XANTHIAS: I'll say I do. All the more reason to flog him: if he's a god he won't feel anything.

DIONYSUS: Well, you're a god too, aren't you, Heracles, old man? Why not let them flog you too?

XANTHIAS: Fair enough. Whichever of us squeals first or even bats an eyelid isn't a god at all.

AEACUS: You're a good sport, sir, I can see that. I call that very fair and proper. [*He takes a rope's end from one of the slaves.*] Right! Bend over, both of you.

XANTHIAS: Wait a minute. How are you going to make sure it's a fair test?

AEACUS: Simple. You each get one stroke at a time, in turn.

XANTHIAS: Good idea.

  [XANTHIAS *bends over, and* DIONYSUS *reluctantly follows his example.*]

AEACUS [*giving Xanthias a good whack*]: There!

XANTHIAS: I bet you I won't even notice it.

AEACUS: I've hit you already.

XANTHIAS [*incredulously*] : No!

AEACUS : Now for the other one. [*He strikes Dionysus.*]

DIONYSUS : Well, get on with it.

AEACUS : I have.

DIONYSUS : Have you, by Jove? Well, you see? I didn't even sneeze.

AEACUS : Well, I don't know, I'm sure. Let's try the other one again.

XANTHIAS : Come on then!

    [AEACUS *whacks him hard.*]

  Holy smoke!

AEACUS : What's the matter? Something hurting you?

XANTHIAS : Most provoking! I'd forgotten all about the Festival of Heracles, up at the Diomeia.

AEACUS : Ah! A pious thought. [*To Dionysus*] Your turn.
    [*He gives Dionysus another good whack.*]

DIONYSUS : Ow! [*He leaps in the air, with his hands clutched to his bottom.*]

AEACUS : What's the matter?

DIONYSUS : Men on horseback, look! [*He continues to prance about, imitating a man on horseback.*]

AEACUS : Funny they should make you cry.

DIONYSUS : There's a smell of onions.

AEACUS : Sure you didn't feel anything?

DIONYSUS : *Feel* anything? No, not a thing.

AEACUS : Ah, well, we'll have to try the other fellow. [*He whacks Xanthias.*]

XANTHIAS : Owch!

AEACUS : Aha!

XANTHIAS [*calmly*] : Would you mind pulling out this thorn for me?

AEACUS : What *is* this all about? Well, here we go again. [*He whacks Dionysus as hard as he can.*]

DIONYSUS : Apollo! – h'm, Lord of Delos' holy isle, and something something in the tumty tum –

AEACUS : That hurt him, did you hear?

DIONYSUS : How does it go, now? And something something in the . . . Wonderful poet, Hipponax.

XANTHIAS : You're wasting your time, there's too much padding down there. Try this place here, just under the ribs.

AEACUS : No, I've got a better idea. [*To Dionysus*] Turn round this way. [*He pokes him in the paunch.*]

DIONYSUS [*screaming*] : Poseidon!

XANTHIAS: Somebody get hurt?

DIONYSUS [*singing at the top of his voice*]: . . . king of the mighty deep,
  Poseidon, lord of the crags and cliffs . . .

AEACUS: I'm blest if I can tell which of you is the god. You'll have
  to come inside. The master and Persephone'll be able to tell all right:
  they're gods themselves.

DIONYSUS: I must say I wish you'd thought of that a bit sooner.

  [DIONYSUS *and* XANTHIAS *go in, followed by* AEACUS *and the*
  SLAVES.]

CHORUS:

  Come, Muse of the holy dancing choir,
  With wit and charm our songs inspire!
  Here sit ten thousand men of sense,
  A very enlightened audience,
  Who expect a lot of a dancing choir
  And set their hopes of honour higher
  Than CLEOPHON – for he has heard
  The warning of a fateful bird,
  A rather enigmatic swallow
  Whose words, though difficult to follow,
  Should not defy interpretation
  When once translated from the Thracian.[130]
  And this is what the mystic fowl
  Like plaintive nightingale doth howl:
  'You always vote "agin", but wait!
  Next time – or next – you're *for it*, mate!'

  [*The* LEADER *comes forward and addresses the audience.*]

LEADER:

  We chorus folk two privileges prize:
  To amuse you, citizens, and to advise.
  So, mid the fun that marks this sacred day,
  We'll put on serious looks, and say our say.
  And first for those misguided souls I plead
  Who in the past to PHRYNICHUS[131] paid heed.
  'Tis history now – their folly they regret;
  The time has come to pardon and forget.
  Oh, yes, they erred, but does it seem quite right,
  When slaves who helped us in a single fight

Now vote beside our allies from Plataea[132]
And put on masters' clothes, like Xanthias here –
Not that I disagree with that decision;
No, no, it showed intelligence and vision;
But if we're going to treat these men as brothers,
Let's be consistent and forgive the others.
When we have been so wise, it seems a pity
That men of our own kin, who've served the City
In many naval battles, not just one,
Should still be paying for this thing they've done.
Come, wise Athenians, swallow down your pride!
We need these loyal kinsmen on our side –
As they will be, if every man who fights
Is a full citizen with all his rights.
But if we choose to strut and put on airs
While Athens founders in a sea of cares,
In days to come, when history is penned,
They'll say we must have gone clean round the bend.

CHORUS:

If I've any knowledge of people at all,
I can tell you with confidence what will befall
A rascal with whom we have long been encumbered,
But whose days on this earth, I assure you, are numbered.
Though in size he is small, as a bore he's colossal;
Of peace and goodwill he is not an apostle.
He's as fly as a monkey, his voice might be quieter,
And he does very well as a wash-house proprietor.
He is Lord of the Earth, for he sells it in pots
For cleaning the woollies and getting out spots;
He makes up detergents that won't even lather,
For he mixes in ashes to make them go farther.
Yes, CLEIGENES[133] knows that his joys will soon cease,
Yet he can't be persuaded to vote for a peace:
He prefers 'the big stick' – for he needs one each night
To protect him from thieves when he's rolling home tight.

LEADER:

I'll tell you what I think about the way
This city treats her soundest men today:
By a coincidence more sad than funny,

182

It's very like the way we treat our money.
The noble silver drachma, that of old
We were so proud of, and the recent gold,
Coins that rang true, clean-stamped and worth their weight
Throughout the world, have ceased to circulate.
Instead, the purses of Athenian shoppers
Are full of shoddy silver-plated coppers.
Just so, when men are needed by the nation,
The best have been withdrawn from circulation.
Men of good birth and breeding, men of parts,
Well schooled in wrestling and in gentler arts,
These we abuse, and trust instead to knaves,
Newcomers, aliens, copper-pated slaves,
All rascals – honestly, what men to choose!
There was a time when you'd have scorned to use
Men so debased, so far beyond the pale,
Even as scapegoats to be dragged from jail
And flogged to death outside the city gate.
My foolish friends, change now, it's not too late!
Try the good ones again : if they succeed,
You will have proved that you have sense indeed ;
And if things don't go well, if these good men
All fail, and Athens comes to grief, why then
Discerning folk will murmur (let us hope) :
'She's hanged herself – but what a splendid rope!'

ACT TWO

SCENE: *Before* PLUTO'S *palace.* XANTHIAS *and an elderly* SLAVE *of Pluto's are engaged on light menial tasks*

SLAVE: Oh, he's a real gentleman, your master is, I can tell that.

XANTHIAS: Yes, you can always tell. There are only two things a real gentleman understands: soaking and poking.

SLAVE: No, but I mean, fancy him not beating you for making out that you was the master and him the slave!

XANTHIAS: He'd have been sorry if he'd tried.

SLAVE: Ah, that's the way I like to hear a slave talking. He, he, he! I love that.

XANTHIAS: Love it, eh?

SLAVE: Why, there's nothing I like better than cursing the master behind his back.

XANTHIAS: Ah, you sly old beggar! I bet you mutter a few things under your breath when he's had a bash at you, eh?

SLAVE: Muttering? He, he, he! Yes, I like a bit of muttering.

XANTHIAS [*encouraging the chuckles*]: And what about prying into his private affairs?

SLAVE: Prying? He. he, he! Yes, I like a bit of prying.

XANTHIAS: Ah, we're going to get along fine, you and me. Have you ever tried eavesdropping when he's got company?

SLAVE: Eavesdropping? Ah, that's real sport, that is.

XANTHIAS: And then you pass it all on to the neighbours, eh?

SLAVE: Well, that's where the fun comes in, ain't it? No end of a kick, that gives me.

XANTHIAS: Put it there, grandpa: give us a hug, that's right. – Listen, my dear old soulmate, my partner in crime, what's all that yelling and shouting and quarrelling going on in there?

SLAVE: That'll be Aeschylus and Euripides.

XANTHIAS: What on earth are they up to?

SLAVE: Oh, there's great goings on among the dead these days, great goings on. Civil war, you might almost call it.

XANTHIAS: What's it all about?

SLAVE: Well, you see, all the fine arts and that, the skilled professions like, there's a sort of custom down here, whoever's the best in each profession, see, he has the right to have his dinner in the Great Hall, with his own chair of honour, up near Pluto, you follow me?

XANTHIAS: I see.

SLAVE: But if somebody else comes along that's better in his profession than what he is, then he has to stand down and let the other feller have the chair.

XANTHIAS: Oh. Well, what is it that's upset Aeschylus so much?

SLAVE: Well, he had the chair for Tragedy, see, because he was the best, like.

XANTHIAS: Who's got it now?

SLAVE: Well, then along comes Euripides, and starts showing off to all the fellers we've got down here – cut-throats, highwaymen, murderers, burglars, regular rough lot they are – and of course he soon has them all twisted round his little finger, with all his arguments and clever talk and that. And they all start saying to themselves, 'He's got something, this bloke,' and getting all worked up, see? So then Euripides, *he* thinks *he* ought to have the chair instead of Aeschylus; so he goes and sits in it, and pushes Aeschylus out.

XANTHIAS: Well, didn't he get flung out on his ear?

SLAVE: Not a bit of it: the people all said *they* had the right to judge which was the cleverest.

XANTHIAS: What people? All those cut-throats and pickpockets you were talking about?

SLAVE: Yes, and a devil of a row they kicked up too.

XANTHIAS: Didn't anyone side with Aeschylus?

SLAVE: Well, you see, there ain't many decent folk down here: just take a look for yourself. [*He indicates the audience.*]

XANTHIAS: What's Pluto going to do about it?

SLAVE: Oh, he's going to have it all done proper, like a contest, see, and both of them showing their skill, and proper judging, all legal, like.

XANTHIAS: Just the two of them? Hasn't Sophocles put in a claim?

SLAVE: Oh, no, when *he* came down here[134] he went straight up to Aeschylus and took his hand and kissed him like a brother. And

Aeschylus says, 'Come on,' he says, 'you must have the chair now,'
he says. But Sophocles, he won't hear of it. But now he's sent a
message: with this contest coming on, he says, he'll stand by for
third man – if Aeschylus wins he'll just go on as before, but if Euripides wins he'll take him on himself.

XANTHIAS: It's really coming off, then?

SLAVE: Any minute now, here where we're standing. [*Confidentially*]
They'll want the scales out here, see, for weighing the poetry.

XANTHIAS: Weighing the poetry? I've never heard of a *poet* trying
to give short weight.

[SLAVES *emerge from the palace, carrying fantastic pieces of weighing
and measuring equipment, and arranging the seating for the contest.
Simultaneously, the* CHORUS *makes an unobtrusive entrance.*]

SLAVE: Oh, yes, it's all got to be weighed and measured up proper,
with rulers and yardsticks for the words, and compasses and wedges
and I don't know what.

XANTHIAS: Regular torture chamber.

SLAVE: Yes, Euripides says he's going to put every line to the test.

XANTHIAS: I reckon Aeschylus must be boiling with rage by this
time.

SLAVE: He's been going round all day with his head down, glaring
like a bull.

XANTHIAS: Who's the judge going to be?

SLAVE: Ah, that was a ticklish problem: hard to find anyone clever
enough. And then Aeschylus said he couldn't see eye to eye with
the Athenians anyway –

XANTHIAS: All those burglars and what not. Quite. I see his point.

SLAVE: – and as for the others, he says, none of them could tell a poet
from the hind leg of a donkey. So in the end they settled on your
master, who's supposed to be a bit of an expert, after all. But we'd
better go in: you never want to get in their way when they're busy,
it just doesn't pay.

[XANTHIAS *and the* SLAVE *withdraw, as* DIONYSUS *emerges from
the palace, looking well feasted and surrounded by* DANCING-GIRLS,
ATTENDANTS, *and a company of the* DISTINGUISHED DEAD,
*who now take their seats in order to watch the contest. A special throne
has been provided for* DIONYSUS, *who is hardly seated before the
sounds of angry altercation are heard from the doorway, and* EURIPIDES
and AESCHYLUS *appear, arguing heatedly. They are eventually hushed*

by the assembled company, become conscious of their surroundings, and pay their respects to Dionysus. The latter motions them genially to take their seats on either side of him. Both are boiling inwardly, however, and during the singing of the ode which follows they continue their quarrel in pantomime. As soon as the ode is finished, EURIPIDES *bursts into his first intelligible speech.*]

CHORUS:

Ah, how impressive the rage that burns in the heart of the Thunderer!
Vainly the fangs of his rival are bared in a gesture of hate!
Note how superbly he raves, with what fine independence his eye-balls
    In divers directions gyrate!
Words are their weapons: watch out, as the armour-clad syllables hurtle,
Helmeted, crested, and plumed, from the lips of the Poet Most High!
Wait for the clash and the din as the metaphors mingle and jumble,
    The sparks as the particles fly!

See the great spread of his mane, as it bristles in leonine fury:
No one can doubt any more that those whiskers are truly his own!
Huge are the words that he hurls, great compounds with rivets and bolts in,
    And epithets hewn out of stone.

Now 'tis the challenger's turn to reply to this verbal bombardment:
Neatly each phrase he dissects, with intelligence crafty and keen;
Harmless around him the adjectives fall, as he ducks into cover
    And squeaks, 'It depends what you mean!'

EURIPIDES [*leaping to his feet*]: I see no reason at all why I should withdraw. I happen to be the better poet.
DIONYSUS: What do you say to that, Aeschylus? No comment?
    [AESCHYLUS *remains speechless with rage.*]
EURIPIDES: Isn't that rather typical of the whole Aeschylean approach? The majestic silence, the pregnant pause?
DIONYSUS: I do feel, Euripides, that you've made rather a sweeping claim, you know.
EURIPIDES: I saw through him years ago. All that rugged grandeur – it's all so *uncultivated.* No restraint. No subtlety at all. Just a torrent

of verbiage, stiff with superlatives, and padded out with pretentious polysyllables.

AESCHYLUS [*on the verge of apoplexy*]: Ohh! Well, I suppose that is about the level of criticism to expect from a person of your rustic ancestry.[135] And what are *your* tragedies but a concatenation of commonplaces, as threadbare as the tattered characters who utter them?

DIONYSUS: Now, Aeschylus, aren't we getting a little heated? Calm down!

AESCHYLUS: Not till I've told this – this cripple-merchant where he gets off.

DIONYSUS: Fetch me a black lamb quickly! Stormy weather blowing up.

AESCHYLUS: Not only do you clutter your stage with cripples and beggars, but you allow your heroes to sing and dance like Cretans. You build your plots round unsavoury topics like incest and –

DIONYSUS: Whoa there, stand back! [*He thrusts Aeschylus firmly back into his seat.*] With all due respect, Aeschylus! Euripides, you poor fellow, wouldn't it be wiser if you moved back out of range a little? I should hate you to get hit on the head by a principal clause and give birth to a premature tragedy. Aeschylus, you must try not to lose your temper. Surely two literary men can criticize each other's work without screaming at each other like fishwives, or flaring up like a forest fire.

EURIPIDES: I'm ready for him! Let Aeschylus have the first word if he likes: I can take it! Criticize what you like – diction, lyrics, plot. I don't care which play you take: *Peleus, Aeolus, Meleager, Telephus* – yes, even *Telephus*.

DIONYSUS: Aeschylus?

AESCHYLUS: I had hoped to avoid having a contest here: it puts me at a considerable disadvantage.

DIONYSUS: How so?

AESCHYLUS: Well, you see, *my* works happen to have outlived me, so I don't have them down here with me. His died with him. But never mind: let's have a match by all means, if you think that's a good idea.

DIONYSUS: Then we must do the thing properly. Bring the brazier and the incense! As the judge of this most, ah, interesting cultural event I must offer up a prayer, before the shafts of wit begin to fly.

[DIONYSUS *rises, takes incense and a libation cup from an attendant and goes to the altar. All present put wreaths on their heads.* DIONYSUS *burns incense and pours a libation.*]

DIONYSUS [*to the Chorus*]: A hymn to the Muses!

CHORUS:

> When men of sage and subtle mind
>   In fierce debate their views do vent,
> And strive some deathless phrase to find
>   To mask each specious argument –
> Then Zeus' virgin daughters nine
> Stand by to watch the sport divine.
>
> Come then today, ye Muses bright!
>   Two grimmer foes ne'er took the field:
> For one is armed with words of might,
>   And one the sword of wit doth wield.
> O heavenly maids, your presence lend!
> The fight is on! Descend! Descend!

DIONYSUS: Now you two must each offer a prayer, before we begin.

AESCHYLUS: O Demeter, that didst nourish my brain, may I prove worthy of thy Mysteries!

DIONYSUS: And now Euripides: take the censer, it's your turn.

EURIPIDES: No, no thank you, I pray to other gods.

DIONYSUS: What, special ones of your own? A private Pantheon?

EURIPIDES: Precisely.

DIONYSUS: Carry on, then; pray to your lay gods.

EURIPIDES: Hail, Ether, my grazing ground! Hail, Pivot of my Tongue! Hail, Mind! Hail, sentient Nostrils! Inspire me with all the right answers, amen!

CHORUS:

> We're expecting, of course, to pick up a few tips
>   From these poets so clever and wise,
> As the elegant vocables fall from their lips
>   And their tempers progressively rise.
>
> Since neither is lacking in brains or in grit
>   It should be a most thrilling debate;
> But while one pins his hopes on his neatly turned wit,
>   The other relies upon weight.

189

For shrewd dialectic he cares not a jot;
  And though traps be contrived for his fall
He'll swoop down like a storm and demolish the lot –
  Quips, quibbles, opponent, and all.

[DIONYSUS *and the* TWO POETS *have resumed their seats, and the
contest begins.*]

DIONYSUS: Right. Off we go. Real, clever, original stuff, mind –
no far-fetched comparisons, no clichés!

[*He invites Euripides to begin.*]

EURIPIDES: Before I deal with my own work as a creative writer, I
should like to say a few words about my opponent. To put it
briefly, he is a mountebank and an impostor. Look at the way he
cheated his audience: brought up on Phrynichus, they were pretty
stupid anyway. The play would begin with a seated figure, all
muffled up – Niobe, for example, or Achilles: face veiled, very
dramatic, not a word uttered.

DIONYSUS: Yes, I remember.

EURIPIDES: Then the Chorus would rattle off a string of odes – four
of them, one after the other: still not a syllable from the muffled
figure.

DIONYSUS: I must say I rather enjoyed the old silent days. Better than
all this talk we get nowadays.

EURIPIDES: That is merely a confession of stupidity.

DIONYSUS: You may be right. But go on. Why did he do that?

EURIPIDES: Well, the whole thing was a swindle, of course. The
audience sat there all tensed up, waiting for Niobe to say something. And she just didn't. The play went on, and Niobe sat and
sat.

DIONYSUS: Oh, the wretch! D'you know, I never tumbled to that!
Now keep still, Aeschylus, what are you fidgeting for?

EURIPIDES: He knows he's beaten. Well, eventually, after a lot more
of this nonsense, about half-way through the play we get a speech.
And what a speech! A dozen great galumphing phrases, fearsome
things with crests and shaggy eyebrows. Magnificent! Nobody
knew what they meant, of course.

[AESCHYLUS *utters a moan of rage.*]

DIONYSUS: What *is* that peculiar noise?

EURIPIDES: One just couldn't make sense of anything, it was all –

DIONYSUS [to Aeschylus]: Oh, it's you, gnashing your teeth! Well, don't do it. I don't like it.

EURIPIDES: Scamanders, fosses, shields with brazen eagle-dragons on them: words that made you dizzy to hear them.

DIONYSUS: Yes, I once lay awake half the night trying to figure out what kind of a bird a tawny hippocock might be.

AESCHYLUS: It was the device painted on the ships, of course. What ignorance!

DIONYSUS: Oh, I thought it must be another name for our friend Eryxis.[136]

EURIPIDES: Is a cock of any kind a suitable theme for tragedy?

AESCHYLUS: And you, you enemy of the gods, what did you put into *your* plays, may I ask?

EURIPIDES: No hippococks or goatstags, for a start – or any other mythical monsters from Persian tapestries. When I took over Tragedy from you, the poor creature was in a dreadful state. Fatty degeneration of the Art. All swollen up with high-falutin' diction. I soon got her weight down, though: put her on a diet of particles, with a little finely chopped logic (taken peripatetically), and a special decoction of dialectic, cooked up from books and strained to facilitate digestion. Then I put her on to monodies –

DIONYSUS: With a pinch of Cephisophon.[137]

EURIPIDES: Well, at least I didn't keep rambling on about the first thing that came into my head; or plunge right into the middle of the story and leave everybody guessing. The first character to come on explained the background and origin of the play, straight away.

AESCHYLUS: Lucky he didn't have to explain yours.

EURIPIDES: Then again, as soon as the play began I had everyone hard at work: no one standing idle. Women and slaves, master, young maiden, aged crone – they all talked.

AESCHYLUS: And didn't you deserve to die for your audacity?

EURIPIDES: Not a bit of it. It was Democracy in action.

DIONYSUS: I should keep off that subject, old man, if I were you.[138]

EURIPIDES [indicating the audience]: And then, you see, I taught *these* people to talk –

AESCHYLUS: You certainly did, by heaven. If only you had been hacked in small pieces first!

EURIPIDES: I taught them subtle rules they could apply; how to turn a phrase neatly. I taught them to see, to observe, to interpret; to twist, to contrive; to suspect the worst, take nothing at its face value –

AESCHYLUS: You did indeed.

EURIPIDES: I wrote about familiar things, things the audience knew about, and could take me up on if necessary. I didn't try to bludgeon them into unconsciousness with long words, or startle them with characters like Cycnus or Memnon, dashing about with bells on their chariots and rings on their toes. You've only got to look at his disciples, and compare them with mine. He's got Phormisius and Megaenetus, the beard-lance-and-trumpet, tear-'em-limb-from-limb brigade: whereas I have Cleitophon and that smart fellow Theramenes.[139]

DIONYSUS: Theramenes? He's clever all right. Up to anything. Runs into trouble – damn near thing – and what happens? A lucky throw, and up pops Theramenes, well outside the danger zone as usual.

EURIPIDES: What I did was to teach the audience to use its brains, introduce a bit of logic into the drama. The public have learnt from me how to think, how to run their own households, to ask, 'Why is this so! What do we mean by that?'

DIONYSUS: That's right: whenever an Athenian comes home nowadays he shouts at the servants and starts asking, 'Why is the flour jar not in its proper place? What do you mean by biting the head off this sprat? What's happened to that cup I had last year? Where is yesterday's garlic, who's been nibbling at this olive?' Whereas before Euripides came along they just sat and stared idiotically.

CHORUS:

> You hear him, famed Achilles:
>   Be careful what you say!
> Beware lest fury seize you
>   And carry you away.
>
> What though he dares denounce you
>   With taunts and foul abuse?
> To fly into a passion
>   Will not be any use.
>
> So leave your angry fuming
>   And shorten sail instead;
> Wait till the wind blows steady
>   And then go straight ahead.

Come, master of the towering phrase, great poet of the age,
Lord of the bosh and balderdash that's talked upon the stage,
The time has come for action, flinch or falter you must not,
So open up the floodgates, and give him all you've got.

AESCHYLUS: It distresses and pains me to have been drawn into an altercation with this fellow. I find the whole situation extremely distasteful. But I suppose I shall have to reply, or he'll say I'm stumped for an answer. Well, I'm going to ask him a question. [*To Euripides*] What are the qualities that you look for in a good poet?

EURIPIDES: Technical skill – and he should teach a lesson, make people into better citizens.

AESCHYLUS: And if you have failed to do this? If you have presented good men, noble men, as despicable wretches, what punishment do you think you deserve?

DIONYSUS: Death. No good asking him.

AESCHYLUS: Well, now, look at the characters I left him. Fine, stalwart characters, larger than life, men who didn't shirk their responsibilities. My heroes weren't like these market-place loafers, swindlers, and rogues they write about nowadays: they were real heroes, breathing spears and lances, white-plumed helmets, breast-plates and greaves; heroes with hearts of good solid ox-leather, seven hides thick.

EURIPIDES: There you are! What did I tell you?

DIONYSUS: I hope he's not going to start hammering helmets here.

EURIPIDES: And how did you show the superiority of these characters of yours?

DIONYSUS: Come on, Aeschylus, there's no need to be pompous and difficult.

AESCHYLUS: By putting them into a martial drama.

EURIPIDES: Such as?

AESCHYLUS: Well, the *Seven Against Thebes*, for example. No one could see that play without wanting to go straight off and slay the foe.

DIONYSUS: Well, that was very naughty of you. You made the Thebans so brave they haven't been the same since.

AESCHYLUS: You Athenians could have trained too, only you

couldn't be bothered. – Then I put on *The Persians*: an effective sermon on the will to win. Best thing I ever wrote.

DIONYSUS: I loved that bit where they sang about the days of the great Darius, and the Chorus went like this with their hands and cried 'Wah! Wah!'

AESCHYLUS [*ignoring this*]: That is the kind of thing a poet should go in for. You see, from the very earliest times the really great poet has been the one who had a useful lesson to teach. Orpheus gave us the Mysteries and taught people that it was wrong to kill; Musaeus showed us how to cure diseases and prophesied the future; Hesiod explained about agriculture and the seasons for ploughing and harvest. And why is Homer himself held in such high esteem, if not for the valuable military instruction embodied in his work? Organization, training, equipment, it's all there.

DIONYSUS: He doesn't seem to have taught Pantacles much. [*Laughter from the stage audience.*] Of all the clumsy, cack-handed – Do you know, I saw him holding a parade the other day, and he found he had put on his helmet without the crest. There he was, on parade, trying to fix that pony-tail in without taking his helmet off – you should have seen him! [*He gives an imitation.*]

AESCHYLUS [*severely*]: But a lot of excellent men did learn. Look at Lamachus.[140] [*Applause.*] And you can see the imprint of Homer on my own work clearly enough. I depicted men of valour, lion-hearted characters like Patroclus and Teucer, encouraging the audience to identify themselves with these heroes when the call to battle came. *I* didn't clutter *my* stage with harlots like Phaedra or Stheneboea. No one can say I have ever put an erotic female into any play of mine.

EURIPIDES: How could you? You've never even met one.

AESCHYLUS: And thank heaven for that. Whereas you and your household had only too much experience of Aphrodite, if I remember rightly. She was too much for you in the end.[141]

DIONYSUS: He's got you there, Euripides. See what happened in your own home, when you made other men's wives behave like that on the stage.

EURIPIDES [*much put out*]: And what harm did my Stheneboeas do to the community, you irritating man?

AESCHYLUS: Why, every decent woman or decent man's wife was

so shocked by plays like your *Bellerophon* that she went straight off and took poison.

EURIPIDES: And did I invent the story of Phaedra?

AESCHYLUS: No, no, such things do happen. But the poet should keep quiet about them, not put them on the stage for everyone to copy. Schoolboys have a master to teach them, grown-ups have the poets. We have a duty to see that what we teach them is right and proper.

EURIPIDES: And you think that the right and proper way to teach them is to write your kind of high-flown Olympian language, instead of talking like a human being?

AESCHYLUS: My poor dear fellow, noble themes and noble sentiments must be couched in suitably dignified language. If your characters are demigods, they should talk like demigods – and, I might add, they should *dress* like demigods. I showed the way in this respect; but you have distorted the whole thing.

EURIPIDES: How?

AESCHYLUS: Well, you dress your kings in rags. You make pitiable creatures of them.

EURIPIDES: But why shouldn't I? What harm does it do?

AESCHYLUS [*still serious*]: Well, nowadays you can't get the wealthier classes to pay their naval-defence contributions. They dress up in rags and tell you how poor they are.

DIONYSUS: With nice fleecy underwear underneath. And the next day you see them buying their dinner at the most expensive fish stall in the market.

AESCHYLUS: And then look how you have encouraged people to babble and prate. The wrestling schools are empty, and where have all the young men gone? Off to these infamous establishments where they practise the art of debating – and that isn't all they practise there either. And now even the sailors argue with their officers – why, in my day the only words they knew were 'slops' and 'yo-heave-ho'!

DIONYSUS: Whereas now they refuse to row, and the ship drifts all over the place.

AESCHYLUS: And think of all the other harm he has done. Hasn't he shown us pimps and profligates, women giving birth in temples and sleeping with their brothers and saying that life is not life? Isn't that why the city is so full of lawyers' clerks and scrounging mountebanks, swindling the community right and left? And not a decent athlete left in the whole city – they're all out of training.

DIONYSUS: How right you are! I nearly died of laughing during the torch race at the Pan-Athenian Games. There was a little, fat, white-skinned fellow plugging along miles behind everyone else, making terribly heavy going of it. And when he got to the Potters' Gate and they all ran out and slapped him, here and here and here, the way they do, you know, with the flat of the hand – well, talk about second wind! He produced enough back-draught to keep his torch alight till the end of the race!

CHORUS:

> Fiercely the fight goes on,
>   Doubtful the ending;
> Well matched these warriors are,
>   Grim their contending.
> When one's in full career,
> The other's quick to veer
> And sneak up in the rear
>   To catch him bending.
>
> Yet though you think your gains
>   Are quite extensive,
> Time spent on digging in
>   May prove expensive.
> Show us what wit can do;
> Vary your tactics too;
> Bring out old tricks and new,
>   Risk an offensive.
>
> As for the audience,
>   You are mistaken
> If you think subtle points
>   Will not be taken.
> Such fears are vain, I vow;
> They've all got textbooks now –
> However high your brow,
>   They won't be shaken.
>
> No talking down to these:
>   That's all outdated!

For native wit alone
   They're highly rated;
But now they've learnt to read
It's real tough stuff they need;
They don't want chicken-feed –
   They're educated!

EURIPIDES: Well now, let's turn to your prologues – first things first, after all – and put your famous skill to the test. I maintain that they fail to give a clear picture of the situation.

AESCHYLUS: Which of them do you propose to criticize?

EURIPIDES: Any number of them. But let's start with the opening lines of *The Libation Bearers*.

DIONYSUS: Silence for Aeschylus.

AESCHYLUS [*reciting*]:
   Earth-haunting Hermes, that with tutelar eye
   Keep'st watch and ward o'er the paternal realm,
   Oh, hear my prayer: save me, and be my friend!
   Lo, to this land I come and do return.[142]

Do you find anything to criticize in that?

EURIPIDES: A dozen points at least.

DIONYSUS: But he's only recited four lines.

EURIPIDES: With a score of mistakes in each.

DIONYSUS: You'd better not recite any more, Aeschylus: it seems you're four lines down already.

AESCHYLUS: What, stop for him?

DIONYSUS: I think it would be wise.

EURIPIDES: You see, he starts off right away with a preposterous blunder.

AESCHYLUS: Nonsense!

EURIPIDES [*as if washing his hands of the whole subject*]: Oh, well, if that's how you feel ... It couldn't matter less to me.

AESCHYLUS [*capitulating*]: What is this mistake I've made?

EURIPIDES: Give me those first two lines again.

AESCHYLUS [*reciting*]:
   Earth-haunting Hermes, that with tutelar eye
   Keep'st watch and ward o'er the paternal realm –

EURIPIDES: And Orestes says this over the tomb of his dead father?

AESCHYLUS: That is correct.

EURIPIDES: Ah! So he is saying that when his father was brutally murdered by his own wife as the result of a secret intrigue, this all happened under the approving eyes of Hermes?

AESCHYLUS: Certainly not. He is addressing himself to Hermes the Helper, 'earth-haunting Hermes', not to Hermes as the god of trickery. This is made quite clear by the words that follow: 'o'er the paternal realm'. His underground function is a perquisite derived from Zeus, his father.

EURIPIDES: That makes it even worse than I had thought.

DIONYSUS: Underground perquisites, eh? Sounds like a rake-off on the tomb offerings.

AESCHYLUS: A remark in the worst of taste, Dionysus.

DIONYSUS: Give him a bit more, Aeschylus. And you, Euripides, watch out for the mistakes.

AESCHYLUS [reciting]:

> Oh, hear my prayer: save me, and be my friend!
> Lo, to this land I come and do return.

EURIPIDES: The great Aeschylus tells us the same thing twice.

AESCHYLUS: What do you mean, the same thing twice?

EURIPIDES: Well, listen. I'll repeat the line. 'Lo, to this land I come', he says, 'and do return.' The 'coming' and the 'returning' are the same thing, surely?

DIONYSUS: So they are: like saying to a neighbour, 'Lend me a looking glass – or a mirror would do.'

AESCHYLUS: The two things are not the same. The trouble with you is, you're obsessed with this verbal juggling of yours. The line is a particularly good one.

EURIPIDES: Please explain.

AESCHYLUS: Anyone can 'come' to his native country, if he belongs there still: nothing need have happened to him at all. But when an exile comes home, he 'returns'.

[Applause from the audience on the stage.]143

DIONYSUS: Well done! What do you say to that, Euripides?

EURIPIDES: I say that Orestes never did 'return' home in that sense: he had to come secretly, he didn't trust the people in power.

[Frenzied applause from the stage audience.]

DIONYSUS [baffled by the applause]: Brilliant! Brilliant! Wish I knew what you were talking about!

EURIPIDES: Come on, let's hear some more.

DIONYSUS: Yes, come along, Aeschylus, get on with it. [*To Euripides*] And you, pounce on the howlers.

AESCHYLUS [*reciting*]:

>   Here on this mound I call on my dead father
>   To hear me, and to listen.

EURIPIDES: There he goes again, the same thing twice: 'to hear me and to listen'.

DIONYSUS: He's calling on the dead, don't you understand? Even three times would hardly be enough.

AESCHYLUS: And how did you construct *your* prologues?

EURIPIDES: I'll show you. And if I say the same thing twice, or if you find a single word of irrelevant padding, you can spit on me for a liar.

DIONYSUS: Carry on, then. I shall listen most carefully to your choice of words.

EURIPIDES [*reciting*]:

>   A happy man was Oedipus at first –

AESCHYLUS: Was he at any time? When even before he was born Apollo had decreed that he should kill his own father? You call that being a happy man?

EURIPIDES: [*reciting*]

>   – But he became the most unfortunate
>   Of mortal men.

AESCHYLUS: He didn't become so, he *was* so all along. Look at his story. First of all, as a new-born baby, he is dumped out in the cold, cold snow in an earthenware utensil, to prevent him from growing up and murdering his father; then he comes limping to Corinth with both his feet swollen: then he marries a woman old enough to be his mother; and then, as though that wasn't bad enough, he finds out that she *is* his mother. And finally he blinds himself.

DIONYSUS: Better to have been an Athenian Commander at Arginusae![144]

EURIPIDES: I still maintain that my prologues are good.

AESCHYLUS: Even without splitting hairs over every word, I assure you I can demolish any prologue of yours with a little bottle of oil.

EURIPIDES: My prologues, with a bottle of oil?

AESCHYLUS: Just one little everyday bottle of oil. You see, the way your prologues are written, you can fit in anything: bottle of oil, pieces of wool, bag of old rag. Tiddly tum. I'll show you what I mean.

EURIPIDES: All right, show me.

DIONYSUS [*to Euripides*]: You must recite one.

EURIPIDES [*reciting*]:

> Aegyptus, who, the oft-told story runs,
> Once put to sea with fifty daughters fair,
> Touching at Argos –

AESCHYLUS: – lost his bottle of oil.

EURIPIDES: What do you mean, lost his bottle of oil? You'll regret this.

DIONYSUS: Recite another prologue. I believe I see the idea.

EURIPIDES [*reciting*]:

> Lord Dionysus of the fawnskin cloak,
> Who leaps with ivy wand amid the pines
> Of fair Parnassus –

AESCHYLUS: – lost his bottle of oil.

DIONYSUS: Two bottles down.

EURIPIDES: He can't keep it up. I've got one here that is guaranteed bottleproof [*reciting*:]

> No one is ever fortunate in all:
> One man, high-born, loses his wealth; another,
> Of lowly birth, has –

AESCHYLUS: – lost his bottle of oil.

DIONYSUS: Euripides!

EURIPIDES: Yes?

DIONYSUS: Reef your sails a bit: this is going to be a storm in an oil bottle!

EURIPIDES: Don't you believe it. This one'll knock it right out of his hand.

DIONYSUS: All right, let's have it: but watch out for bottles!

EURIPIDES [*reciting*]:

> Leaving his native town of Sidon, Cadmus,
> Son of Agenor –

AESCHYLUS   – lost his bottle of oil.

DIONYSUS: If I were you, I'd make him an offer for the sole rights in his bottle; otherwise you won't have any prologues left.

EURIPIDES: *His* bottle! I like that! Anyway, I've got lots of prologues he *can't* fit it into.

[*Reciting*:]
>   Pelops the Tantalid, with his horses swift,
>   Riding to Pisa –

AESCHYLUS: – lost his bottle of oil.

DIONYSUS: You see, he's done it again. Sell it to him, Aeschylus, for heaven's sake. You can get a beautiful new one for an obol.

EURIPIDES: No, no, I've got a lot more prologues yet.

[*Reciting*:]
>   'Tis said that Oineus –

AESCHYLUS: – lost his bottle of oil.

EURIPIDES: You might at least let me finish one line.
>   'Tis said that Oineus, offering to the gods
>   Firstfruits of harvest –

AESCHYLUS: – lost his bottle of oil.

DIONYSUS: What, in the middle of a sacrifice? How very awkward for him. Who took it, I wonder?

EURIPIDES: Don't encourage him. See what he can do with this one:
>   Almighty Zeus, so Truth herself relates –

DIONYSUS [*anxious to forestall this blasphemy*]: You're beaten, and you know it. That bottle of oil keeps turning up like a stye on the eye. It's time you turned your attention to his lyrics.

EURIPIDES: Ah, yes, those lyrics! Well, I hope to demonstrate that he is a bad lyric writer. His lyrics are all the same.

CHORUS:
>   What, Aeschylus not write good lyrics?
>   You'll have the old boy in hysterics!
>   I do not know much
>   About dactyls and such
>   (Though I know a good song when I hear it);
>   But I had the idea
>   That this gentleman here
>   Was perfection, or something damn near it.
>   What, Aeschylus not write good lyrics?
>   Great heavens, what will he say next?
>   It seems a bit hard
>   On the Eminent Bard –
>   No wonder he's looking so vexed.

EURIPIDES: They certainly are amazing lyrics, as you'll soon see. I'm going to sing you the whole lot, all in one.

DIONYSUS: And I'll keep the score with these pebbles.

[*Music: flutes, punctuated by deafening crashes on the cymbals.*]

EURIPIDES [*singing*]:

Fiercely the battle is raging: Achilles, thy comrades await thee!
[*Crash!*] Come quickly and help us,
I fear we can hold out no longer!

We who dwell by the lake are proud of our ancestor Hermes –
[*Crash!*] Come quickly and help us,
I fear we can hold out no longer!

DIONYSUS: Two nasty crashes for you, Aeschylus!

EURIPIDES [*singing*]:

Hearken great lord of the Greeks, and listen to me, Agamemnon:
[*Crash!*] Come quickly and help us,
I fear we can hold out no longer!

DIONYSUS: That makes three.

EURIPIDES [*singing*]:

Silence! The temple doors open; the virgin priestesses are chanting:
[*Crash!*] Come quickly and help us,
I fear we can hold out no longer!

Proudly today we march forth, a great and invincible army:
[*Crash!*] Come quickly and help us,
I fear we can hold out no longer!

DIONYSUS: Which way is the bathroom? I fear I can hold out no longer. You'll have to excuse me – these crashes are bad for my kidneys.

EURIPIDES: You can't go away till you've heard the next part. It has a wonderful lyre accompaniment.

DIONYSUS: Well, get on with it, and no crashes this time, please.

EURIPIDES [*singing*]:

What though the prophet bird with vengeful spear
Flat-a-thrat-a-flat-a-thrat
The twin-throned kings in muted mockery send
Flat-a-thrat-a-flat-a-thrat
A fox to dog the Sphinx, a Sphinx to fox the dog
Flat-a-thrat-a-flat-a-thrat

That through the skies his milky way doth wend
  Flat-a-thrat-a-flat-a-thrat
And, bearing down on Ajax, foxeth *him* –
  Flat-a-thrat-a-flat-a-thrat.

DIONYSUS: What *is* all this flat-a-thrat? A bit of Persian you picked
up at Marathon, Aeschylus? Where do you collect all these rope-
makers' shanties?

AESCHYLUS: If I make use of traditional elements in my lyrics, I do
at least take them from a respectable source and make them serve an
artistic purpose. There is more than one kind of flower in the garden
of the Muses – why should I have to pluck the same ones as Phrynichus, or anyone else? But this man flings in bits and pieces from
all over the place. He gets his inspiration from the brothel or the
drinking-club; his lyrics are full of the rhythms of the dance-floor,
the dirge-like wailings of these Carian trumpeters. I'll show you
what I mean. Bring me a lyre – no, a lyre's too good for this sort of
thing: where's that girl with the castanets?

[*A saucy-looking* DANCING-GIRL *comes forward.*]

Aha! The Muse of Euripides! Come along, my dear, stand over
here. Just the right accompaniment for this kind of lyric.

DIONYSUS: *Not* in the Lesbian mode, I take it.

[AESCHYLUS *produces a scroll containing his parody of Euripides, evidently prepared beforehand. As he sings the lyric – mimick-
ing the 'modern' style without quite losing his patriarchal dignity – the*
CASTANET GIRL *girl dances.*]

AESCHYLUS [*singing*]:

      Sea birds
Over the wavetops wheeling, chattering,
      Wee birds!
  Wing tips dip,
  Splashing in the –
  Plashing in the –
See how their feathers glisten in the sea-spray –

      Spiders
Up in the rafters, underneath the ceiling,
      Why does
  Each little foot go

Twiddling and
Twiddling and –
Busy little weavers working at the loom!

    Dolphin
Plunging, leaping, everybody knows it's a
Good luck dolphin
Very fond of music,
Leaping in the bows of a big blue ship.

    Tendrils
Twining, twining, luscious hang the
Clusters on the –

            [*the rhythm and tune become repetitive*]
Vine is a –
Grapes on the –

            [*here the rhythm changes entirely*]
And I flung my arms around him, and said –
Did you notice that foot?

DIONYSUS [*erotically, his eyes on the castanet girl*]: Yes! What impudence!

AESCHYLUS: Yes, I thought you would appreciate that. [*He is pointing out the place in his scroll, but* DIONYSUS *is unaware of this.*] That initial anapaest breaks the rhythm completely.

DIONYSUS [*suddenly realizing*]: Oh, yes! Quite. Absolutely.

AESCHYLUS: A man who can descend to that sort of thing in his own verse has no right to criticize mine. Well, so much for his choral songs. Now I want to give you some idea of what his lyrical monologues are like.

[*Sings:*]

    O shining darkness of the Night
    Walking forth from the dim shadows of Hades
    What is this dream you have sent me?
    It has life and yet it has no life
    It is a child of the black night
    And its face is terrible.
    Wrapped in a black shroud it glares at me
    Murder, murder in its eye
    And it has remarkably long claws.

Light the lamp O my servants
And in your little buckets
Fetch me the limpid liquid
That flows in the mountain streams.
Heat this water (for that is what it is)
I will wash away this dream
That the gods have sent me.

Hearken, O mighty God of the sea –
No, never mind. Hearken, O members of my household,
These are great marvels that you have witnessed!
Glycé has stolen the cock from my henhouse
And done a bunk.
Ah, ye nymphs of the mountains –
Or perhaps *you'd* better do it, Manya dear,
Catch her
And bring her to me.

Ah me, unhappy wretch that I am,
I was just sitting spinning
(Nimble fingers at work on the flax)
And the wheel whirled round and round
And round.[145]
I was going to go out early
While it was still dark,
And sell my thread in the market,
When ah! he did depart, my cock, my treasure;
His soul took to flight,
Winging, winging, into the empyrean
And I was left bereft
To grieve bereaved,
And from my eyes falling, falling,
Tears, the falling tears
Fell, the tears fell, from my eyes fell
Tears.

O Cretans, children of Ida, mighty archers,[146]
Speed to my aid,
Get your bows and arrows
And come round here at once, please, this is urgent,
And throw a cordon round the building.

And thou too, daughter of Dictynna,
Fair Artemis, lover of the chase,
Come with your hounds
And we'll track her down yet
If we have to ransack the whole place.
Come then, Hecaté, daughter of Zeus,
With twin torches flaming,
Light me the way across to Glycé's house:
I want to catch the bitch red-handed.

DIONYSUS: I think we've had enough lyrics now.

AESCHYLUS: I've had enough of them too. And I now propose that we settle this matter once and for all by a simple test. Let the scales be brought; then we shall be able to judge whose poetry is the weightier, his or mine.

[*An enormous pair of scales is brought out, or let down from above. Meanwhile* PLUTO *appears at an upper window.*]

DIONYSUS: Come over here, then, both of you, and I'll be the grocer, weighing out your verses like pieces of cheese.

CHORUS:

How thorough these geniuses are!
But these are the cleverest by far.
　　Did ever you hear
　　Such a brilliant idea,
So simple, and yet so bizarre?

I'd not have believed it, I swear,
If a man that I met in the square
　　Had said that a friend
　　Of a friend of his friend
Had known of a man who was there!

DIONYSUS: Now, each of you stand by one pan of the scales.

[AESCHYLUS *and* EURIPIDES *take up their positions.*]

AESCHYLUS: Right.

EURIPIDES: Right.

DIONYSUS: Now you must each take hold of your own pan and hold it steady, and each recite one line; and when I call 'Cuckoo!' you'll both let go. Ready?

AESCHYLUS: Ready

EURIPIDES: Ready.

DIONYSUS: All right, speak your lines into the scale.

EURIPIDES: 'Would that the Argo ne'er with wingèd sail . . .'

AESCHYLUS: 'Spercheios' watery vale, where cattle graze . . .'

DIONYSUS: Cuckoo!

AESCHYLUS }
EURIPIDES } [letting go]: Right!

DIONYSUS: Oh, look, this side's going *right* down.

EURIPIDES: Now why should it do that?

DIONYSUS: He put in a river. Like the wool merchants: they wet the wool to make it weigh more. Whereas you with your 'wingèd sails' . . .

EURIPIDES: Well, let's try again. See what he can do this time.

DIONYSUS: Right, take hold again.

AESCHYLUS }
EURIPIDES } : Ready.

DIONYSUS: Fire away, then.

EURIPIDES: 'No temple hath Persuasion, save in words.'

AESCHYLUS: 'Alone of all the gods, Death takes no gifts.'

DIONYSUS: Let go. Now, let's see – yes, it's this one again. You see, he put in Death; that's a heavy word if you like.

EURIPIDES: Well, what about Persuasion, doesn't that carry any weight? A beautiful line, too.

DIONYSUS: No, Persuasion won't do: mere empty words without sense. You'll have to think of something really ponderous, to weigh your side down. Something strong and big.

EURIPIDES: What have I got that's strong and big? [*A thought strikes him but he rejects it.*] – Umm, let me think.

DIONYSUS: What about that stirring line 'Achilles threw two singles and a four'? Well, come on now, this is the last round.

EURIPIDES [*triumphantly*]: 'He seized his mighty bludgeon, ribbed with iron.'

AESCHYLUS [*triumphantly*]: 'Chariot on chariot, corpse on corpse was piled.'

DIONYSUS: He's licked you again.

EURIPIDES: I don't see why.

DIONYSUS: All those chariots and corpses – a hundred Egyptians couldn't lift that lot.

AESCHYLUS: As far as I am concerned, this line against line business is too easy by far. Let Euripides get into the pan himself, with his children, and his wife, not forgetting Cephisophon[147] of whom we have heard so much, and the whole of his collected works into the bargain. I undertake to outweigh the whole lot with two lines of mine.

DIONYSUS: You know, I like them both so much, I don't know how to judge between them. I don't want to make an enemy of either. One of them is so *clever*, and the other is so *good*, don't you think?

PLUTO [*sepulchrally*]: In that case you've been rather wasting your time down here, haven't you?

DIONYSUS: Well, supposing I do make a choice?

PLUTO: You can take one of them back with you: whichever you prefer. No point in coming all this way for nothing.

DIONYSUS: Bless you! Well now, listen, you two. I came down here for a poet.

EURIPIDES: What do you want a poet for?

DIONYSUS: To save the City of course. If the City isn't saved, there won't be any more drama festivals, and then where shall I be? Now, whichever of you can think of the best piece of advice to give the Athenians at this juncture, he's the one I shall take back with me. Now, here's my first question: what should be done about Alcibiades? Athens is in a very tricky situation, you know.

EURIPIDES: What do the Athenians think about it, themselves?

DIONYSUS: Ah. You may well ask. They love him. But then again they hate him. And then again, they want him back. But you tell me what *you* think, both of you.

EURIPIDES [*after consideration*]:
>Quickness and brains are what we seek, I know:
>He's quick – to harm, but when we need him, slow;
>Brilliant enough to plan his own escape,
>But useless when the City's in a scrape.

DIONYSUS: That's neat. I like that. Very good. And Aeschylus, what's your opinion?

AESCHYLUS:
>It is not very wise for city states
>To rear a lion's whelp within their gates:
>But should they do so, they will find it pays
>To learn to tolerate its little ways.

DIONYSUS: Honestly, I can't decide between them, when one's so clever that you can't tell what he means, and the other's about as clear as the purest mud. We'll try one more question. I want each of you to tell me how you think the City can be saved.

EURIPIDES [*raising his hand*]: I know, sir, please sir, can I speak now, sir?

DIONYSUS: Well, Euripides?

EURIPIDES [*very rapidly*]:

> Believe the unsafe safe, the safe unsure,
> Mistrust what now you trust, and fear no more.

DIONYSUS: The unsafe safe – I'm afraid that's a little bit beyond me, Euripides. Couldn't you give us something a wee bit clearer, not quite so epi — epig— epepig— something not quite so damn clever?

EURIPIDES: It seems perfectly plain to me. If we are now putting our trust in [*mysteriously*] certain persons, and *not* putting our trust in certain other persons, and the City is *not* being saved, then it seems to me that the only reasonable hope of saving the City lies in reversing the procedure. Elementary, my dear Dionysus.

DIONYSUS: Amazing, my dear Palamedes.[148] Well now, Aeschylus, what's your advice?

AESCHYLUS: Tell me, what kind of people *is* the City using nowadays? Presumably they are honest, capable, patriotic –

[DIONYSUS *begins to laugh, gently and not unkindly, but uncontrollably. Soon everyone on the stage except* AESCHYLUS *is helpless with laughter.*]

DIONYSUS: You *are* out of touch, aren't you! No, those are the people she hates most of all.

AESCHYLUS: You mean she prefers dishonest people?

DIONYSUS: She doesn't prefer them, of course not. But she has no choice.

AESCHYLUS: Well, if the City doesn't know its own mind, I don't see how it *can* be saved.

DIONYSUS: You'll have to think of something, if you want to come back with me.

AESCHYLUS: I'd rather reserve my opinion till I get there.

DIONYSUS: Oh, no, you don't: fair's fair. You must send them your good advice from here.

AESCHYLUS: Well, in my day everyone knew the answer:

Treat enemy soil as yours, your own let go:
Your ships are wealth, all other wealth is woe.[149]

DIONYSUS: That's all right, except that the 'other wealth' all goes to the jurymen these days.

PLUTO: Now please decide.

DIONYSUS: Well, in my heart of hearts I have known all the time. No question about it, the man for me is –

EURIPIDES: Now remember you swore by the gods to take me home! [*Emotionally*] Our old friendship ... you can't go back on an oath!

DIONYSUS [*quoting that fatal line*] : 'My tongue it was that swore ...' Come, Aeschylus.

EURIPIDES: What? – Why, what have you done, you unspeakable monster?

DIONYSUS: What have I done? I have declared Aeschylus the winner, that's all. Any objections?

[*Loud applause, in which* PLUTO *joins.*]

EURIPIDES: Can you dare to look me in the face after playing such a low-down, shameful trick?

DIONYSUS: I appeal to the audience.

EURIPIDES: 'Oh, heart of stone, wouldst leave me here to die?' Well, to go on being dead, anyway.

DIONYSUS [*quoting that other fatal line*][150] : 'Who knows if death be life and life be death?' – And fork be knife, and knife be fork and spoon.

[EURIPIDES, *struggling wildly, is removed by* ATTENDANTS.]

PLUTO [*in his usual sepulchral voice*] : Dionysus and Aeschylus, kindly step inside my palace –

DIONYSUS [*dismayed*] : Why, what have we –?

PLUTO: – where I propose to offer you the hospitality the occasion seems to demand. One for the road, gentlemen, won't you come in?

DIONYSUS/AESCHYLUS [*together, in the same sepulchral tones*] : That's extremely kind of you, Pluto; I don't mind if I do!

[*They enter the palace, followed by the rest of the assembled company.* SLAVES *clear away the seating, etc. The* CHORUS *remain on stage.*]

CHORUS:

How very uncommon it is to find
A man with a shrewd and intelligent mind,

A man with a sense of proportion!
If you look at the stuff that is written today
And the stupid things our statesmen say,
You would think that people had lost the knack
Of telling the white from the utterly black –
    They've thrown away all caution!

They sit at the feet of Socrates
Till they can't distinguish the wood from the trees,
    And tragedy goes to POT;
They don't care whether their plays are art
But only whether the words are smart;
They waste our time with quibbles and quarrels,
Destroying our patience as well as our morals,
    And making us all talk ROT.

So altogether we're glad to find
That a man with a shrewd and intelligent mind
    (A man with a sense of proportion)
Is returning to Earth, as this comedy ends,
To the joy of his colleagues, relations, and friends –
Is returning to Earth, in this decadent age,
To save the City and save the stage
    From politics, lies, and distortion.

[PLUTO *and his* GUESTS *come out of the palace, and the* 'DEAD' *who have formed the audience on the stage gather round to see them off.*]

PLUTO: Good-bye, then, Aeschylus, off you go with your sound advice and save the City for us. Educate the fools – you'll find a good many. And give this [*he hands him a vicious-looking knife*] to Cleophon with my compliments, and these [*a pair of nooses*] to the Tax Commissioners, and here's one for Myrmex and another for Nicomachus; and this [*a bowl labelled 'Hemlock'*] is for Archenomus: and tell them all to hurry up and come down here to me. Otherwise I shall brand them and tie them together by the feet along with Adeimantus,[151] and have them packed off underground before they can say knife.

AESCHYLUS: Very well, I will. And will you, please, ask Sophocles to take over my Chair of Honour and look after it while I am away? I declare that the second place is his by right. And on no account

must that wicked, lying, foul-mouthed scoundrel ever be allowed
to sit on my chair, even inadvertently.

PLUTO [*to the Chorus*]: Guide him, then, with your sacred torches,
escort him with his own songs and dances.

[*The* CHORUS *form up as an escort for* AESCHYLUS, *and the
procession moves off, singing.*]

CHORUS:

> Spirits of the darkness,
>   Speed him on his way;
> Safely may he journey
>   To the light of day.
>
> To the City's counsels
>   May he wisdom lend;
> Then of war and suffering
>   There shall be an end.
>
> If those doughty warriors,
>   Cleophon and Co.,
> Want to keep on fighting,
>   They know where to go.
>
> In their distant homeland
>   They can do less harm;
> Let them wage their warfare
>   Back on father's farm.

Notes

THE WASPS

1. After being sent off fairly early in the play (p. 53), the boys probably reappeared in the trial scene, first as the Cooking Utensils and then as the Puppies.

2. The Corybants, devotees of the Phrygian Earth-mother Cybele, were famous for the orgiastic rites in which they worked themselves into a state of trance or delirium.

3. Cleonymus, a satellite of Cleon's, was reputed to have dropped (or thrown away) his shield during a battle. In the original the pun is neater, since *aspis* means both 'asp' and 'shield'.

4. Adapted from the traditional riddle: 'What creatures can be found on land, in the sea, and in the sky?' (Answer: the Bear, the Dog, and the Serpent. The three Greek words each served as the name both of a land and of a sea creature, and also of a star or constellation.)

5. Xanthias correctly identifies the whale-like monster as Cleon the tanner. The sheep, of course, are the citizens of Athens.

6. Theorus: known only from Aristophanes. In the original, Alcibiades' 'lisp' makes him pronounce *korax* (raven) as *kolax* (toady, flatterer): a hopeless problem for the translator.

7. The Megarians claimed to have been the originators of comedy. Aristophanes' actual words mean 'nor any laughter stolen from Megara', which, in view of the context here, is usually taken to imply that Megarian comedy was crude and vulgar.

8. The Greek word is *philoxenos*, which was also the name of a well-known homosexual of the day. I have had to translate freely.

9. The *clepsydra*, used for timing speeches in the lawcourts.

10. Demos: a young aristocrat, much admired for his physical beauty. (Socrates twits one of his admirers in Plato's *Gorgias*.)

11. See note 2.

12. Jokes about figs and figwood are frequent in Aristophanes There is probably a reference to the first element of the word *sykophantes* (an informer, literally 'a revealer of figs').

13. A topical reference: but this particular Dracontidҽs cannot be identified.

14. The story of Odysseus and the Cyclops had recently been made into a satyr-play by Euripides.

15. The city of Scione, which had revolted to Brasidas in 423, was now being blockaded by the Athenians.

16. The superb portmanteau adjective used in the original (*archaio-melisidonophrynicherata*) cannot be imitated in English. The *sidono* element shows that the songs sung by the old men were from Phrynichus' *Phoenician Women* (476 B.C.), which had a chorus of Sidonian maidens.

17. Laches had been sent to Sicily in command of twenty ships in 427. He had accomplished little during his brief period of command, and passages in this comedy suggest that Cleon had accused him of accepting bribes from the Sicilian cities.

18. A reference to her Cretan name of *Dictynna* (from Mount *Dicte*), which the Greeks tended to derive from *dictyon*, a net.

19. The point is obscure: other references to Diopeithes in Aristophanes' comedies indicate that he was a crazy soothsayer, but the ancient commentator on this passage says that the reference is to 'a rhetorician noted for a certain frantic courage'.

20. This would be a replica of the image in the shrine of Lycus, which stood near the door of one of the lawcourts, and was no doubt a familiar landmark. It seems to have been treated as a bit of a joke, rather as the Albert Memorial used to be; and, as the context shows, the shrine tended to be used for purposes unconnected with worship.

21. This chorus could be sung to the 'March of the Men of Harlech'.

22. Apparently a teacher of rhetoric and a disciple of Gorgias. He is here described, possibly figuratively, as 'son of Gorgias'. Nothing is known of his trial.

23. Cecrops, the legendary founder of Athens, was always depicted with a serpent's tail instead of legs. The Dracontidae ('sons of the serpent') were an Athenian family very proud of their ancient origins. Thus Procleon addresses Cecrops as 'a Dracontides as to the leg part': I have paraphrased this.

24. Literally, 'men whom I've taught to weep four to the quart'. The phrase *four to the quart* was roughly equivalent to our *nineteen to the dozen*; but there is here a pun on the word for *quart*, which also means *the stocks*.

25. Aeschines, an associate of Cleon's, was notorious for empty talk and boasting. His nickname was 'Kapnos' (smoke).

26. i.e. Cleonymus (see note 3). Nothing is known of Evathlus except he was one of Cleon's informers.

27. For Theorus, see note 6. Euphemius is unknown, but the inference is clearly that he was even more of a lickspittle than Theorus.

28. Silver obols were still being coined at this time. They were very small, and Athenians habitually carried their small change in their mouths.

29. A quotation from Euripides' lost tragedy *Bellerophon*.

30. See note 28. Lysistratus crops up again at the drinking party in Act Two. He is also mentioned in *The Acharnians*.

31. See note 3.

32. 'The Dog' was apparently one of Cleon's nicknames, and Cydathenaeum was the *deme*, or ward, of Athens from which he came. Laches (see note 17) was from the deme of Aexone.

33. Cheeses were encased in plaster to keep them fresh.

34. Thucydides: not the historian, but one of the aristocratic leaders who had opposed Pericles in the forties.

35. Aristophanes' earliest plays were not produced under his own name. See Introduction, page 16.

36. *The Knights*, produced at the Lenaean Festival in 425, was a savage attack on Cleon.

37. These very abusive lines are repeated word for word in *Peace*, which was produced in 421, after Cleon's death. For the actual performance of *The Wasps* they had probably been replaced by a milder version.

38. In *The Merchantmen* (Lenaean Festival, 423) Aristophanes had attacked Cleon's satellites.

39. The Polemarch was the official who dealt with resident aliens. Aristophanes is constantly hinting that Cleon's hangers-on were not of true Athenian birth.

40. *The Clouds* (Dionysian Festival, 423) had been a failure. The text we have is of a revised version.

41. At the battle of Marathon, 490 B.C.

42. At the battle of Salamis, 480 B.C.

43. This sounds like a popular catch-phrase of the day. The line probably had more point than it appears to have.

44. i.e. as a rower in the navy.

45. See note 25.

46. The words of the original catch are not known: they have probably been distorted to make them apply to Aeschines. There may have been a recent official mission to Thessaly with Aeschines (and Amynias – see p. 91), among the delegates.

47. The guests at a drinking party brought their own food, the host supplying the drink.

48. I have followed Zielinski and other editors in reversing the respective positions of this chorus (lines 1450–73) and the 'second parabasis' (lines 1265–91).

49. A challenge at law could be delivered personally by the injured party provided a witness was present. It was then the duty of the witness to give evidence of the issue of the challenge, and to summon the accused to appear in court.

50. Two dithyrambic poets of the sixth century B.C.

51. Unfortunately the text is garbled at this point, and the brilliant joke for the sake of which Chaerephon has been dragged into the play is quite unintelligible. It is clear, however, that Procleon is reverting to the 'comparison game' which he learnt at the party. The point of the joke *may* have been roughly on the lines indicated here.

52. A conviction on a charge of 'hybris' (serious and malicious injury or outrage) involved a heavy fine (which went to the State and not to the complainant) or sometimes even death. But the complainant himself was liable to a fine of 1,000 drachmas if he obtained less than one fifth of the jury's votes.

53. See note 48.

54. In the translation, the reference to his mania for dice has been borrowed from the opening scene (p.42). For the 'Thessalian jaunt', see note 46. The *Penestae* ('paupers') were a subject tribe treated as serfs by the ruling caste of Thessaly. Jokes about diplomatic missions in Aristophanes' plays often contain a reference to the lavish subsistence allowance received by the delegates.

55. The attack on Ariphrades sounds rather more venomous (and more obscene) in the Greek. There are other references to his sexual propensities in *The Knights and Peace*.

56. See Introduction, page 28.

57. Thespis (sixth century B.C.), a semi-legendary figure, was regarded as the father of tragedy. Procleon's version of a 'Thespian dance' would probably have been based on imagination rather than research, though it is possible that the general style of the dances had been handed down from one generation of dancers to the next.

58. An actor and dancer who had apparently scored a great success in Euripides' satyr play *The Cyclops*. – The reference can hardly be to Phrynichus the tragedian, who died before most of the audience were born. Certainly the final chorus (p. 94) seems to imply that he and his 'high kicks' were well known to the audience. The Phrynichus at the drinking party (p. 86) was probably the same man.

59. Carcinus, we are told by an ancient commentator, actually had four sons, three of them dancers and one a tragic poet. The tragic poet was

Xenocles, a frequent victim of Aristophanes' satire. (See *The Poet and the Women*, pp. 106, 114, and *The Frogs*, p. 159.)

THE POET AND THE WOMEN

60. In 411 B.C., when this play was produced, Euripides was seventy-four. At this time he was still living in Athens: he may well have been in the audience.

61. Agathon, one of the most celebrated tragedians of the day, was about forty-one when this play was produced. None of his works has survived.

62. The phrase is a literal translation from the Greek. (Perhaps the only phrase from Aristophanes to have found its way into English.)

63. A famous tragedian who had flourished in the early part of the century. His *Phoenician Women* was produced in 476 B.C., when Euripides was nine years old. (The other three poets mentioned lived in the sixth century B.C.)

64. All three were dramatists, contemporaries of Aristophanes, and often ridiculed by him.

65. From Euripides' *Alcestis*, line 691.

66. In the Greek: 'the tenement of Hippocrates'. Presumably a reference to an architectural innovation that had caused comment – or perhaps to the size of Hippocrates' family. (He cannot be identified for certain with any known Hippocrates.) Euripides' disbelief in the established gods, and preference for deities of his own, such as 'Ether', was a stock joke (cf. *The Frogs*, p. 189).

67. A reference to the notorious oath sworn by Hippolytus in Euripides' play of that name (cf. *The Frogs*, p. 210).

68. The joke appears to have been along these lines, but the text is garbled at this point.

69. The phrase probably occurred in the formal 'curse' regularly pronounced before sessions of the Assembly, but this was a sensitive point with the Athenians just at the moment. They had recently been persuaded, against their better judgement, to apply to the Persian satrap Tissaphernes for aid against Sparta. The negotiations had fallen through, and Tissaphernes was now in fact on the point of renewing his treaty with the Spartans.

70. It wouldn't have been his either, but the point is the substitution of one child for another. Compare Mnesilochus' taunt to First Woman on page 118.

71. A reference to the stock joke about Euripides' mother having kept a market garden and sold potherbs in the market. Nobody knows how it originated.

72. A reference to a passage in Euripides' *Stheneboea* (a lost play).

73. From another lost play, *The Phoenix*. I have borrowed Rogers' translation of the line.

74. See note 59.

75. Myrtle wreaths were worn at drinking parties as well as at sacrifices: this accounts for the other half of Second Woman's business, which was still flourishing.

76. Probably a reference to the drinking party that would be given in honour of the winning playwright after the performance (cf. *The Frogs*, p. 168).

77. The festival at which Athenians had their sons enrolled as citizens when they reached the age of seven. Lambs were sacrificed by the proud fathers and the meat shared out among the congregation.

78. Ships were regularly hauled across the Isthmus of Corinth on rollers.

79. The episode that follows is a parody of a scene in Euripides' lost play *Telephus*, in which the hero snatches the infant Orestes from his cradle, and threatens to kill the child if his enemies move against him.

80. In the Greek, a nice example of the figure of speech known as *zeugma*: 'set up a shout and a trophy'. The remark sounds like a topical reference (some battle, perhaps, when a relieving force had stopped to erect a 'trophy' after a minor skirmish, and had consequently arrived too late to be of any use?) – but I have failed to trace it.

81. Four neat lines in the Greek, in mock-heroic style: possibly a parody of some passage by Euripides.

82. There was a serious shortage of these, as of other naval supplies.

83. Presumably a parody of the corresponding passage in *Palamedes*.

84. I have assumed that some such occasion as the *dekate* (naming-party for a ten-day-old child) is referred to.

85. Charminus and Cleophon were real people: the women's names, except Salabaccho, are chosen for their meaning. Salabaccho is mentioned in *The Knights* (424 B.C.): *une poule*, but evidently no chicken.

86. The point of all this is very obscure, and the Greek of the last two couplets is itself open to several interpretations. I suspect that 'stealing a measure of corn' from one's husband (the phrase used in the Greek) may have been a euphemism for cuckolding him.

87. I am not sure whether any vase-paintings showing the structure of Greek umbrellas (or parasols) exist, but it is clear from *The Knights*, lines 1347–8, that they could be opened and shut. In *The Birds*, Prometheus shelters under an umbrella so as not to be seen by Zeus.

88. Lamachus, once a butt of Aristophanes, had died a hero's death in Sicily. The demagogue Hyperbolus, exiled by the Athenian Assembly in 417 B.C., had been assassinated in Samos in 412. The point

of the attack on his mother is completely obscure: it is not known whether she was really a moneylender or to what extent a woman could engage in such activities. In *The Clouds*, Aristophanes had criticized other comic poets for their attacks on Hyperbolus 'and his mother'.

89. Euripides' *Helen* had been produced, with the *Andromeda*, at the previous year's Dionysia. The scene which follows is a close burlesque of a scene in Euripides' play.

90. i.e. the seaweed. Another reference to the old, old joke (see note 71).

91. More precisely, a *Prytanis*, or 'member of the Praesidium of the State Council'. ('Commissar' might perhaps be the best translation, but it has the wrong kind of associations.)

92. The *sanis*, a plank, or cross of planks, to which the offender was bound: an ancient equivalent of stocks or pillory. Its exact construction is not known: from the text of this play it would appear that the cords could be tightened by means of a peg or screw. (See p. 136.)

93. An artist (an animal painter, according to one ancient source), who had apparently been a familiar figure in the market place for some years: he is mentioned in Aristophanes' *Acharnians* (425 B.C.). The reference to his 'fasting' sounds like a stock joke based on some well-remembered anecdote rather than a gibe at his poverty.

94. Scurrilous lampoons on well-known citizens were often introduced into the lyrics accompanying the dances (cf. *The Frogs*, pp. 172–3).

95. Both are epithets of Apollo.

96. Euripides' *Andromeda* has, unfortunately, not survived, but one does not need the text to appreciate the burlesque that follows.

97. She probably did not appear in person in the original production. If, as seems probable, the part of Echo was doubled with that of Euripides, the actor would already be wearing his Perseus costume; so presumably Echo's part was spoken behind the scenes, and possibly in a voice that could be recognized by the audience as that of Euripides. In any case the scene is full of opportunities for 'business': my stage directions are, of course, only suggestions.

98. In the *Andromeda* (412 B.C.): this shows that *The Poet and the Women* was produced in 411.

THE FROGS

99. See note 114.

100. The image of Dionysus was brought to the theatre each year for the dramatic performances at the City Dionysia. Thus the operative words are *more than*.

101. All the slaves who took part in the Athenian victory at Arginusae in 406 B.C. were given their freedom and the rights of citizens.

102. See note 67. Dionysus does not quote the line, but paraphrases it clumsily.

103. Hemlock took effect from the feet upwards.

104. Charon's traditional fare was one obol, but prices go up in wartime. In 410 B.C. the demagogue Cleophon had introduced a daily cost-of-living allowance of two obols a day for citizens who had been deprived of their livelihood by the occupation of Decelea. Two obols was also the daily pay of a soldier or sailor, and the price of a ticket for the theatre.

105. Cinesias was a dithyrambic poet, frequently mocked by Aristophanes; Morsimus, grand-nephew of Aeschylus, wrote tragedies.

106. Interesting evidence that women, as well as men, could be initiated into the Eleusinian Mysteries.

107. i.e. 1½ drachmas.

108. The pun in the original is on the name 'Charon' and the greeting 'Chaire'.

109. See note 101.

110. The reference is to the Anthesteria, an annual festival held in the precinct of 'Dionysus in the Marshes'. Wine-drinking competitions were an important feature of the celebrations.

111. One of the more horrific bogies believed in by the superstitious.

112. The actor Hegelochus had apparently made nonsense of his part on some occasion by giving a word the wrong intonation. I have tried to achieve a similar effect by making him mispronounce a letter.

113. A notorious atheist who used to make fun of the Mysteries.

114. Probably the women initiates were played by a subsidiary Chorus of boys, and appeared only in this scene. The same boys may have been used for the Chorus of Frogs.

115. The island of Aegina, lying between the mainland of Attica and the Peloponnese, provided a good base for illicit trade with the enemy. The Greek text specifies some of the forbidden exports, and mentions the official concerned, a certain Thorycion, by name.

116. The fee payable to the author out of State funds had been reduced, perhaps on the proposal of some influential person who had been a victim of Aristophanes' satire.

117. Another reference to Cinesias (see note, 105), one of whose claims to fame was that he had once 'defiled a shrine of Hecate'.

118. The luckless Thorycion (see note 115) is again mentioned by name.

119. The Temple of Demeter at Eleusis, twelve miles from Athens, where the Mysteries were celebrated.

120. The wearing of torn clothes seems to have been a feature of certain rites, but the poet hints that their use in this case may have had an economic motive. It is known that in this year (406–405 B.C.) there had

been great difficulty in finding anyone to finance the productions at the dramatic festivals, and in the end the expenses had had to be shared, two people being responsible for each chorus instead of one.

121. Archedemus, known as 'the Blear-Eyed', was one of the demagogues who had been instrumental in bringing about the cruel and senseless vote of the Assembly by which the commanders who had been victorious at Arginusae (406 B.C.) were sentenced to death. This was very recent history.

122. Cleisthenes was one of a group of Athenians who had made fortunes out of political blackmail after the abortive revolution of 411 B.C. This, rather than his sexual morals, must be the real reason for Aristophanes' attack. Compare his role as an informer in *The Poet and the Women.*

123. Callias, son of Hipponicus (here changed to the indecent form 'Hippobinus'), was notorious as a spendthrift and womanizer. Too little is known about him for the full point of the joke to be clear.

124. Interesting evidence in support of the idea that the Eleusinian initiates were bound by some kind of code of behaviour. The use of the terms *idiotai* (kinsmen, fellow-citizens) and *xenoi* (strangers, guests) reminds one of the 'laws' of the blood-feud as practised right up to fairly recent times in parts of the Balkans: fellow-clansmen had to settle their feuds by arbitration and not by 'blood-taking', and even a legitimate victim could not be touched so long as he was a guest on the territory of the clan which was at feud with his own.

125. The usual formula used when a libation (drink offering) was poured.

126. Known as 'the Buskin' – the boot that fits either foot. He had helped to organize the abortive oligarchical revolution of 411, had survived the downfall of the régime then set up, and in the restored democracy had led the outcry against the Arginusae commanders (see note 121).

127. Cleon (see Introduction, p. 28) had died in 422; Hyperbolus (see note 88) in 412. Comic poets had long memories.

128. See note 121.

129. The evidence of slaves was valid only if given under torture.

130. The whole passage does, as a matter of fact, 'defy interpretation'. The main point of the attack on Cleophon here is obscure, apart from the familiar innuendo that he is not of pure Athenian birth. The final threat, though, is clear enough; and the prophecy was to be fulfilled very soon, for Cleophon was executed early the following year.

131. One of the leaders of the oligarchical revolution of 411. When democracy was restored in 410, he was assassinated, and his slayer was enfranchised and treated as a national hero. At the same time many

people who had supported the revolution had been deprived of their citizenship.

132. The Plataeans had been made citizens of Athens in 427, after the destruction of their city by the Spartans.

133. Cleigenes, like Cleophon, was an extreme democrat and opposed to peace negotiations with Sparta. Like Cleophon again, he had been one of those responsible for the disfranchisement of the supporters of Phrynichus.

134. Sophocles had died in 406, a few months after Euripides.

135. See note 71.

136. Not known.

137. A member of Euripides' household, possibly a slave or a lodger, who was rumoured to have had an affair with Euripides' wife. One of the stock jokes of the day was that Cephisophon had also helped Euripides to write his plays (perhaps by providing him with a dramatic situation in real life!).

138. Euripides had left Athens (perhaps wisely) in 408 and settled at the court of Archelaus, King of Macedon.

139. See note 126.

140. See note 88.

141. See note 137.

142. These lines are missing from the extant MSS. of *The Libation Bearers*, so we are indebted to Aristophanes for their preservation.

143. The most distinguished exile at the time was Alcibiades, and Aeschylus' last remark would certainly have been understood as a covert reference to him.

144. See note 121.

145. The word 'round' should be sung to a long run of notes each time it occurs, so as to achieve an effect similar to that of the repeated syllable in the Greek.

146. The policemen of Athens were known as 'the archers'.

147. See note 137.

148. Palamedes, hero of one of the lost tragedies of Euripides, was noted for his sagacity.

149. Aeschylus is still thinking in terms of the war against Persia (he fought in the battle of Marathon, 490 B.C.).

150. Dionysus' appeal to the audience, just above, is a brilliant adaptation of yet another 'fatal line': 'Is an act shameful, if it seem not so to the doers?' By altering the first two letters of the word for *doers*, Dionysus turns it into *audience*.

151. Adeimantus was one of the military commanders for the current year. Next to nothing is known of Myrmex, Nichomachus, and Archenomus.